More Praise for the First Edition

"Packed with rock-solid evidence, disturbing statistics and moving stories, this short but passionate plea for connectedness at work and in life delivers a wake-up call. How connected you feel to other people at work turns out to be the primary driver of your sense of engagement as an employee, but Americans in particular have let relationships and community suffer. Experts Michael Lee Stallard, Jason Pankau and Katharine P. Stallard explain why people need to connect. getAbstract recommends this quick read to leaders who want to build places where the best people want to work and connect." —getAbstract

"*Connection Culture* really captures the why and how to mobilize an organization to work together toward a compelling vision. The insights about the unique contributions of the leader and the leadership team are especially useful." —Alan Mulally, Retired CEO, Boeing Commercial Airplanes and The Ford Motor Company

"Every manager needs to read this book—it will foster healthier work environments and make my job a lot easier!" —Ted George, MD, Clinical Professor, George Washington University School of Medicine; Senior Investigator, National Institute on Alcohol Abuse and Alcoholism

"Our organization has benefited greatly from the principles in *Connection Culture*. The book creates an engaging framework for leaders who want more for their businesses and employees. It is a must read for anyone leading an organization." —Mike Cunnion, Chief Executive Officer, Remedy Health Media

"*Connection Culture* lays out a compelling case for a culture of connection in every organization and provides a framework for leaders who want to apply positive personal values in practice in their organizations and teams." —John Young, Group President, Chief Business Officer, Pfizer

"*Connection Culture* captures the profound truth that people come first and provides the framework, language, and practices every leader needs to achieve a sustainable, superior performance. A great leadership guide for leaders at every level." —Frances Hesselbein, President and CEO, The Frances Hesselbein Leadership Institute

"A wonderful book . . . *Connection Culture* isn't a very long or wordy book, but it's loaded with lessons." —*Small Business Trends*

"At the end of the day leadership is all about the human experience. *Connection Culture* provides ideas, actions, and pathways that servant leaders can use to not only enhance performance, but more importantly to build a strong culture." —Howard Behar, Former President, Starbucks International

T0273677

"The message of *Connection Culture* is profoundly personal yet ultimately universal. If you think you know what connection really means, you'll come away with a whole new perspective once you have read this gracefully written book." —Bruce Rosenstein, Managing Editor, *Leader to Leader*, Author, *Create Your Future the Peter Drucker Way*

"Leadership is about relationships. *Connection Culture* reveals the art and science of creating a culture that builds relationships and drives performance." —David Burkus, Author, *The Myths of Creativity* and *Under New Management*

"Engaging, while offering real solutions to human challenges that occur in the workplace! As someone who has researched and published in the field of organizational psychology, I can honestly say that *Connection Culture* is right on target and a book that every leader should race to get their hands on." —Karla R. Peters-Van Havel, Chief Operating Officer, The Institute for Management Studies

"Thank you, Michael, for reminding us again that people—customers and employees— are the most important ingredient of any business. Leaders place so much emphasis on the operations and financials, but people connecting and working together is the key to success." —Jay Morris, Vice President, Education, Executive Director, Institute for Excellence, Yale New Haven Health

"*Connection Culture* grabbed my attention from the beginning and had me jumping on the phone to share its ideas with friends and colleagues. We have to do better as leaders and as teachers of leadership development to be intentional in creating and sustaining connection cultures. Even when you think you've got it all in place (the surveys, training, recognition awards, and celebrations), disconnection creeps in. You must read this book." —Janis Apted, Associate Vice President, Faculty and Academic Development, The University of Texas MD Anderson Cancer Center

"Too many leadership books focus on developing work experience without acknowledging the rest of our lives. *Connection Culture* demonstrates how the positive habits, relationships, and character we've developed in the workplace can serve us well at home and in our communities. Not only does this deep exploration of connection culture explain the positive effects of using these skills, it also offers ways to get started on the journey." —James daSilva, Senior Editor, SmartBrief on Leadership

"Connection works when we work on connection. Michael Stallard draws us in with his stories, convinces us with his evidence, and guides us with his recommendations. He concludes by inviting us to mark the day we finish the book as the start of a new outlook, focused on establishing a thriving work culture through freshly enlivened, engaged, and enriched connections." —David Zinger, Founder, Employee Engagement Network

MICHAEL LEE STALLARD

TODD W. HALL, KATHARINE P. STALLARD, AND JASON PANKAU

SECOND EDITION

CONNECTION CULTURE

· THE ·
COMPETITIVE
ADVANTAGE OF SHARED
IDENTITY, EMPATHY,
AND UNDERSTANDING
AT WORK

24 23 22 21   2 3 4 5

Parts of this book are adapted from articles in *Leader to Leader* from the Frances Hesselbein Leadership Institute.

The Via Institute Classification of Character Strengths is copyright 2004-2014, VIA Institute on Character. All rights reserved. www.viacharacter.org

ATD Press is an internationally renowned source of insightful and practical information on talent development, training, and professional development.

ATD Press
1640 King Street
Alexandria, VA 22314 USA

Ordering information: Books published by ATD Press can be purchased by visiting ATD's website at td.org/books or by calling 800.628.2783 or 703.683.8100.

Library of Congress Control Number: 2020936302

ISBN-10: 1-950496-52-X
ISBN-13: 978-1-950496-52-5
e-ISBN: 978-1-950496-53-2

ATD Press Editorial Staff
Director: Sarah Halgas
Manager: Melissa Jones
Community Manager, Management: Ryan Changcoco
Developmental Editor: Kathryn Stafford
Production Editor: Hannah Sternberg
Text Design: Michelle Jose
Cover Design: Emily Weigel, Faceout Studio; Michelle Jose, ATD

Printed by BR Printers, San Jose, CA

Contents

Contents

Foreword

Connection Culture presents a new way of thinking about leadership, employee engagement, and organizational health. It shares the stories of many different organizations that found tremendous success by nurturing connections—from Costco to the U.S. Navy to the Duke University men's basketball team. Combining an array of data and research findings as well as examples from real-life experiences, Michael Lee Stallard makes the compelling case that a culture of connection provides a clear competitive advantage for organizations and individuals. *Connection Culture* provides powerful tools for enriching and transforming organizations.

Texas Christian University (TCU) is proud to be one of the organizations profiled in *Connection Culture*. At TCU, our goal is to produce graduates who can deal with change, motivate others, and think and act responsibly in a global community. These are the qualities most needed for leadership and thriving in the future.

And we want to do more.

Some years ago, I was intrigued to learn that Stallard, the father of two of our students, was an expert on leadership and organizational culture. What he wrote on connection culture resonated with me. During my career in higher education, I've seen students thrive when supportive relationships make them feel connected, and I've seen how they struggle when they feel lonely. I was pleased to see how TCU's culture resonated with Stallard's connection culture theory—the university's culture is rooted in a long history of valuing service to others and inclusiveness, both of which increase connection.

TCU's connection culture has always been led by the people who become part of the TCU community. This focus on personal connectivity is modeled at all levels of faculty, staff, and student leadership—on campus and around the globe.

In an effort to strengthen our culture of connection even further, TCU has partnered with Stallard to create the TCU Center for Connection Culture. It begins at home as we equip our faculty, staff, and students with the skills to be more intentional about connection. We are committed to embracing connection programs and activities for our entire university as well as for community participants. We desire to be a beacon of connection and a model for other institutions that strive for community, inclusion, and ethical leadership.

While reading *Connection Culture*, I was reminded of Moore's Law, which states that the processing power of computers will double every two years. I find this to be an apt metaphor for the rapidly evolving environment—one for which we must prepare our TCU graduates. This book provides positive ways of thinking and acting that can help them—and us all—navigate the future.

Our World Has Changed and Our Perspectives Have Broadened

Even now, as I write this update to the foreword for the second edition, a worldwide pandemic is unfurling and information on COVID-19 is spreading as quickly as the virus itself. We are in the midst of enacting sweeping measures: distance learning, working remotely, and the cancellation of gatherings that make being a Horned Frog so meaningful.

This historic season has tested not only life here at Texas Christian University, but life as we know it everywhere. The global COVID-19 pandemic suddenly challenged the way we live and learn, radically altering the way we relate to one another.

Or did it?

When our beautiful campus resembled a ghost town, the tulips kept right on blooming, and the sharing of ideas and resources flourished right along with them. I watched with gratitude as a new normal unfolded for a spirited Horned Frog family that can never truly be separated, even when apart.

What we are experiencing right now makes the elements of this book even more relevant. Because TCU has long fostered a sense of community, our emotional connection is strong and we were able to build upon those relationships for the betterment of our students.

Our rallying cry is #TCUTogether, a campaign launched to share the many stories of Frogs Helping Frogs. Almost immediately, student affairs began hosting virtual events to bring students closer together and combat feelings of isolation. I launched a video series direct to students and receive (and respond to) hundreds of emails per week. I can't count the number of live online events, Zoom calls, and touchpoints TCU has created to grow our connection and support our community, even in this time of social distance.

These unprecedented times have taught us all that although we are apart, a Horned Frog will never be alone.

Victor J. Boschini Jr.
Chancellor, Texas Christian University
April 2020

Introduction
to the Second Edition

My interest in workplace culture sprang from a desire to understand what was going on in my own work life and to discern what I should do as a leader to establish and maintain an environment in which the people I led could consistently do their best work. I took a break from working on Wall Street so I could focus on studying and addressing the widespread problem of employee disengagement and workplace burnout. Gathering and assimilating research and the perspectives of academics and experts, and conducting research on people in the trenches of modern organizational life led me to write and speak about what I discovered, and eventually to found a company to bring these insights to organizations.

Now, almost 20 years later, my colleagues and I have had the privilege of sharing our work with groups ranging in size from a medical software start-up of fewer than 20 employees to every Costco warehouse manager worldwide. Early on we worked with the engineering section of the NASA Johnson Space Center. More recently, we've spoken to leaders at the U.S. Air Force, Federal Reserve Bank of San Francisco, Memorial Sloan Kettering Cancer Center, and Yale New Haven Health. In education, we've worked with Utah's largest public school district and have an ongoing relationship with Texas Christian University (TCU), which established the TCU Center for Connection Culture. Other clients have been centered in the technology, construction, and finance industries.

What I've learned about connection applies beyond the realm of our work lives. The principles are relevant for individuals, families, community groups, sports teams, and even nations. Knowing that a connection deficit negatively affects our own health and well-being, the health of organizations, and the health of society, I've become concerned observing how the pace and stress of life threaten to squeeze out time for supportive, lifegiving relationships and endeavors. The United States and countries around the world are experiencing an epidemic of loneliness. In recent years, the news has been full of reports of incivility and active shooter incidents. There has been a rise in suicide rates, even in those as young as elementary school age. As I update this introduction, protests are taking place across the United States calling out systemic racism. It is a time of entering into honest, open, and productive dialogue that is very necessary if we are to be a country that values the dignity and inherent value of each individual. In all of these social issues, we must go beyond just talking and take action to make lasting change. I believe we can collectively turn the tide if we are willing to be intentional about connection.

New Research, Case Studies, and Connection Practices

This updated and expanded edition of *Connection Culture* builds on our understanding since the first edition was published in 2015 and since our book that introduced connection culture, *Fired Up or Burned Out: How to Reignite Your Team's Passion, Creativity, and Productivity*, was published in 2007. For instance, recent research has found that:

- Individuals with stronger social connections were associated with a 50 percent reduced risk of early death, whereas individuals who were lonely or socially isolated were associated with a risk of early death that is equivalent to the risk from smoking 15 cigarettes a day (Holt-Lunstad et al. 2010; Holt-Lunstad et al. 2015).
- America and many other nations are experiencing an epidemic of loneliness, with three in five (61 percent) American adults self-reporting loneliness (Holt-Lunstad 2017; Cigna 2020).
- Greater loneliness in the workplace results in poorer task, team role, and relational performance (Ozelik and Barsade 2017).

You'll find new practices that boost connection and a five-step process to operationalize connection culture. You'll learn about common obstacles that get in the way of cultivating a connection culture and how to overcome them. This edition also broadens the diversity of leaders and types of groups highlighted, including Lin-Manuel Miranda and the team that developed the award-winning Broadway musical *Hamilton*, German Chancellor Angela Merkel, Steph Curry and the Golden State Warriors basketball team, the Mayo Clinic, Oprah Winfrey, and Tricia Griffith of Progressive Insurance. We've also added features that encourage you to pause and reflect on your own experience and how the material applies to your life and work environment.

In chapters 1 and 2 you will learn about the three cultures of connection, control, and indifference, and why a culture of connection helps individuals and organizations thrive.

In chapter 3 you will learn the Vision + Value + Voice model that is essential to create and sustain a connection culture.

At the close of parts I and II, you'll find a section we call Profiles in Connection. Here you'll read about leaders and groups that dramatically differ in the nature of the tasks they perform yet share commonalities in their social cultures. Perhaps you'll spot some best practices of connection in action that you can implement.

Chapters 4 and 5 will arm you with interesting and relevant research supporting the case for connection from a wide variety of fields, including psychology, sociology, neuroscience, and organizational behavior. You will also see how a lack of connection affects wellness, well-being, and longevity, and how connection provides six specific benefits to teams and organizations that add up to a powerful performance and competitive advantage.

Chapters 6 and 7 will equip you with a process to operationalize connection culture, including specific, practical, and actionable ways to boost connection in your group's culture.

The Perfect Storm: Stress, Loneliness, and the COVID-19 Pandemic

As the editing process for this second edition of *Connection Culture* neared completion, a novel coronavirus that causes the illness COVID-19 emerged in the city of Wuhan in China. As the highly transmissible virus began to spread worldwide in the early months of 2020, life as we had known it abruptly changed. On July 16, 2020, as I revise this introduction one final time, the statistics are sobering. To date, the virus has been found in nearly every country in the world, 13.7 million positive cases of COVID-19 have been publicly reported, and 588,023 individuals have died. In the United States alone, at least 138,255 people have died (*New York Times* 2020a, 2020b). The numbers continue to rise. Thankfully, the majority of people who contract COVID-19 are able to recover.

Because there wasn't (and as of this writing still isn't) a vaccine to protect people from contracting the virus, public health and government officials began to focus on strategies to slow the spread of transmission and "flatten the curve" so as not to overwhelm health systems. Many different strategies were used, including "social distancing," wearing face masks while in public, and quarantining at home (which could be voluntary or mandated by law, depending on where you lived). The social distancing strategy called for people to maintain a physical distance of at least six feet in an effort to reduce the risk of disease transmission. Additionally, many local governments put restrictions on the number of people who could be together at one time, which meant that people could no longer gather as they would have for weddings, funerals, worship services, or birthday parties. Because of social distancing restrictions, public spaces were closed, and conventions, vacations, and live performances were canceled or moved into the virtual space. In addition, school buildings and college campuses closed, and education moved to being delivered through distance learning. School plays, spring sports, and the prom were canceled, and students couldn't walk across the podium to receive their diplomas in a graduation ceremony.

Office workers became remote workers, doing their jobs from home. Other employees were furloughed or let go as organizations were forced to adapt to a sudden drop in activity. The millions of people who rely on income from gig work or having a side hustle were especially hit hard. According to an article in the *New York Times* on May 8, "The Labor Department said the economy shed more than 20.5 million jobs in April, sending the unemployment rate to 14.7 percent as the coronavirus pandemic took a devastating toll" (Schwartz et al. 2020). This was the highest U.S. unemployment rate since the Great Depression.

Alongside the feelings of loss and disappointment were feelings of fear and anxiety. Many worried that they or a loved one would contract COVID-19, they would lose their job due to the economic recession, they would be financially vulnerable due to the declining value of their savings, or that they would be unable to pay their bills.

Individuals worldwide were already struggling with high levels of stress and loneliness before the pandemic arrived. The physical distancing required to reduce virus transmission only add to our social isolation, contributing to a perfect storm of factors that increase physical and emotional health problems. A Kaiser Family Foundation poll of American adults conducted a few months after the COVID-19 outbreak began found the mental health of nearly half (45 percent) of respondents was negatively affected due to worry and stress over the virus (Kirzinger et al. 2020).

To help individuals and organizations, Katharine Stallard and I wrote "Connection Is Critical During the Coronavirus Pandemic," which was published in a number of media outlets in late March. In that article, we shared key points about connection: Social connection makes us smarter, happier, and more productive; makes us more resilient to cope with stress; and appears to improve cardiovascular, endocrine, and immune system performance, which may provide physical and emotional resources to fight the virus. We observed that the convergence of factors—high stress, the current loneliness epidemic, and increased social isolation from the COVID-19 pandemic—made boosting connection an even more urgent matter. Acknowledging that the need for physical distancing makes it more difficult to connect in conventional ways, we recommended a number of practices to boost human connection under these conditions.

How long increased social isolation from COVID-19 will last is difficult to tell. It likely won't end until a vaccine is developed, which may take one or more years. And once that happens, what will the lingering effects of having faced this traumatic event be? In the years immediately following the Spanish Flu, a particularly deadly pandemic that swept the globe in 1918–1919, there continued to be a fear of social connection when having done so in the midst of the prolonged crisis proved fatal for more than 600,000 individuals in the United States alone (Kenner 2018).

And how will the way we work change? For one, I expect to see a larger percentage of individuals working remotely, no longer benefiting from social connection in a shared workplace. In addition, many social distancing practices—such as wearing masks, plexiglass sneeze shields, and workstations that are more physically spread out—will likely continue, which will make connection in the workplace more challenging.

Going Forward, Together

Despite these concerns, I'm optimistic that the COVID-19 pandemic will bring about the post-traumatic growth that often comes after people experience times of adversity. This growth could come in the form of a renewed appreciation for human connection. If I'm right, we could see the emergence of a new anthropomorphic age that ushers in greater creativity, productivity, and well-being as the trials we face lead to greater human connection and a renaissance of the human spirit.

Getting through the COVID-19 pandemic and minimizing the loss of human life will require unprecedented levels of connection. Not only will connection be necessary to protect people until a vaccine is developed, it will also fuel the collaboration and creativity needed to crack the code and identify that vaccine. This became clear to me after I read a *New Yorker* article by Dr. Atul Gawande (2020), the noted surgeon and author. Gawande's hospital system, Mass General Brigham, was able to keep COVID-19 cases at a minimum among its 75,000 employees despite being in Boston, which was a hot spot for the disease. In the article he observed that in addition to his hospital's four pillar combination strategy—hygiene, distancing, screening, and masks—it was a fifth element, culture, that moved people who knew what to do, to actually do it.

Now more than ever, it is an essential time in history to cultivate cultures of connection. I hope you will join me by taking action to increase connection in your home, your workplace, and your community. As you will learn through reading this book, our future depends on it.

Michael Lee Stallard
July 2020

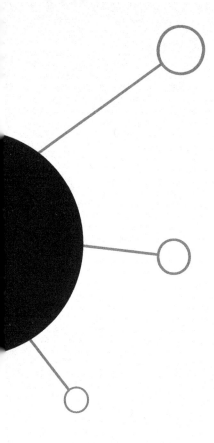

PART I
A New View of Leadership and Organizational Culture

If a leader's sole focus is on seeing that tasks are accomplished, then success will be unsustainable. Leaders must create an environment where people thrive. What does it take for you to thrive at work, and what is the role that culture plays in whether or not you are able to give your best effort?

In part I, you will learn about seven universal human needs required for people to thrive at work and three types of culture everyone should know about, including the type of culture that best promotes the health and productivity of individuals and organizations. You will learn a vocabulary of culture and a simple, memorable, and actionable model to create the best culture. This knowledge will help you understand what type of culture you need to thrive, and it will begin to equip you to cultivate a workplace culture that brings out the best in the people you are responsible for leading or whom you lead through your influence. Part I concludes with eight profiles of diverse individuals and organizations that are cultivating cultures of connection.

1

The X Factor

Is there a "best" team and organizational culture? Is there an X factor in cultures that brings out the best in people and propels the success of groups? Countless books, podcasts, webinars, and workshops offer dos and don'ts for leading people. The sheer volume of opinions and approaches available reinforces the lack of consensus on the definitions or a general model for leadership or organizational culture despite a century of scientific inquiry.

In recent years, however, two trends have emerged. The first is that scholars are finding organizations comprise a web of relationships best captured by theories of complexity. The second trend is that effective leaders care about people and foster positive relationships. "Connection" is cited as an emerging general theory of leadership and organizational culture that integrates these trends, according to "The Connection Value Chain: Impact of Connection Culture and Employee Motivation on Perceived Team Performance," a published doctoral dissertation by Jon Rugg (2018).

Applying a one-size-fits-all culture isn't realistic in today's increasingly diverse and global working world. That said, organizations that have sustainable high performance will have common elements to their culture that enable them to be their best. Although the tasks will differ depending on the industry, when it comes to the relational aspects, there is a best culture: *a culture that has a high degree of human connection.*

To understand the power of human connection in a team and organizational culture, it helps to see examples of leaders who care about people and cultivate connection in their group's culture. Let's begin by looking behind the scenes at the group that created a groundbreaking Broadway musical. Meet Lin-Manuel Miranda and his key collaborators, and notice how their manner of working together brought out the best in each of them and together they brought something remarkable to the world of musical theater.

How "Harmony" Sparked *Hamilton*

Hamilton took Broadway by storm when it opened on August 6, 2015, and has not let go. What makes this show a must-see? *Hamilton* recounts the American Revolution through the life of Alexander Hamilton via a hip-hop mash-up that includes rap, R&B, jazz, and pop, depending on the character or the message of the song. It casts a multiethnic group of actors dressed in 18th-century attire to portray historical characters, most of whom were white. In 2018, the annual Kennedy Center Honors departed from its tradition of solely recognizing individual artists or bands for their contributions over their careers and gave a special award to *Hamilton* as a piece of work. The four key collaborators who brought the show into being were celebrated as "trailblazing creators of a transformative work that defies category." Introducing the award, Gloria Estefan proclaimed, "*Hamilton* turned the conventions of musical theater upside down, forever changing the look and sound of Broadway" (Jensen 2018).

Early Connections

Lin-Manuel Miranda, who wrote the music, lyrics, and script of *Hamilton* as well as originated the role of Alexander Hamilton, is a MacArthur Fellowship Genius Grant recipient and has also been honored with Grammy, Emmy, Drama League, and Drama Desk awards. Clearly, Miranda is extraordinarily talented. What many people may not know is that he is also an outstanding connector with his family, community, and artistic collaborators; connection enhances his life and work.

Miranda was raised in New York City by parents who immigrated from Puerto Rico. Considered highly empathetic from a young age, he attuned to the emotions conveyed in songs like Stevie Wonder's "I Just Called to Say I Love You," Simon and Garfunkel's "Bridge Over Troubled Water," and "Feed the Birds" from *Mary Poppins*. Today, Miranda credits his ability to connect by empathizing with characters as key to his success as a writer and actor. Empathy, he says, is "the number 1 tool in an artist's tool box" (Winfrey 2017b).

Miranda attended Wesleyan College in Connecticut and majored in theater. Early on at Wesleyan, he met Anthony Venazile, and together with other friends they founded an improvisation hip-hop group named Freestyle Love Supreme, which still performs periodically and was on Broadway for a limited engagement in fall 2019. Every performance is one of a kind as the performers react to audience suggestions and work them into riffs and musical numbers created on the spot. Think of how quick and clever and fearless you would need to be to do that!

While a college student, Miranda began writing a musical about the community around Washington Heights in northern Manhattan. True to the sounds of the streets, he wove in hip-hop, freestyle rap, merengue, and salsa numbers. Miranda said his intention in making *In the Heights* was that it would be a "love letter" to the community he grew up in, a musical that shows the hopes and dreams, the work ethic, and sacrifices of immigrant parents for their children rather than the stereotypical portrayal of drugs and violence (Ball and Read 2016). Miranda has said, "The overwhelming majority of residents in Washington Heights are not involved with crime or drugs. It would be inauthentic for me to write about drug deals and domestic abuse. It wasn't my experience" (Low 2007).

Instead, he was motivated by fond memories he had of growing up, including his relationship with Edmunda Claudio, whom he called *abuela* (grandmother), and walking with her through the neighborhood, hearing Latin music, and visiting the bodega. Although she was not his biological grandmother, Abuela Mundi looked after Miranda and his sister while their mother and father worked, just as she had looked after Miranda's father when he was a boy growing up in Puerto Rico. About her, Miranda says, "I could do no wrong in her eyes, she gave me unconditional love" (Low 2007). He based the *In the Heights* character Abuela Claudia on her.

In the Heights opened off-Broadway in 2005 and had its Broadway debut in 2008, with Miranda in a leading role. The show earned 13 Tony nominations and won four, most noticeably Best Musical. At 28, Miranda was the youngest person to ever win a Tony for Best Original Score. The cast recording of *In the Heights* took home the Grammy for Best Musical Show Album that year.

Miranda's vision for his next Broadway musical of original material came from reading Ron Chernow's bestselling biography *Alexander Hamilton*, a book he picked up to read while on vacation. The story goes that as he was reading poolside in Mexico, he was hooked. He felt the emotions in hip-hop expressed the relentless energy of the immigrant striver Hamilton, who had come alone to New York as a teenager and rose to become an aide to General George Washington in the Revolutionary War and served as the first secretary of the treasury of the United States. Here was another immigrant story to shine a light on.

As a start, Miranda composed a song he called "The Hamilton Mixtape." When he performed it at the White House in 2009, rather than a song from *In the Heights* that was probably expected, the video of Miranda's performance went viral. For the next two years, Miranda primarily worked on projects related to other musicals and movies, and he married Vanessa Nadal, a scientist and lawyer he first met when they were in high school. In 2011, when Freestyle Love Supreme performed at a benefit concert, Miranda sang another song he had written based on Alexander Hamilton titled, "My Shot." Thomas Kail, a co-founder and the director of Freestyle Love Supreme, noticed the audience's enthusiastic reaction. Miranda had been talking with Kail about Hamilton for three years. Following Miranda's performance, Kail approached him and said they both needed to start working regularly on the "Hamilton" project. They agreed to a schedule in which Miranda would write and Kail would provide feedback.

Connecting With Vision, Value, and Voice

Great leaders connect with people when they communicate an inspiring vision, value people as human beings rather than treating them as means to an end, and give them a voice to express their ideas and opinions. Vision, value, and voice create connection.

Miranda has a group of close collaborators he has known for years and worked with on *In the Heights, Hamilton,* and other projects: director Thomas Kail, music director Alex Lacamoire, and choreographer Andy Blankenbuehler. He enjoys interacting with them, trusts them, and respects their talents. Miranda says the group has been through a lot of experiences together. He says it's like a marriage or band, and that his favorite thing to do is to bring a new song to the group because he knows they're going to make it better.

Vision, value, and voice are clearly at work in the culture that these collaborators have established and in which they are able to do great work together. Kail refers to the dynamic among the group as "harmony," evoking the blending of individual voices into one in a way that results in a fullness and richness that a solo line does not have. He also observed that the way the group operates is that they collaborate yet each individual has autonomy to run his own department where he has specialized expertise. The show, he says, is a sum of their parts. Kail says he hopes the resulting harmony among the people involved in *Hamilton* becomes part of the show's legacy. Miranda has said *Hamilton* is "a culmination of . . . a lot of people putting a lot of hard work in, and particularly Tommy Kail, who got all of the art forms involved in making a musical and made them into one cohesive thing called *Hamilton*" (Espana 2017).

Lacamoire has stated, "I never worked with [Lin-Manuel, Tom, and Andy] because 'I want to make art and I want to make something that's going to be really important.' I just wanted to hang out with these guys and do what I feel I do best . . . and have some fun and have a dialogue . . . and contribute" (Kail et al. 2018). After hearing the songs Miranda was writing, Lacamoire shared that it began to fill him with pride in America and that the energy, passion, and perseverance of the Founding Fathers awakened his understanding of American history.

Miranda has explained that the creative team was very deliberate about choices made: "Our goal in every aspect of the production from costumes to choreography is to eliminate any distance between a contemporary audience and the story which took place [more than 200] years ago. So to that end, casting the show the way our country looks today helps" (Low 2015). As Kail says, "This is a story about America then, told by America now" (Miranda and McCarter 2016).

When asked about the casting choices in an interview, Miranda replied: "When I started reading [Chernow's *Alexander Hamilton*], I was picturing hip-hop and R&B artists singing these songs. So they were always people of color. It's the most natural fit for this genre of music. So part of it stems from the initial impulse of writing the show, and Tommy continued the impulse" (Low 2015). On another occasion Miranda said, "We have every color represented on that stage. It eliminates distance between us and the story of our founders. It helps them feel more human to us, because it's what our country looks like now" (Ball and Reed 2016). The actor Daveed Diggs, who originated the dual roles of Thomas Jefferson and the Marquis de Lafayette and won a Tony Award for his performances, explains, "*Hamilton* allows us to see ourselves as part of history that we always thought we were excluded from. . . . Rap is the voice of the people of our generation, and of people of color, and just the fact that it exists in this piece, and is not commented upon, gives us a sense of ownership" (Mead 2015).

To convey the vision of *Hamilton* to a new company that will perform the show around the world, Kail said that by helping the cast members understand the storytelling—the where and why of a certain idea—they catch the vision and bring their A game to the performance: "Everybody onstage and offstage in this company is working at the absolute top of their game" (Espana 2017).

Valuing one another is an element of the group's culture. It's been observed about Kail that he cares about people. It comes through in many ways. He gets to know the actors offstage so he can adapt to the way each actor is wired. Kail has said, "My job is to try to create an environment where the writer can feel nurtured and supported and alive . . . and find other people . . . to try to realize the show" (Espana 2017). He refuses to work with people who are not kind. He has said, "There are a lot of talented people in the world" and "you can find talented people who are kind and good and decent" (Jennings 2015). He observed how respectful the people he works with are to one another and that each of them believes "you can develop something of high quality without acrimony or raising your voice" (Kail et al. 2018). One of Kail's rules is he doesn't raise his voice. "I'm gonna ask [actors] to do things they don't wanna do," he says. "So I'm gonna be transparent with them. I'm in the business of really sensitive people with a lot of feelings. If I can make them feel safe, I can make them feel their best" (Jennings 2015).

Making sure everyone has a voice to express their opinions and ideas is another essential element of the culture cultivated by Kail as director. Miranda has stated about their meetings, "I'm more the editor than the writer—Alex will have 50 musical ideas, Andy will have 50 staging ideas, and Tommy and I will sift [through them]" (Miranda and McCarter 2016). He says, "We respond to each other's energy in a way that's really positive" (Kail et al. 2018). Kail has a way of cultivating an environment where the best ideas emerge.

The group also recognizes that their best work is influenced by a wide variety of ideas. Their attitude is to bring in all the ideas and then sort through them together to find the best. Some of the many influences reflected in *Hamilton* include lyrics from hip-hop numbers; the works of Stephen Sondheim and Rodgers and Hammerstein; elements of choreography by Jerome Robbins; Broadway shows including *Rent, Fiddler on the Roof, Sweeney Todd, Evita, Chicago, Gypsy,* and *Oklahoma*; and films like *The Matrix* and *Ratatouille*.

Reflecting on giving people a voice, Kail said that it's important to make people feel safe so they will share their ideas, and then to consider everyone's ideas. He pointed out that collaboration has much to do with having a person's contribution recognized and heard, adopting a posture of "Maybe. Let me see [what you had in mind]" rather than "No." Doing so "opens the door to possibility that doesn't exist when you already have the idea locked in your mind as to what it has to be" (Kail et al. 2018). He believes that giving people a voice is what *Hamilton* does for everyone involved.

Lacamoire summed up the contrast between isolation and connection, and how connection affects him: "A lot of what we do can be so solitary . . . When we get in a room and they finally get to hear [what I've been working on] and it sparks something . . . even if it starts that dialogue, that's what I live for . . . that's why I do theater, it's to be able to get in a room with other people and not be alone, and to be able to talk and have that link" (Kail et al. 2018).

Connection and Sustainable Superior Performance

Connection among the group of individuals who brought *Hamilton* to life sparked a creative energy that propelled the show to the pinnacle of success. It is now recognized as the most successful musical of the modern Broadway era.

Hamilton received a record 16 Tony Award nominations and won the categories Best Book of a Musical, Best Score, Best Orchestrations, Best Choreography, Best Costume Design of a Musical, Best Lighting Design of a Musical, Best Leading Actor in a Musical, Best Featured Actor in a Musical, Best Featured Actress in a Musical, Best Direction of a Musical, and, the most coveted award, Best Musical. It also received the 2016 Pulitzer Prize for Drama and the Grammy for Best Musical Theater Album.

Hamilton is connecting with people across differences of race and age. Kail has spoken of being surprised at how young the fans can be. I've seen that too. A Korean-American friend told us that when her son was nine years old, he would spend school recess with his friends learning and memorizing lyrics to some of the songs. Soon his six-year-old brother was singing along.

Another indicator of the broad appeal of *Hamilton*, the kindness of the people in the cast, and the type of connector Lin-Manuel Miranda is came in early spring 2020. As Americans were coming to grips with how social distancing measures to slow the spread of COVID-19 had upended normal life and upcoming plans they may have had, actor John Krasinski started recording a weekly 15-minute show from his home called "SGN" (short for Some Good News). He described the show, which he posted on YouTube, as "a news show dedicated entirely to good news" at a time when "somehow the human spirit came through and found a way to blow us all away" despite people going through so much change, anxiety, and isolation (Krasinski 2020a).

Krasinski had learned of a nine-year-old girl named Aubrey whose exciting birthday plans to see a performance of *Hamilton* in Florida had been dashed. And so, in SGN's second episode, Krasinski and his wife, actress Emily Blunt, surprised her with a video call. When asked how much of a *Hamilton* fan she was on a scale of 1 to 10, Aubrey answered, "a million." They promised to send the superfan and her mom to New York City to see *Hamilton* when it reopened on Broadway (Krasinski 2020b).

But the biggest surprise was still to come when Lin-Manuel Miranda popped onto the screen. The young girl's response was priceless: her eyes opened extra wide and her hands flew up to her face covering her mouth, which had dropped open in shock.

"Hi, Aubrey. How are you?" said Miranda. "I'm sorry you didn't get to see *Hamilton*. I'm so glad to meet you." She was too stunned to reply.

Soon more members of *Hamilton*'s original Broadway cast joined the video call, serenading her with the opening number from their own homes. Since Aubrey couldn't go to the theater to see the show, they brought a bit of the show to her. As the song finished, performers called out "Happy Birthday, Aubrey. We love you!" In the first month, that episode had more than 12 million views on YouTube (Krasinski 2020b).

Extending *Hamilton* out to young people who might not have the opportunity to see the show otherwise, Miranda and *Hamilton* producer Jeffrey Seller partnered with the Gilder Lehrman Institute of American History and the Rockefeller Foundation in 2015 to create the *Hamilton* Education Program (often referred to as "EduHam"). The program, designed to integrate the study of American history with the performing arts, incorporates material about Alexander Hamilton and America's founding into classroom studies and culminates in students going to the theater for a special performance of the show. Begun in New York City, to date, more than 160,000 students from almost 2,000 Title I-eligible high schools across the United States have taken part in the program (Dembin 2017; American Theatre Editors 2020).

Even the temporary closure of theaters due to the COVID-19 pandemic did not slow down *Hamilton*'s momentum and continued success. In June 2016, director Tom Kail spent three days filming the show's original Broadway cast: Two full performances were recorded in front of a live audience; 13 additional audience-less numbers were captured via Steadicam, crane, and dolly (Lee 2020). The resulting film was then acquired by the Disney corporation and initially intended to release in October 2021 in movie theaters. However, in light of the pandemic, Disney moved the release date up dramatically—to July 3, 2020—and made the decision to release it digitally, on the Disney+ platform. On the movie's opening weekend, there were more than 2 million tweets about *Hamilton* and U.S. downloads of the Disney+ app increased by 72 percent (Katz 2020). About the film, Disney executive chairman Bob Iger said, "In this very difficult time, this story of leadership, tenacity, hope, love, and the power of people to unite against adversity is both relevant and inspiring" (Paulson 2020).

The leaders who developed *Hamilton* care about people and cultivated a culture of connection. In examining how the team members communicate, collaborate, and cooperate, we see the influence a connection culture can have in bringing out the best in individuals, as well as the group as a whole.

Connection: The X Factor That Brings Out the Best

Group cultures, including the cultures of teams, departments, and organizations, can be viewed as either having the effect of connecting people or isolating them. Why do leaders need to care whether the individuals they are responsible for leading are connected? Research has found that social connection is a primal human need that appears to improve the performance of the body's cardiovascular, endocrine, and immune systems (Uchino et al. 1996). Viewed from the opposite side, research has shown that lacking sufficient connection is associated with a host of negative outcomes including poorer cognitive performance, impaired executive control and self-regulation, decreased sleep quality, lower levels of self-rated physical health, more intense reactions to negatives and less uplift from positives, greater feelings of helplessness and threat, substance abuse, depressive symptoms, and suicidal ideation (reviewed in Cacioppo and Patrick 2008). Employees who feel regularly left out, lonely, or out of the loop are not going to be able to do their best work and may not wish to.

In the research my colleagues and I conducted, we found that isolation typically results from excessive control behaviors or from excessive busyness and indifference to the human need for connection. Cultures that connect people (which we have termed "connection cultures" or "cultures of connection") are best for individual well-being and for helping organizations thrive. Specifically, cultures that intentionally connect people to their work, their colleagues, and the organization as a whole convey several performance advantages upon those organizations, including a cognitive advantage that makes people smarter and more creative, higher employee engagement, tighter strategic alignment, better decision making, a higher rate of innovation, and greater agility and adaptability to cope with faster changes taking place today. These benefits combine to provide a significant performance and competitive advantage.

How About You?

To appreciate the importance of culture in the workplace, consider your own experiences. During the course of your career, have you experienced times when you were eager to get to work in the morning, you were so immersed in your work that the hours flew by, and by the end of the day you didn't want to stop working? What was it about the job that made you feel that way?

How about the opposite? Have you experienced times when you struggled to get to work in the morning, the hours passed ever so slowly, and by the end of the day you were exhausted? Again, what was it about the job that made you feel that way?

If you are like most people, you've experienced those extremes during your career. I have too. As I reflected on my experiences, I realized I hadn't changed—the culture I was in was either energizing me or draining the life out of me.

Thus, I began a quest to identify the elements of workplace cultures that help people and organizations thrive for sustained periods of time. When the practices my team and I developed to boost employee engagement contributed to doubling our business's revenues during the course of two and a half years, I knew we were on to something. A few years later, I left a career on Wall Street to devote my full attention to understanding group culture so I could help others improve the cultures they were in. In this book, I'll share what my colleagues and I have learned during nearly 20 years focusing on this topic.

Connection Culture provides a new way of thinking about leadership and organizational culture. In the pages ahead, you will learn about this new approach and discover how to tap into the power of human connection.

Making It Personal

✓ Reflect on a time when you were energized by your work. What factors were present that contributed to your energy?

✓ Reflect on a time when your work felt draining. What factors were present that contributed to your fatigue or your feelings of being burned out?

✓ How would you describe the current culture you're in? Does it draw you in and connect you with your colleagues and the organization, or does it push you away and leave you feeling disconnected? Have changes occurred since the COVID-19 pandemic began that have affected your energy?

2

Three Cultures You Need to Know: Connection, Control, and Indifference

What type of culture are you in right now? I believe you can decode a culture by looking at the predominant attitudes, uses of language, and behaviors. As we explore what it takes to establish and strengthen connection cultures, it is instructive to understand how cultures differ in ways that affect the health and performance of individuals and organizations.

There are primarily three types of relational cultures: cultures of control, cultures of indifference, and cultures of connection. The first two have the effect of disconnecting people and organizations. Let's start with those.

Cultures of Control

In cultures of control, people with power, influence, and status rule over others. A culture of control breeds an environment in which people fear making mistakes and taking risks. It is stifling—killing innovation because people are afraid to speak up. Employees may feel left out, micromanaged, unsafe, hyper-criticized, or helpless.

Cultures of control tend to exhibit a number of common attributes. I've observed that this type of culture is often hierarchical and formal in nature. An inner circle develops comprised of favored individuals who have the most power, influence, and status, and receive the most recognition, responsibility, and compensation. This favored group makes the most important decisions while rarely sharing information with, seeking, or considering the opinions of others outside the inner circle. Individuals in the inner circle may expect those outside it to obey their commands without understanding or questioning their decisions. Questioning is viewed as disloyal and, if continued, may be punished by coercion, degradation, intimidation, and isolation through gradual marginalization (such as not being invited to attend meetings, being ignored in meetings, getting passed up for promotions, or being moved into less important roles with lower power, control, influence, and status). Eventually, most marginalized individuals leave on their own or are forced out.

Individuals outside the inner circle who appease the inner circle are likely to be rewarded over time with greater recognition, more responsibility, promotions, and higher compensation. Like those in the inner circle, they may develop an attitude of superiority, hubris, and a false sense of infallibility. Some individuals in this group are eventually invited to join the inner circle.

Most individuals on the outside go along with the decisions of the inner circle, yet they are not enthusiastic, energized, or engaged. They may be able to give their best efforts for a short period of time but because they are not inspired or energized they are not able to perform at the top of their game for a sustained period of time.

Those outside the inner circle suffer from a lack of autonomy and input that may lead them to develop what Martin Seligman has described as "learned helplessness" (and, I would add, hopelessness). They come to believe that they don't have the power or authority to make a difference, so they adopt a passive survivor mentality and simply do what is necessary to keep their job (and paycheck). Some will secretly sabotage organizational efforts as a means to exact revenge on a system they view as unfair.

Sometimes cultures of control are led by overly critical perfectionists who have trouble giving others autonomy or seeing others' perspectives. This type of leader may be so hyper-critical that people feel beaten down, and negativism pervades the workplace. In other instances, the leader of a culture of control may have a strong desire for power, control, status, or money that drives them to extreme measures to achieve those ends.

Two thought leaders who influenced my thinking on cultures of control are Art Kleiner and his book *Who Really Matters: The Core Group Theory of Power, Privilege, and Success* and Edgar Schein's ideas about coercion in organizations.

Cultures of Indifference

Cultures of indifference are predominant today. In this type of culture, people are so busy with tasks that they fail to invest the time necessary to develop healthy, supportive relationships. I have also observed that some leaders don't see value in the relational nature of work. Whether they voice it or not, their attitude is "You are being paid to do a job. I don't care how you feel or if you have friends here. All I care about is your work." People in cultures of indifference often come to feel like they are thought of and treated as mere means to an end rather than as human beings who are valuable in and of themselves. They may feel like a cog in a machine, unimportant, underappreciated, uncertain, or invisible. Many people struggle with a lack of connection.

Leaders may have good intentions but suffer from blind spots. For instance, they may be insecure and the anxiety they experience compels them to want to perform a large number of tasks to prove themselves. This leads to a lack of organizational focus and workloads for those under them that are unreasonable and may cause people to feel overwhelmed. Instead of having the confidence to focus on a reasonable number of priorities and implement them with excellence, leaders of cultures of indifference expect people to do too much and, as a result, actions are executed in a mediocre way that produces lackluster results.

Cultures that disconnect people also can reflect a hybrid of the attributes of a culture of control and culture of indifference. A distinguishing feature of an unhealthy culture is a sole focus on task excellence. Leaders may openly dismiss the need for relationship excellence. Others may give it lip service and occasional attention or see its value without knowing how to bring it about. In disconnecting people rather than drawing them together, these cultures sabotage individual and organizational performance. Feeling consistently unsupported, left out, or lonely takes a toll. Without the psychological resources to cope with the normal stress of modern organizational life, employees may develop unhealthy attitudes and behaviors, many of which are addictive and destructive.

Cultures of Connection

To achieve sustainable superior performance, every member of an organization needs to intentionally develop both task excellence and relationship excellence. A connection culture produces task and relationship excellence.

In a connection culture, people care about others and care about their work because it benefits other human beings. They invest the time to develop healthy relationships and reach out to help others in need, rather than being indifferent to them. They embrace that every individual has something to bring to the table based on their experiences and background, and that a diverse marketplace of ideas and perspectives is a strength. This bond of connection helps overcome the differences that historically divided people, creating a sense of community and unity that is inclusive and energized, and spurs productivity and innovation.

A Major Opportunity for You

Understanding the factors that create a connection culture and enable us to thrive is extremely important. According to the Gallup organization's employee engagement research, just 33 percent of employees in the United States are engaged and a mere 15 percent globally are engaged (Clifton and Harter 2019). The rest are either not enthusiastic and energized at work or they are at times actively working against their organization's interests. Disengaged people show up for the paycheck but don't perform anywhere near what they are capable of if they were in a culture that energized and engaged them.

This lack of employee engagement is a problem that has serious ramifications. The business world is becoming a much more global and competitive place, with standards going up all the time. Organizations with a large percentage of disconnected and disengaged employees may not survive. Individuals who fall behind thanks to poor work cultures will also be in trouble. Unable to work up to their potential, their organizations may peg them as mediocre or poor performers and thus limit their opportunities for advancement. Potential future employers also may not recognize that they are capable of much more.

This may sound bleak but you should consider it a major opportunity. Reading this book will help you gain the knowledge to become part of the turnaround story and create cultures that help people thrive, whether you are a leader in a formal position of management or authority, or if you informally lead others through your influence and desire for change. It will give you the tools to become more intentional about putting yourself in a healthy culture;

creating a culture to boost employee engagement, productivity, innovation, and performance; and implementing actions that increase and sustain the health of the culture you work in.

Although *Connection Culture* is focused on organizations and the workplace, it also applies to the culture in your family, volunteer group, and community. For many individuals today, home and work environments have blended with the increase in remote work following the COVID-19 pandemic, so having a connection culture in their home will have a positive impact on their work.

The Competitive Advantage of Connection

One of the most powerful and least understood aspects of successful organizations is how employees' feelings of connection, community, and unity provide a competitive advantage. Employees in an organization with a high degree of connection are more engaged, more productive in their jobs, and less likely to leave for a competitor. They are also more trusting and cooperative; they are more willing to share information with their colleagues and therefore help them make well-informed decisions.

Connection in the workplace is an emotional bond that promotes trust, cooperation, and esprit de corps among people. It is based on shared identity, empathy, and understanding that moves individuals toward group-centered membership. Without that sense of connection, employees will never reach their potential as individuals. And if employees don't reach their potential, the organization won't either. Connection is what transforms a dog-eat-dog environment into a sled dog team that pulls together.

When interacting with people, we generally find a connection with some but not with others—"we really connected" and "we just didn't click" are common phrases in our daily conversations. Connection describes something intangible that we sense in relationships. When it is present, we feel energy, empathy, and affirmation, and are more open; when it is absent, we experience neutral or even negative feelings.

Although we know what it's like to feel connected on a personal level, few understand the effect connection has on us, our families and friends, and our co-workers and the organizations we work in.

Epiphany

I left Wall Street in May 2002 and spent the next several years researching and writing *Fired Up or Burned Out: How to Reignite Your Team's Passion, Creativity, and Productivity*, which introduced the concept and practices of a connection culture. In addition to researching organizational behavior, psychology, sociology, history, political science, and systems theory, I did a great deal of reflecting about my own life experiences. To my surprise, some of the things I learned about the power of connection came from unexpected places.

In late 2002, my wife, Katie, was diagnosed with breast cancer. During her treatments, we were comforted by the kindness and compassion of healthcare workers at Yale New Haven Health's Greenwich Hospital, some of whom were cancer survivors themselves. The connection we felt with them boosted our spirits.

Twelve months later, tests indicated that Katie might have ovarian cancer. January 7, 2004, was one of the most sobering days of my life—after her three-hour surgery, we found out that it was ovarian cancer and that it had spread. I still remember the surgeon telling me that he was sorry. That night I took our daughters (Sarah, 12, and Elizabeth, 10) and Katie's mom to visit her in the ICU. Seeing her so weak and pale scared the girls. Sarah backed up against a wall and began to faint. After an ICU nurse helped us revive her, we knew it was time to head home. As we walked through the deserted hospital lobby, Elizabeth began to sob. Sarah and I wrapped our arms around Elizabeth until she calmed down. Later that night, looking at our daughters who had fallen asleep on Katie's pillow, I felt alone and afraid of what the future might hold for our family.

After six chemotherapy treatments and a short break, Katie started a second regimen of chemotherapy, this time at Memorial Sloan Kettering Cancer Center in New York City. On our first visit, as we got within sight of the 53rd Street entrance in midtown Manhattan, a larger-than-life friendly doorman named Nick Medley locked eyes with Katie and smiled at her. This was the first of many happy surprises—few make eye contact with a passerby in New York City, let alone smile! I realized that Nick was probably a seasoned wig-spotter and, recognizing that Katie was a cancer patient, was intentionally reaching out to connect with her. In the lobby, the receptionist called everyone "honey" (again, very unlike Manhattan). Each person we encountered was friendly. Katie's oncologist, Dr. Martee Hensley, spent an hour educating us about treatment options and answering our long list of questions. Her warmth and optimistic attitude gave us hope.

By the end of the visit, I had two reactions. First, I had done the research and knew this was one of the best teams in the world to treat ovarian cancer—that was my rational reaction. Second, I believed that they cared. Even though I knew Katie's chance of survival was less than 10 percent, I was hopeful that these amazing people would get her through the difficult season ahead.

One day while Katie was undergoing treatment, I stumbled upon a meeting in a lounge where employees who worked at that location were discussing the results of an employee survey. Nick was there, and I overheard him say that he loved working at the center because he loved his colleagues, the patients, and their families—and most of all he loved the cause, which is to provide "the best cancer care, anywhere." (This got my attention. "Love" was not a word I was used to hearing in the workplace.) It was apparent that Nick's co-workers also felt a connection with one another, their patients, and their patients' families. During the time we spent at Sloan Kettering, it struck me how much more joy and esprit de corps I felt in a cancer treatment center than I experienced while working on Wall Street. I wasn't at all surprised when I saw a segment about Nick on ABC's *World News Tonight*—that this cancer survivor gave hundreds of hugs a day to patients and their families.

Although many factors are involved, the human connection that provides emotional support is one factor research has found to be associated with positive patient outcomes (Bloom et al. 2001; Devine et al. 2003; Lekander et al. 1996; Levy et al. 1990). According to the American Cancer Society, one of the worst things for cancer patients is to feel alone. Katie and I rarely felt alone. When people stopped by to visit us, which happened regularly, it wasn't a somber occasion—we talked, laughed, and enjoyed one another's company. Christian, Jewish, and Muslim friends told us they were praying for Katie and our family, and an atheist friend said he was sending positive thoughts our way. I'm convinced that the connections we felt with healthcare workers, friends, and family helped Katie go into remission and protected our family's spirits.

We know that connection is just one piece of the puzzle when it comes to combating illness. We had a friend with an abundance of connection in her life who valiantly battled cancer for a number of years before passing away. She inspired countless people with her determination and optimism and even joy in the midst of her struggle. Regardless of the medical outcome, there's no denying the comfort and strength connection can provide to those who suffer and to their caregivers.

Having had such a good experience at Memorial Sloan Kettering Cancer Center, we enthusiastically recommended it to a friend of ours who was diagnosed with a different type of cancer. The physicians in that specialty were located in a different building, and surprisingly, her experience was completely at odds with ours. After the initial consultation, she felt alone and unwelcome and decided to seek treatment elsewhere.

Reflecting on these experiences made me realize three things about connection:

- It is a powerful force that creates a positive emotional bond between people.
- It contributes to bringing out the best in people and energizes them, making them more trusting and more resilient to face life's inevitable difficulties.
- It can vary dramatically across teams, units, and even locations of organizations, depending upon local culture and leadership.

As an aside, in 2014, Katie was diagnosed with a new episode of breast cancer that was different from the one in 2002. When we returned to Memorial Sloan Kettering Cancer Center, we found that the connection was just as strong as ever. Katie's surgeon, Dr. Alexandra Heerdt, her oncologist, Dr. Tiffany Traina, and their teams were upbeat and optimistic. On the day of Katie's surgery, we arrived at the hospital at 7 a.m. and found Dr. Heerdt waiting for us in the reception area. She gave Katie a big hug and asked if we had any questions. After the surgery, Dr. Heerdt told me that she had removed the tumor and it appeared that it hadn't spread (which was later confirmed by lab results). When we met with Dr. Traina later to discuss adjuvant treatment options, she was personable and compassionate. We were optimistic Katie would overcome this cancer too. And she did. In the fall of 2019, we celebrated Katie's fifteenth year of being free from ovarian cancer and her fifth year of once again being free from breast cancer.

Backed by Science

As I continued my research for writing *Fired Up or Burned Out*, it was exciting to see hard evidence corroborate what I was seeing anecdotally. Neuroscientists and endocrinologists have discovered that human connection:

- reduces the levels of the stress hormones epinephrine, norepinephrine, and cortisol in the blood so we are more likely to engage the cortex region of the brain where we make rational decisions
- triggers the release of the enzyme telomerase, which heals damage to the telomeres on the tips of our chromosomes caused by stress
- increases the neurotransmitter dopamine, which enhances attention and pleasure
- increases serotonin, which reduces fear and worry
- increases the levels of oxytocin or vasopressin, which makes us more trusting of others (Hallowell 1999a; Sapolsky 2008).

Other research establishes that connection improves wellness, well-being, and performance throughout our lifetime, indicating that we are biochemically hardwired for connection. It enhances the quality and length of our lives. Conversely, disconnection (social isolation or exclusion) brings about dysfunction and depression.

This is also supported by the observations of psychiatrists. For example, Edward Hallowell, a practicing psychiatrist and former instructor of psychiatry at Harvard Medical School, has written that most of the business executives he encounters in his practice are deprived of connection. They report loneliness, isolation, confusion, distrust, disrespect, and dissatisfaction, so Hallowell helps them identify ways to increase connection in their lives (Hallowell 1999b).

Human Beings, Not Machines

Why is connection so powerful? Because humans are not machines—we have emotions, hopes and dreams, and a conscience.

Humans also have universal needs that must be met to thrive. It's important to understand that these are needs, not just wants (or desires). The work context has seven specific needs: respect, recognition, belonging, autonomy, personal growth, meaning, and progress. This list is derived from personal research as well as research and insights from A.H. Maslow on the hierarchy of needs and need deficits, Mihaly Csikszentmihalyi on flow and optimal experience, Richard M. Ryan and Edward L. Deci on autonomy, Viktor E. Frankl on meaning, and Teresa Amabile and Steven Kramer on progress. The resulting sense of connection from having these needs met makes us feel connected to our work, the people we work with, and the organization we work for.

The first three needs (respect, recognition, and belonging) are relational needs. When these needs are met, we feel connected to the people we work with. The next two (autonomy and personal growth) are task mastery needs, which affect how connected we feel to the work we are doing. The sixth need, meaning, is an existential need and it is linked to the seventh need, progress.

Respect

When we first join a group, we expect people to be courteous and considerate. If they are patronizing, condescending, or passive-aggressive, it makes us feel threatened and keeps us from thriving.

Recognition

As we spend more time with the group, we expect people to recognize and voice our task strengths ("you're a great manager") or character strengths ("you persevere to overcome obstacles"). It's almost as if we have a recognition battery that periodically needs to be recharged—except that the outlet is on our back, where we can't reach, so we have to rely on those around us to charge it for us. If it's not charged, we feel threatened and emotionally and physically drained.

Belonging

As additional time passes, we expect to develop a sense of belonging to the group, and that the group has our back. This makes us more resilient to cope with life's inevitable difficulties. And don't worry, everyone has them—sickness, death, job loss, divorce, and depression, for example, are part of life. The people in our group help us through hard times because they care. (And they also tell us when we have food on our chin or are doing something unwise.) They care enough to tell us what we need to hear and are there for us when we need them.

Autonomy

We need the freedom to do our work. Being micromanaged or slowed down by red tape, bureaucracy, or control-obsessed personalities prevents us from thriving.

Personal Growth

When we are engaged in a task that is a good fit with our strengths and provides the right degree of challenge, we experience a state that psychologists describe as flow. It is like being in a time warp—time flies by when we are immersed in a task. Unchallenged, we feel bored. Over-challenged, we feel stressed out. The optimal degree of challenge invigorates us.

Meaning

When we are engaged in work and feel connected to it because it is important to us in some way, we are energized and put additional effort into it. When our work has meaning, we feel a sense of significance.

Progress

Finally, when we see progress and positive results in work that is meaningful to us, it encourages and energizes us to continue our efforts.

Connection Is Critical to Organizations

It follows that the effect of connection on individual performance will have an influence on an organizational level. There is an extensive amount of research showing that connection provides a competitive advantage, which we'll review in greater detail in chapter 5. For now, consider this:

- Compared to business units with engagement and connection scores in the bottom 25 percent, the top 25 percent's median averages were:
  - 20 percent higher sales
  - 17 percent higher productivity
  - 21 percent higher profitability
  - 40 percent fewer quality defects
  - 70 percent fewer employee safety incidents
  - 41 percent lower absenteeism
  - 10 percent higher customer metrics (Gallup 2017).

- Employees who feel engaged and connected are:
  - 20 percent more productive than the average employee
  - 87 percent less likely to leave the organization (CLC 2004).

Fostering connection in the workplace is a win-win for individuals and for organizations. Given the evidence, it is irrational not to be intentional about connection because it is the key to help you thrive personally and professionally. It affects the health of your family, workplace, volunteer organizations, community, and nation. You cannot thrive for long without it.

The following chapters demonstrate how you can bring out connection in the workplace by creating a connection culture—a culture with the necessary elements to meet our human needs.

Making It Personal

✓ Describe a time when you truly connected with another person or a group. How did that make you feel?

✓ Describe a time when you were being treated as a means to an end. How did that make you feel?

✓ Is your current work environment an example of a culture of control, a culture of indifference, or a connection culture? Why?

✓ Which of the seven universal human needs necessary to thrive at work are being met in your workplace? Which are not being sufficiently met?

✓ What steps can you take to help meet the seven universal needs for others in your workplace? Commit to taking two actions in the next week to meet others' needs (for example, affirm a colleague for a job well done).

3

The Vision + Value + Voice Model

People occasionally ask about the name of the first company we started to help leaders improve organizational cultures, E Pluribus Partners. It is a nod to "E pluribus unum," the original motto of the United States, which means "out of many, one" in Latin. We chose this unusual-looking and tricky to pronounce phrase because it reflects how connection enables the best of what the many bring for the benefit of the collective one.

It's interesting to note how other languages capture a similar notion. The French phrase esprit de corps, for example, literally means "the spirit of the body." In certain countries in Africa, *ubuntu* refers to one's connection to the community. At one of our seminars, a Japanese woman taught us that the Japanese call connection *ittaikan*, which means "to feel as one body of people." Connection is a universal phenomenon.

As I shared in the previous chapter, in our work with organizations, we define connection in the workplace as a bond among people based on shared identity, empathy, and understanding that moves individuals toward group-centered membership. Let's unpack these concepts.

Identity is how people think of themselves—it's their story or narrative, including their values, reputation, and mission, if they have one. When people share an identity that inspires them and makes them feel proud, it creates a sense of connection, community, and unity among the members of the group.

Shared empathy is increased when people get to know and care for one another. Valuing people in and of themselves, rather than as a means to an end, is key. Emotions are contagious, so as empathy increases people become more sensitive to the feelings of others, and as a result become more considerate and compassionate (Hatfield et al. 1994).

Shared understanding arises when members of a group are in the know, so to speak. They are informed on matters important to them, and their opinions and ideas are sought and considered. In other words, when there is an abundance of conversation and communication within a group, it produces a high degree of knowledge flow that results in shared understanding.

One of our goals early on was to come up with a model that would help leaders at any level of an organization cultivate a healthy workplace culture. We knew it had to be simple, memorable, and actionable. People could remember the formula of Task Excellence + Relationship Excellence = Sustainable Superior Performance, but when it came to the Relationship Excellence piece, the terms shared identity, shared empathy, and shared understanding weren't sticking in the minds of some of our clients. To address that, our colleague Carolyn Dewing-Hommes distilled it down to three Vs that represent the same ideas for the primary elements of a connection culture. Hereafter we will refer to shared identity, empathy, and understanding as vision, value, and voice, respectively.

Assessing the Health of Your Work Culture

When we first began researching employee engagement and organizational effectiveness, we interviewed individuals and asked them to consider their own work (or volunteer) experiences in answering the following:

> Think of a time when you felt fired up at work. Now list the elements in the work culture that made you feel that way. After you've completed your list, consider a time when you felt like you were burning out. Write down the elements in the culture that made you feel that way.

More often than not, individuals described an emotional reaction (how they felt). The following are typical responses, along with commentary explaining the rationale for categorizing them under vision, value, voice, or task excellence and results. As you read through the lists, you might want to put a check mark next to statements that resonate with you in the context of your current job.

Vision

The positive responses in the table below reflect a sense of shared experience and identity. People felt connected to their work because of the group's focused effort, and their individual contribution made a meaningful difference. In the most powerful connecting experiences, the work improved the lives of others. A sense of shared identity develops among group members as their attitudes, language, and behaviors communicate the importance of the work, how the work is done in a way that reflects shared values, and how the work is producing positive results.

Positive	Negative
• "Creating something new or doing something bigger than ourselves."	• "Our work had no purpose."
• "We created something of lasting value."	• "Hard to see value of work."
• "We had a clear strategy and direction with a common mission and goals."	• "There were too many priorities that were constantly changing."
• "Having a shared vision about how we could succeed."	• "There were unrealistic goals and expectations."
• "I could make a difference in my role."	• "There was a lack of focus and goals were not aligned."
• "We had values I cared about and that we lived up to (not just window dressing)."	• "Feeling uncertain about the organization's future."
• "I felt proud to tell my family and friends that I worked at this organization."	• "We weren't told where our team was going, why it was important, how we were going to get there, and what our individual roles were."

Value

The positive responses show that people feel valued as human beings, rather than being treated as a means to an end. They had supervisors and leaders who cared about them, took time to get to know them, and helped them get into the right roles so they could continue to learn and grow. These leaders encouraged people when they did good work, gave them autonomy, and kept them challenged but didn't chronically overload them with so much work that they had no work-life balance. The people they worked with valued them too. A sense of shared empathy develops among group members as their attitudes, language, and behaviors communicate that they are valued as individuals and not merely for their work.

Positive	Negative
• "There was mutual respect and leaders cared about people first."	• "There was a lack of recognition."
• "Leaders did the right thing . . . they were ethical."	• "We were overworked and had little work-life balance."
• "We had autonomy and were trusted and empowered to make decisions."	• "I was micromanaged."
• "My role fit my interest and strengths."	• "The work was repetitive. It was not challenging enough."
• "My supervisor cared about me as a person and helped me learn, develop, and grow."	• "There was no clear career progress."
• "We had fun."	• "No team support."

Voice

The positive responses reflect people who believed that they were kept informed about important matters and had a voice—their opinions and ideas were sought and considered. They also appreciated the openness of their culture and the open-mindedness of leaders. A sense of shared understanding develops among group members as their attitudes, language, and behaviors increase communication and bring greater clarity to issues that are important to individual members.

Positive	Negative
• "It was safe to speak, to disagree, to try new things, and to be myself."	• "We were kept in the dark; there was a lack of communication."
• "My opinion counted."	• "I was expected to follow orders; my opinion wasn't considered and didn't matter."
• "It was a creative and innovative work environment."	• "People competed rather than collaborated with one another."
• "There were no hidden agendas."	
• "We were kept in the loop."	• "Lack of open-mindedness."
• "People were open and spoke the truth."	• "Feedback was infrequent. Poor communication."
	• "Not being listened to."

Task Excellence and Results

The positive responses reflect a passion for excellence. When people worked with competent colleagues, their work was held to high standards and they produced positive results. This contributed to the sense of connection among employees.

Positive	Negative
• "We could see that we were making progress in our work."	• "There was no sense of accomplishment."
• "Our work was done with excellence. We had high standards."	• "We were not stretching ourselves."
• "We delivered positive results."	• "People I worked with didn't care."
• "We hired talented people."	• "Uncommitted management."
• "Completing tasks, getting stuff done."	• "I didn't have the resources and training I needed to do my work well."
• "Celebrating milestones."	• "My supervisor wouldn't deal with obstacles that prevented me from doing my work well."
	• "Excessive process, red tape, bureaucracy, and politics that impede progress."

When vision, value, and voice are all present in an organization, it creates a connection culture. Let's dive deeper into what each of these elements looks like in practice.

Vision + Value + Voice

The first element of a connection culture is vision. It exists in a culture when everyone is motivated by the mission, united by the values, and proud of the reputation. When people share a purpose or set of beliefs, it unites and motivates them. At Memorial Sloan Kettering Cancer Center, they are united and motivated by the aspiration stated in their tagline, "The Best Cancer Care, Anywhere," and the organization's reputation as one of the leading cancer centers in the world.

The following is one of my favorite examples of a brilliant leader's desire to instill vision in a company. During World War II, U.S. president Franklin D. Roosevelt traveled to Seattle, Washington, to meet with 18,000 aircraft workers at Boeing Corporation. He brought along Hewitt Wheless, a young airplane pilot from Texas who had escaped death thanks to the resilience of the bullet-riddled B-17 plane he flew out of harm's way. His plane had been built at that very Boeing plant. Seeing and hearing that young pilot thank them for saving his life connected the aircraft workers to a common cause. It transformed those welders and riveters into freedom fighters. From 1941 until 1945 American aircraft companies out-produced the Nazis three to one, building nearly 300,000 airplanes (Kearns Goodwin 1994).

Vision is more than identifying and articulating a mission. It also includes understanding how an organization goes about accomplishing its mission. In other words, vision encompasses the organization's values or beliefs about what is right and, by implication, what isn't right in how it conducts its business. An organization's mission and values, including how it lives up to them or doesn't, produces a reputation that employees are proud of, indifferent to, or embarrassed by. When employees are proud of their organization's reputation, they feel more connected.

Vision + Value + Voice

The second element of a connection culture is value. It means that people are truly valued as individuals, not merely for what they produce. Value exists in a culture when everyone understands the needs of people, appreciates their positive unique contributions, and helps them achieve their potential.

In leading the turnaround of Dun and Bradstreet, Allan Loren established a rule that no meeting would be scheduled on Mondays or Fridays if it required people to travel over the weekend (Hanessian and Sierra 2005). He cared for people enough to protect their personal time. Loren also wanted to see people grow, so he implemented a program that matched everyone in the organization with a mentor who would provide continuous performance feedback. Mentors were selected based on their strengths in the areas that a particular employee wanted to improve upon.

Head of the Tata Group until he retired in 2012, Ratan Tata's response to the November 26, 2008, terrorist attack on the Tata-owned Taj Mahal Palace and Tower Hotel in Mumbai, India, showed how much he valued employees. Dependents of the 80 employees who were affected were flown to Mumbai and housed for three weeks. Tata personally visited all their families and attended the funerals of those who died. He also provided counseling for his employees and their families and forgave any outstanding loans to the affected employees. In addition, he established a trust fund so that dependents of those who died would continue to receive the deceased person's salary for life, the education of their children and dependents would be paid for, and the families would receive healthcare for the remainder of their lives.

Founded in 1877 and based in Mumbai, the Tata Group is one of the most respected organizations in the world. The "Tata family" comprises more than

700,000 people working in more than 100 countries across six continents. It conducts business the "Tata Way," which prioritizes people and social responsibility over profit maximization. Tata was one of the first businesses to institute an eight-hour workday and distributes so much of its profit to philanthropic causes that some critics have questioned whether this generosity is wise. In answer to this criticism, Ratan Tata responded, "I would like to think this is the best part of what Tata stands for. . . . We really do care" (Rajgopaul 2010; Tata 2019; Tata Group 2014).

Vision + Value + **Voice**

The third element of a connection culture is voice. It exists when everyone seeks the ideas and opinions of others, shares opinions honestly, and safeguards relational connections. In a culture in which voice exists, decision makers have the humility to know that they don't have a monopoly on good ideas, and they need to seek and consider the opinions and ideas of others in order to make the best decisions. When people's ideas and opinions are sought and considered, it helps meet the human needs for respect, recognition, and belonging. Being in the loop makes people feel connected to their colleagues, whereas being out of the loop does the opposite.

Over the course of her remarkable 34-year career at Xerox, Anne Mulcahy's leadership roles were varied, giving her a broad understanding of the organization and an ever-expanding network of relationships with colleagues. When she was appointed CEO of Xerox Corporation in 2001, the company was nearly broke and the company's lawyers and financial advisers told her to file for bankruptcy protection. She refused. Instead, she hit the road to meet with Xerox employees and customers, logging 100,000 miles of travel her first year. She was open and told them what she thought had to be done, even telling Wall Street analysts that the Xerox business model was unsustainable, which precipitated a 26 percent drop in the value of Xerox stock the following day.

Mulcahy shared the good, the bad, and the ugly with employees, solicited their ideas and opinions, and implemented the best ones. During the next decade, Mulcahy and her colleagues brought Xerox back to life. One Xerox board member described it as a miracle. When she retired in 2010 as Chairman and CEO, the first woman in the company's history to hold either role, Xerox had been transformed into an innovative digital technology and services enterprise. Years later, I spoke with Anne about connection culture and her time at Xerox. She shared that, for her, voice is about "having an active, participative role where people see themselves in the picture and they know what to do, they know how to be part of the solution and not part of the problem. That interactive relationship of dialoguing with . . . people is a huge part of people feeling engaged and therefore being able to have impact" (Mulcahy 2012).

Connection Character

As part of gathering and reviewing the research for *Fired Up or Burned Out*, I studied the field of positive psychology. Positive psychologists reviewed religious and philosophical systems and identified six virtues that have 24 underlying character strengths (descriptions can be found in appendix I). Positive psychologists believe that these character strengths improve mental and physical health and favor the survival of civilizations.

It was an aha moment for me when I saw a clear link between these character strengths and the elements of a connection culture. These character strengths also favor the survival of organizations. For example, when individuals possess bravery, creativity, curiosity, honesty, humility, judgment, love of learning, perspective, and prudence, the connection culture element of voice is present in a culture. The Character > Connection > Thrive Chain (Figure 3-1) shows how everything fits together.

As an aside, the 24 character strengths are found in belief systems that have been sustained for long periods of time, including Christianity, Judaism, Islam, Taoism, Buddhism, and Humanism. Unfortunately, most belief systems have renegade branches that promote hate rather than live out the character strengths. These hate groups often masquerade as a major belief system in name but certainly not in deed. For example, Adolf Hitler's Nazi movement promoted "Positive Christianity." However, his message and actions were utterly at odds with Jesus's teaching to love, serve others, and be humble. Hate groups may thrive for a time, but eventually collapse for a lack of human value (the very heart of a connection culture).

FIGURE 3-1. THE CHARACTER > CONNECTION > THRIVE CHAIN

24 Character Strengths	Create the Connection Culture	That Meets Universal Needs	That Help People and Organizations Thrive	
			Individuals Thrive	Organizations Thrive
Appreciation of Beauty and Excellence, Hope, Leadership, Perseverance, Self-Regulation, Spirituality, Zest	Vision	Respect Recognition Belonging Autonomy	Wellness Well-Being Trust Cooperation	Employee Engagement Strategic Alignment Better Decisions
Fairness, Forgiveness, Gratitude, Humor, Kindness, Love, Social Intelligence, Teamwork	Value	Personal Growth Meaning Progress	Empathy Enthusiasm Optimism Energy Creativity	Innovation Agility and Adaptability Productivity Profitability Customer Satisfaction
Bravery, Creativity, Curiosity, Honesty, Humility, Judgment, Love of Learning, Perspective, Prudence	Voice		Superior Problem Solving	Employee Retention Safety

Many individuals have observed the importance of character to human flourishing. David McCullough (1991), the Pulitzer Prize–winning author and historian, wrote: "While there are indeed great, often unfathomable forces in history before which even the most exceptional of individuals seem insignificant, the wonder is how often events turn upon a single personality, or the quality we call character." In one of his most memorable speeches, the Reverend Martin Luther King Jr. shared that he dreamed of a day when his four young children would "live in a nation where they will not be judged by the color of their skin but by the content of their character."

The late Stephen Covey, author of *The 7 Habits of Highly Effective People: Powerful Lessons in Personal Change*, held up Frances Hesselbein as an extraordinary leader, calling her "a model for living one's values" (Diversity

Woman 2014). The former CEO of the Girl Scouts of the USA, Hesselbein defined leadership as "a matter of how to be, not how to do." She underscored this by explaining, "We spend most of our lives learning how to do and teaching other people how to do, yet it is the quality and character of the leader that determines the performance, the results" (Hesselbein 2012).

John Wooden, the legendary coach of the UCLA men's basketball team, frequently taught his players that "ability may get you to the top, but only character will keep you there" (Wooden 1997). His observation that both ability and character are necessary to perform at the top of your game is similar to the connection culture model: task excellence + relationship excellence (connection) = sustainable superior performance. When coaching, Wooden used a system called the "Pyramid of Success," which included the building blocks of industriousness, enthusiasm, friendship, loyalty, cooperation, self-control, alertness, initiative, intentness, condition, skill, and team spirit. He taught his players that believing and behaving in a way that is consistent with these values produced poise and confidence that resulted in competitive greatness (that is, the desire to continuously challenge oneself in life). Patience and faith make up the mortar that holds the blocks together. Once the pyramid was built, it meant that the player met Wooden's standards, and he earned the right to be called a member of the UCLA basketball team.

Organizations also have character. They reflect the collective character of the people who work in them and especially the character of their leaders. An organization's annual report may state values such as integrity and honesty, but if the people who are part of the organization don't follow those values, they are either frauds or, more likely, blind to their own character issues. Great leaders are not only intentional about connecting, they are intentional about developing their own character and the character of the people they are responsible for leading.

The people who bring vision, value, and voice into a culture and make it happen are the enablers of the connection culture model. Prior to this second edition, we used the terms of committed members and servant leaders. To simplify matters, we've moved to calling them connected members and connected leaders. Connected members are committed to task excellence, promoting the connection culture, and living out character strengths and virtues. They may be senior managers, receptionists, salespeople, engineers, information technology experts, or customer service representatives. Connected leaders are those connected members who have the authority to coordinate task excellence, facilitate the connection culture, and model and mentor others in connection character.

Individuals can only become connected leaders after becoming connected members. In other words, there needs to be proof of a commitment to achieving task excellence and a connection culture, and of the requisite connection character, before being given the authority to lead. With leadership authority comes the responsibility for modeling connection character, as well as mentoring others. Connected leaders are serious about modeling and mentoring others because they were shaped by the individuals who modeled leadership and mentored them.

Connected members and connected leaders develop task excellence and relationship excellence that includes vision, value, and voice. As a result, people feel connected, are more productive and energetic, give their best efforts, align their efforts with organizational objectives, and fully communicate and cooperate. This leads the organization to achieve sustainable superior performance (Figure 3-2).

FIGURE 3-2. THE CONNECTION CULTURE

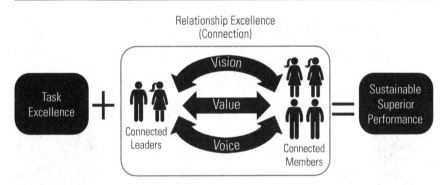

Much has been written about the culture of Southwest Airlines. It is the largest domestic U.S. airline and still has an enviable record of profit in an industry that Warren Buffett once joked hadn't made a cumulative profit since the Wright brothers' first flight at Kitty Hawk in 1903. Southwest Airlines prides itself on its culture of putting people first and treating passengers like family. Its leaders learned from experience that connection affects performance.

Southwest Airlines' culture services department has 30 full-time employees whose efforts help ignite employees' passion and pride for Southwest. Additionally, the company's culture committee encompasses more than 200 individuals from across the airline who are passionate about inspiring employees to own, strengthen, and promote Southwest's renowned culture. Committee members have the opportunity to connect with one another at an annual culture summit, influence change by sharing their insights on a variety of topics, and serve as culture advocates in their locations. Together, culture services employees and committee members work to foster an environment where employees feel appreciated. And in the spirit of appreciation, numerous awards, both at the local and corporate levels, are given to employees who've been recognized by their peers for living out the company's values. Southwest knows the value of a strong company culture and invests in their people and programs to ensure the unique culture continues to flourish (Crabtree 2019).

What happens without a connection culture? While task excellence may be present for a while, in cultures of control or indifference most managers and employees put up self-protective barriers that keep them from performing at the top of their game. The disconnection sabotages task excellence and the organization suffers too (Figure 3-3).

FIGURE 3-3. CULTURES OF CONTROL AND INDIFFERENCE

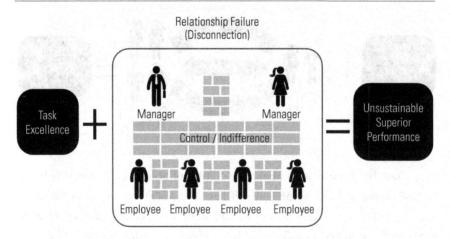

Leaders who foster cultures of control or cultures of indifference may succeed for a while, but their success is built on feet of clay that will inevitably crumble. History is filled with examples of this. Our heroes are the individuals who cultivate connection and bring vision, value, and voice to cultures they influence. Wherever you find great nations, companies, nonprofits, and sports teams, you will find these great individuals who cultivate cultures of connection.

Making It Personal

✓ Write a list of the elements in a culture that would fire you up, then write out a list of the elements in a culture that would burn you out. Look through each list to see if you can identify elements that fall under vision, value, and voice as well as task excellence and results.

✓ Read through the descriptions of the 24 character strengths in appendix I. Which character strengths are most important for your team to do its work well? Are there character strengths on the list that you believe your team needs to strengthen? Consider how you might strengthen those areas and start taking action.

Profiles in Connection

Consider the wind. We cannot see it, but we can see its effect on trees when the wind blows through them. Similarly, we see the effect of connection on individuals, teams, and organizations. When connection is present, people are more enthusiastic, cooperative, creative, and productive. When connection is absent, they lack these traits.

Once you begin to truly understand connection, you'll see it everywhere. When you examine success stories through the lens of the connection culture framework, you'll be inspired by what leaders are doing in other sectors. The stories featured here are about inspiring leaders from business, government, healthcare, higher education, sports, media and entertainment, and the social sectors.

Restoring Navy Pride

A leader in government and the military who intentionally developed a connection culture is Admiral Vernon Clark, the chief of naval operations (CNO) from 2000 until his retirement in 2005.

The CNO is the head of the U.S. Navy and the principal naval adviser to the U.S. president on the conduct of war. When Admiral Clark assumed the CNO role, the navy was not meeting its sailor retention goals, which is problematic when you consider the navy's sophisticated surveillance, navigation, and weapons systems, and the importance of maintaining the readiness of national defense. Concerned about how this would affect military preparedness, Clark made winning the war for talent his number 1 priority.

Admiral Clark increased vision by reminding sailors that the navy's mission is to take the war-fighting readiness of the United States to any corner of the world at a moment's notice. He said that it was time to build a modern navy that would be "strategically and operationally agile, technologically and organizationally innovative, networked at every level, highly joint [with the other branches of the military], and effectively integrated with allies" (Clark 2002).

Admiral Clark would tell sailors: What we do matters. What we do is hard work. We intentionally put ourselves in harm's way. We are away from our loved ones for months on end. We do it because it's important and we are people of service. We are committed to something larger than ourselves: the protection of America's interests around the world and democracy (U.S. Navy 2005). This made them feel proud and connected to him as their leader. Rear Admiral Frank Thorp, who served on Admiral Clark's personal staff, recounted an occasion when he spotted a sailor with tear-filled eyes after hearing Clark speak. Thorp approached the young man to see what was wrong. The sailor said he was going to ask his commanding officer to rip up the discharge papers he had recently submitted because for the first time a leader had told him why he should stay in the navy (Herdt et al. 2008–2010).

Admiral Clark strongly supported an increase in pay that was approved by the president and Congress. When navy budget officials proposed cuts related to training and developing people as part of the annual planning cycle, Clark wouldn't allow it. Instead, he increased the training budget. As part of what he called the revolution in training, Admiral Clark established the Naval Education and Training Command and required everyone in the navy to have a personal development plan. He changed the performance appraisal system to provide constructive feedback for everyone, and added the requirement to leaders' performance appraisals that they help sailors learn and grow. He valued personal growth and continuous improvement, saying, "If you are not growing, in my view, you are of little value to the institution. . . . if you are not growing, you're dead" (Clark 2003).

In the navy, enlisted sailors sometimes feel like second-class citizens compared to the officers. Admiral Clark made it one of his priorities to blur some of the lines between the officers and enlisted sailors while still maintaining the necessary decision-making chain of command. When he traveled to commands and bases around the world, Clark met with commanding officers, as well as the master chiefs, their enlisted counterparts. He intentionally reached out to the master chiefs because he valued them and what they could do for the sailors under their leadership. He told them: These young sailors under our command swear to support and defend the U.S. Constitution from all enemies, and we as leaders need to make promises in return. We need to give them the training and resources to enable them to fulfill their promise.

We need to give them an opportunity to prove what they can do (Herdt et al. 2008–2010).

Admiral Clark recognized the importance of the enlisted leaders because of his own experiences as a sailor. He often told a story of his first experience on a ship following officer candidate school.

> I didn't know the pointy end of the ship from the blunt end. It was scary, really. But, fortunately, there was a master chief there who took a liking to me, Master Chief Leedy. For some reason, I don't know what possessed him, but after I had been there about a week he came up to me, and put his arm around me, and he said, "Mr. Clark, I'm going to help make you into a fine officer." (Herdt et al. 2008–2010)

The advice and encouragement from Master Chief Leedy helped make Clark a better officer. He said that he, and the country, needed the master chiefs to mentor and encourage today's young sailors in the same way. They listened—Master Chief Petty Officer of the Navy Jim Herdt once said that master chiefs around the world had the general attitude that "Old Vern is counting on us and we can't let him down" (Herdt et al. 2008–2010). He made them feel valued, and when they reached out to help those under their command learn and grow, the sailors felt valued too.

Clark also worked to change the legacy systems that devalued sailors, such as the navy's job assignment process. Under Clark and a program he dubbed "the revolution in personnel distribution," the system was changed to a job-bidding approach, with incentive compensation for the jobs and locations that were least in demand. As a result, the percentage of sailors forced into positions or locations was reduced from 30 percent to around 1.5 percent.

In group meetings with leaders, Admiral Clark encouraged participants to speak up. His own approachable, conversational style set the tone for others to share their ideas and opinions. He asked everyone to "challenge every assumption," "be data driven," and "drill down" into the details. He challenged them to "have a sense of urgency to make the navy better every day" in order to deliver greater efficiencies and readiness for the dollars America invested in the navy (Herdt et al. 2008–2010).

Clark was more concerned about getting it right than being right himself. He had observed over the course of his career that people tended to tell the boss what they believed he wanted to hear rather than what they really thought. Clark wanted to minimize the risk that would happen so he encouraged "constructive friction." By recognizing and embracing that there will be honest disagreement because people have different perspectives that require talking through to arrive at the best answer, he made it safe for people to disagree and express views that were outside the consensus. As a result, Clark's leaders felt connected with him and the U.S. Navy, and they emulated his leadership style, which made the sailors under their command feel more connected.

Admiral Clark is quick to say that he's not perfect. Nonetheless, the navy achieved some impressive gains during his tenure as CNO, and many naval leaders have praised his leadership and positive influence. In a little more than a year after Clark became CNO, first term re-enlistment soared from less than 38 percent to 56.7 percent (Herdt et al. 2008–2010).

As the navy improved sailor retention and developed greater alignment with Admiral Clark's vision, it became faster and more responsive. Within a matter of hours following the terrorist attacks on September 11, 2001, aircraft carriers, Aegis destroyers, and cruisers were in position to protect America's shores. This was partially because naval leaders anticipated what had to be done and took action before they received orders. After the Pentagon was attacked, communications and the navy's decision-making process were quickly re-established, and planning for America's response began while the embers of the fire still smoldered a short distance away.

Making It Personal

✓ "Winning the war for talent" was Admiral Clark's number 1 priority when he took the helm as Chief of Naval Operations. What is your number 1 priority this year? How does it support your organization's overall vision? What steps in the areas of vision, value, and voice could you take that will aid in achieving the goal?

✓ Admiral Clark was upfront about the challenges inherent in being a sailor—it's hard work, they put themselves in harm's way, they are separated from their loved ones for stretches of time. He reminded sailors of the "why" behind the sacrifices they were making. Think of a time when you were asked to move outside of your comfort zone. Were the challenges or risks acknowledged by others, especially your supervisor? If not, what difference might it have made in your attitude to receive that acknowledgment?

✓ To increase voice and be sure that any opposing opinions would come up for consideration, Admiral Clark encouraged "constructive friction." If you were introducing this concept to a team, what ground rules would you put in place?

Connecting on and off the Court

Steph Curry, point guard for the NBA's Golden State Warriors, stands out in many respects. One commentator observed that Curry doesn't fit the stereotype—he's slight, has no killer instinct, isn't alpha—but that Curry is the best player in the world when it comes to ball handling, shooting, and leadership (Cowherd 2019). *Fortune* magazine declared Curry and Warriors' Head Coach Steve Kerr together among the 50 best leaders in the world (Ballard 2016).

Curry has been defying expectations throughout his life. As a high school player, the major colleges passed on recruiting him. Yet he has gone on to become a force in pro basketball, being named the NBA's Most Valuable Player twice, becoming a six-time NBA All Star, and acting as leader of a team that has won three out of the four NBA championships they've played in with Curry on the floor. He is arguably the best leader in professional basketball today.

At 5 foot 6 inches and a mere 125 pounds as a high school sophomore, Steph Curry was so small that he had to shoot the basketball from his waist. Eventually, with some physical growth and encouragement from his dad, he changed to a more conventional shooting style of releasing the ball over his head.

Adjusting his style was difficult. Curry's younger brother, Seth, remembers seeing him in their backyard taking shot after shot and crying from being so discouraged at his lack of progress. Still, he persevered and ended his junior year of high school averaging just under 20 points per game. The major colleges he'd hoped to attend said he was too small to make an impact. "I turned it into motivation and continued to work on my game even more," he said (Dunkyard 2016).

Curry, who grew up in Charlotte, North Carolina, received a basketball scholarship from Davidson College, a small liberal arts school of fewer than 2,000 students located less than a half hour's drive from his family's home. A Division 1 school in athletics, the Davidson Wildcats compete in the Atlantic 10 Conference, not in the ACC with Duke or University of North Carolina at Chapel Hill. Davidson men's basketball coach Bob McKillop had begun recruiting Curry when he was a freshman in high school. In Curry, McKillop saw what he described as "brilliance" (Dunkyard 2016). Curry said he responded to the confidence Coach McKillop expressed in him and McKillop's belief that Curry would have an immediate impact on the team. In his second game as a college player that freshman year, Curry lit up the court and scored 32 points in a nonconference game against the University of Michigan on the Wolverines' home court in Ann Arbor. When McKillop saw Steph's parents afterward, he predicted their son would go on to a successful career in the NBA. They weren't so sure. McKillop, it turned out, was right.

Curry had an outstanding college career. In his sophomore year, Davidson made it to the Elite Eight round of the NCAA tournament, beating Gonzaga, Georgetown, and Wisconsin before losing to Kansas, the team that went on to win the tournament. To put that accomplishment in perspective, it had been 39 years since Davidson had won a single game in an NCAA tournament. Of that year's March Madness, former Davidson teammate Jason Richards said, "People around the basketball world knew how good Steph was, but that put him on the map, because everyone watches the NCAA tournament. We became the darlings of that year, with Steph being our guy, our leader. He took the nation by storm and ran with it" (Lopresti 2018).

In his junior year, he led the nation in scoring. Following that year, he declared for the NBA draft. Once again, the critics said he was too small and not strong enough to make an impact. The Golden State Warriors thought otherwise and drafted him in the first round as the seventh overall pick in the 2009 NBA Draft.

In 2010, his first year with Golden State, Curry finished second in rookie of the year voting. The following two seasons, however, he missed many games from ankle problems that required two surgeries. After rehabbing at home, with the support and encouragement of his family, he came back in

2012, set a new NBA single season three-point record, and led the Warriors to the playoffs.

Steph Curry has benefited throughout his life from the connection of a loving and supportive family. His father, Dell, played in the NBA for 16 years. His mother, Sonya, was a college athlete at Virginia Tech, where she and Dell met. A tearful Curry thanked them in his acceptance speech after being named the NBA's Most Valuable Player in 2015. Specifically, he expressed his gratitude for his mom's spiritual leadership and discipline, and his father's example on and off the court. Curry is close to Seth, who is also a player in the NBA. Their sister, Sydel, played volleyball for Elon University and is married to NBA player Damion Lee, who joined the Golden State Warriors and became a teammate of Curry's in the 2018 season. In 2011, Curry married his wife, Ayesha, whom he had met in high school, and they now have three children.

As a player and leader on the Warriors, Curry uses his skills to connect in ways that lift the performance of his teammates. He's humble and doesn't need to be in the spotlight. He had no problem becoming the number 2 scorer when the superstar Kevin Durant joined the Warriors and was named NBA Finals MVP in 2017 and 2018 (Peter 2019). Durant says about Curry: "The stuff you hear about Steph—as far as sacrificing, being selfless, caring about his teammates, caring about other people—is real, it's not a fake, it's not a facade. . . . He really is like that" (Piotrekzprod 2017).

The players around Curry know that he looks out for them and makes sure they feel included, whether it's welcoming them when they are new to the team, passing the ball to them so they can take shots even when he could have taken the shot himself, or encouraging them. Quinn Cook said, "[Steph's] happy for you when you do well. He's always building you up if you're going through anything." Alonzo McKinnie observed, "If [Steph] sees us down, he's coming to uplift us. He cheers up guys and gets guys in that good spirit. . . . It shows his character and the type of guy he is on and off the court." Commenting on Curry's ability to come alongside teammates who may be at odds with each other, Klay Thompson says that he is "a very great voice of reason during times of turbulence." DeMarcus Cousins, who played for the Warriors from 2018 to 2019, stated "everything about [Steph] is A-plus." Damion Lee has said, "For any leader, it's about understanding what someone is going through and trying to help them and empathize as much as you can. [Steph] tries to build that and keep everyone together" (Medina 2019).

Curry's teammates and coaches praise him for engaging in individual and group conversations about how to make the team better. This includes helping individual players perform better or considering things the team can do together to improve their performance over the season. Coach Steve Kerr observes, "Steph leads with his example, his work ethic, his humility. The players all love him. They love playing with him. They appreciate him so much" (Peter 2019). *San Jose Mercury News* sportswriter Mark Medina wrote that Curry brings joy to the team, noting "[Steph] will take half-court shots at the end of practice. He will leap out of his seat when a teammate completes a highlight reel. He will say or do things that will make people laugh."

Looking back at the end of the 2018–2019 season, in which the Warriors lost in the NBA Finals to the Toronto Raptors, Curry shared in a *New York Times* article that the "regular season was the hardest one we've ever had in terms of keeping everything together. Not because of anything more than it's just mentally challenging to perform at this level every single night." Injuries aside, he noted that the playoffs were "as fun, if not more, than years past. Because one, we were challenged. Two, there was constant communication in the locker room like, 'this is what we live for'" (Deb 2019).

Making It Personal

✓ Have you worked on a team in which colleagues competed with one another rather than connected? How did that make you feel? What drove that behavior?

✓ In what ways does Steph Curry make his teammates better? What can you implement from Steph Curry's example that will help your colleagues perform their best?

✓ Is there one person on your team who gets the most attention? (It might be you!) What can that person do to foster connection?

Principled Pragmatist

Angela Merkel, Chancellor of Germany since 2005, is recognized as Europe's most powerful and longest-serving elected leader. Her ascent has been nothing short of remarkable; her longevity as chancellor has been surprising, given the many predictions of her demise. What has led her to be considered among the best leaders in the world?

Merkel grew up in East Germany. On paper, the German Democratic Republic, the official name of the new state created in 1949 after the end of World War II, was democratic, but in reality it was under oppressive Communist rule emanating from the Soviet Union. Her father, Horst Kasner, was a Lutheran minister who had been raised in Berlin and attended university and seminary in western Germany. He was passionate about preaching the Word of God—serving a cause greater than self—and it was this calling that led him to say yes in 1954 to taking the helm of a small Lutheran parish in the new state. At a time when hundreds of thousands of Germans were fleeing the east while they still could, and the number of ministers remaining in the Soviet-occupied zone was dropping, Pastor Kasner stepped forward. Angela Merkel was an infant at the time.

Her father's occupation made her family outsiders under a government that officially embraced atheism. Her mother, Herlind, whom she is reported to have been very close to, has been described as a woman loved by everyone. She had been a schoolteacher prior to the move but had to give up her occupation because the subjects she taught, Latin and English, "were perceived as counter-revolutionary and bourgeois" (Qvortrup 2016). When Merkel was three years old, her father was promoted to head a newly established seminary for training future Lutheran pastors. The family moved to a larger town and lived in a complex that included a school for children with special needs. The Kasner family worked together, with periodic help from the special needs children, to restore the complex's buildings that had fallen into disrepair. Merkel's interactions with special needs children (whom the Soviet state and other children kept their distance from) may have helped shaped her belief in human rights and valuing all human beings.

Merkel joined the communist youth organization so that she could access a university education and job. She earned a doctorate in quantum chemistry and worked as a researcher in that field. In communist East Germany, people learned to keep their opinions to themselves for fear of persecution. Later it was discovered that the Stasi, the East German secret police, had files on her father and a memo on Merkel that stated she privately admired the freedom of the West and resented that she could not access research or interact with researchers there.

Following the Soviet Union's collapse and German reunification in 1990, Merkel began volunteering in politics. Her quiet, modest, analytical style and work ethic gained the attention of leaders who made her a government minister. Once again, she was an outsider—a woman from East Germany among predominantly male West German political leaders. Male leaders tended to be condescending toward her. For example, German Chancellor Helmut Kohl used to refer to her as his *mädchen* (little girl). When the press uncovered a secret slush fund Kohl used to reward loyalists, Merkel challenged his leadership. Not long thereafter, Merkel became the first female chancellor of Germany and, at 51 years old, the youngest to serve in that role.

For many years, the German people have referred to Chancellor Merkel as *Mutti*, which means *mom*. Many are comforted that she is never rash about making decisions. Instead, she takes the time to gather information and knowledge by seeking the ideas and opinions of others, thinks through possible scenarios and outcomes, then makes a decision when she believes it is the proper time. This measured approach gives people around her a voice and shows she values them, even though it can take more time and be frustrating for some. (Her critics began using "merkel" as a verb to cast her careful, deliberative decision-making style as indecisiveness.)

Unlike many politicians who wear flashy clothing and exude charisma, Merkel doesn't attract attention. That can be said of her speaking style as well. In private and when the cameras are off, she can be cheerful and personable, with a good sense of humor. When the cameras are on, however, she communicates in the unemotional and rational manner you would expect from a scientist who grew up in a culture in which it was safer to keep your head down and opinions to yourself. When she became chancellor, she refused to move into the chancellor's opulent penthouse apartment and instead chose to live in an ordinary flat with her husband.

Although Chancellor Merkel has a reputation for taking moderate positions on issues, occasionally she takes a clear stand on principles and her values become evident (one observer described Merkel as a "principled pragmatist"; CFR 2015). Two incidents reveal Merkel's core values. Following the 2011 Fukushima Daiichi Nuclear Power Plant disaster in Japan, she banned nuclear energy in Germany. This created a tangle of litigation, but she did it to protect people from the risk of a nuclear accident on German soil. In 2015, she allowed an influx of hundreds of thousands of immigrant refugees who were being persecuted in other countries, including war-torn Syria. Both were decisions against her political interest, yet they showed that Angela Merkel values human beings and places their protection from harm above her own political interest.

In his book *Angela Merkel: Europe's Most Influential Leader*, Matthew Qvortrup (2016) described an incident in August 2015 when the chancellor faced an angry crowd confronting her over her position on allowing in refugees. Rather than ignore them and walk past, or be drawn into angry rhetoric, she took another tack. She put a positive vision in front of them. "Welcoming people who flee tyranny is part of what we are all about, part of our understanding of who we are," she declared. "There is no tolerance for those who question the worth of other people, no tolerance for those who are not willing to help, when helping is right and humane." In this statement, "she was not only standing for dignity, she was also upholding Germany's self-respect; she was personifying the new, open and tolerant country—one that distanced itself from its dark history of genocide, tyranny and the unspeakable horrors of the Nazi concentration camps."

Although the integration of immigrants has been challenging, the situation is improving. Merkel has continued to defend her decision, saying, "It was right and it was important for us to take these people in during this extraordinary situation" (Hill 2018).

In her commencement speech delivered at Harvard University on May 30, 2019, she gave this exhortation to the graduates and those in attendance:

> I have learned that answers to difficult questions can be found if we always see the world through the eyes of others; if we respect the history, tradition, religion, and identity of others; if we firmly stand by our inalienable values and act accordingly; and if we do not always follow our initial impulses, even with all the pressure to make snap decisions, but instead stop for a moment, keep quiet, think, take a break. Of course, that takes a lot of courage. Above all, it requires being truthful to others and perhaps most importantly to ourselves.

During the COVID-19 pandemic, Chancellor Merkel connected with and united the German people. As is typical of her approach, Merkel developed a command of the facts related to COVID-19 then decided on a course of action. On March 18, to unite Germans behind the plan, she gave an address on national television for the first time since becoming chancellor in November 2005, other than her annual New Year's message (Dempsey 2020). At the outset, Merkel placed the evolving situation in context, stating, "This is serious. . . . Since German reunification—no, since the Second World War—no challenge to our country in which our acting together in solidarity matters so much" (News Wires 2020). She acknowledged how hard it is to be apart from family and friends in such a time, and asked Germans to be self-disciplined in preserving social distancing practices. Germans listening to this call for self-sacrifice knew that their chancellor valued freedom: "For someone like myself, for whom freedom of travel and movement were hard-won rights," she said, "such restrictions can only be justified when they are absolutely necessary." She thanked healthcare workers and first responders, and recognized that "those who sit at supermarket cash registers or restock shelves are doing one of the hardest jobs there is right now" (Davidson 2020).

Observers cited Merkel's leadership as one reason Germany had one of the lowest COVID-19 death rates in the world. Her popularity and approval ratings soared (Gallu and Delfs 2020). Nearly 90 percent of Germans thought their government handled the pandemic well (News Wires 2020).

Praising Chancellor Merkel's leadership, Professor Hans-Georg Kräusslich, head of virology at University Hospital in Heidelberg, one of Germany's leading research hospitals, concluded, "Maybe our biggest strength in Germany is the rational decision-making at the highest level of government combined with the trust the government enjoys in the population." (Bennhold 2020). Media worldwide also took note of Merkel's leadership during the pandemic. As one observer summed it up, Angela Merkel "may someday be remembered [as] . . . the political leader who executed, celebrated, and personified evidence-based thinking when it mattered most" (Miller 2020).

Making It Personal

✓ How would you describe your decision-making style? How would your colleagues describe it? When announcing a decision you have made that impacts others, how often do you explain the rationale and welcome questions?

✓ If you've made a decision that was met with criticism, how did you handle it?

✓ During your formative years, was there a particular person or event that had a profound influence on your values?

The Soul of Starbucks

At the 2018 *Seattle Business* magazine's Lifetime Achievement Award dinner to honor Howard Behar, Starbucks Executive Chairman Howard Schultz introduced his former colleague of more than two decades, proclaiming that Behar taught the organization guiding principles and values that have been forever imprinted on the organization's culture. Howard Behar, he explained, "taught us the universality of longing for human connection, for being respected and valued—not for ringing the register or trying to get the money out of a customer's hand—but by touching [customers'] hearts and celebrating the people who do the work" (Schultz 2018).

Howard Behar began at Starbucks in 1989 when it had 28 stores and was beginning to expand outside of the U.S. Pacific Northwest. During his 21-year tenure, he served as executive vice president of sales and operations, as president of Starbucks North America, as the founding president of Starbucks International, and on the Starbucks Board of Directors. He worked so closely with Howard Schultz and the late Orin Smith, who held several senior positions, that people at Starbucks referred to the three as "H2O" (two Howards and one Orin). They had dinner together most Monday evenings.

Much can be learned about Behar's leadership philosophy and practices by reading his excellent books, *It's Not About the Coffee: Leadership Principles From a Life at Starbucks* and *The Magic Cup: A Business Parable About a Leader, a Team, and the Power of Putting People and Values First*. Like all great leaders, Howard Behar communicates an inspiring vision about serving others, he values people as human beings and doesn't think of or treat them as mere means to an end, and he gives people a voice by seeking their ideas and opinions then considering them.

Behar is passionate about serving others; he is a trustee emeritus of The Robert Greenleaf Center for Servant Leadership. In his acceptance speech for the Lifetime Achievement Award, he gave the credit for the success of Starbucks to all the partners (the term Starbucks uses for employees). The role of H2O, he explained, was to "set the tone, live the values, and knock down the hurdles. In essence, our job was to serve our people on the journey of creating the Starbucks you see today. The better we served, the better the results. It was really that simple." Driving the point home as he came to the end of his remarks, he told the audience: "Being of service is the key in this life. At the end of the day, the success that Starbucks has had is directly attributable to serving people. . . . That begins and ends with the commitment of leadership" (Schultz 2018).

Behar has talked about the importance of connecting people who work in business to how they are serving others (in other words, the element of vision). He explains it this way:

> It doesn't make any difference what your job title is. There's only one reason for being. . . . Even the lowly widget-maker's job is about serving people—the widget-maker that makes a widget that goes into a printing press, the printing press gets sold to a publisher, the publisher produces a magazine or newspaper that gets delivered to somebody's home to inform or entertain them. The widget-maker is making a difference in people's lives. The key is figuring out that connection. . . . Staying focused on that connection, you will never get burned out or bored. You may get tired, but that's all it will be. (Schultz 2018)

Behar says the little things matter too. He tells the story of an elderly Starbucks customer named Big Jim who lived in a nursing home across the street from a Starbucks store. Every day, about the same time in the afternoon, Big Jim came in and ordered a small drip coffee and a blueberry muffin. Big Jim and the Starbucks staff became like family, not a transactional relationship of customer and employee. The Starbucks baristas often wrote little notes to him on the coffee cup or on the bag they put the muffin in. One day, Big Jim didn't show up. Concerned, they sent a barista across the street with a drip coffee and blueberry muffin to check on him. The receptionist at the nursing home informed him that Big Jim had passed away in his sleep. The next day, one of Big Jim's children stopped by the store and asked the manager if all the baristas and the manager could possibly attend Big Jim's funeral because he loved them and it would have meant a lot to him to have them there. The store manager said yes and arranged for others to cover for them. When they walked through the front door of the funeral home, there on display, covering three big tables, were Starbucks cups and bags with the handwritten notes to Big Jim that he had held onto. Behar wondered, "Who would have ever thought a small thing, just saying 'I love you' basically every day, would mean so much to another human being? But it does. . . . How many times do you walk down the hallway in your companies and don't look up . . . and say 'Hi, how are you doing?' [to the people you are passing]? Get in the habit of doing that" (Schultz 2018).

Rather than drawing attention to himself, Behar likes to tell stories about the times that Howard Schultz demonstrated that he values people. When Behar had been at Starbucks for three months, he received a call from a store manager in Seattle named Jim who wanted to meet with him and Schultz in person. "So, Jim, what can we do for you?" was Howard Behar's opening question when they got down to business. Jim told them he was dying of AIDS. This was 1989, in the early days of the AIDs epidemic when there was a lot of uncertainty and fear about the disease. "So, Jim, what can we do for you?" was the immediate question of Howard Schultz. Jim told them he would like to continue working for as long as his health permitted. Behar recounts that, without blinking an eye, Schultz promised Jim he could work as long as he was able to and after he could no longer physically work, his salary and benefits would not run out. Schultz's promise came at a time when Starbucks was still losing money and its future was shaky (Schultz 2018).

Behar also tells the story of receiving a call in the middle of the night at his home in Seattle when he was president of Starbucks North America, alerting him that three Starbucks employees at the Georgetown store in Washington, D.C., had been shot and killed, including an 18-year-old who had just recently begun at Starbucks as his first job. Behar immediately called Howard Schultz, who was in New York City on vacation. Schultz didn't call Starbucks' public relations people or lawyers for them to make the initial response or to consult on what the next steps should be. Instead, he chartered a plane and headed straight to Washington, D.C., himself. When he arrived, he spoke with the police then proceeded to the store to get the addresses of the three murdered Starbucks employees. He went to each of their homes, told their families he was sorry, and shared in their tears. He showed courage by expressing the grief he felt. Doing so contributed to helping the victims' families, friends, and colleagues as they reeled from the shock and began to process what had happened. As awful as grieving the loss of a loved one or friend is, it's far worse to grieve alone.

Howard Schultz's empathy and compassion spoke loudly to Behar, a leader who has a huge heart. The message it conveyed to him was that at Starbucks he could "do anything I need to do in service to another human being." Behar had left his former employer and joined Starbucks in part because the previous CEO he had worked for advised him he "shouldn't wear his heart on his sleeve." Schultz was the type of leader Behar wanted to work for, a leader he could respect and admire because of his courageous and compassionate heart, a leader he wanted to give his best efforts to serve.

Howard Behar shows people he values them and gives them a voice by "walking the halls," which is all about getting out of your office, getting to know the people you are responsible for leading, and listening to them. When traveling to connect with the people he was responsible for leading, he began the practice of holding open forums. In *It's Not About the Coffee*, Behar explains, "We use Open Forums to deal with changes or bring up issues where there is conflict or potential conflict." His approach was to raise the issue and be silent so that people would speak up. If no one responded within the first minute or two, he would ask someone to share their point of view in public then patiently hear the person out. Behar has said that he's seen how anxiety is reduced by getting people to express their point of view without fear of retaliation or being disrespected. "Those clear channels, that culture of listening and being heard, has made a huge difference in our ability to constantly keep our organization moving forward. . . . There are no negative thoughts, there are just thoughts. It's all positive. It's all feedback. You learn from all of it" (Behar and Goldstein 2007).

Behar was a safe leader for people to speak honestly to. In 1993, Greg Rogers, an assistant manager at a Starbucks store in Santa Monica, California, noticed how well cold drinks were selling at another shop in the area, and he came up with a frozen drink concoction that he thought might spur sales on a warm afternoon. Attempts to share the idea up the chain of command stalled. At the time, Starbucks strictly made hot coffee and espresso beverages. His district manager reached out to Behar, and he traveled to the Santa Monica store to try the new drink for himself. He loved it and advocated for it to Howard Schultz. The Frappuccino was born and became a huge success.

Behar had an enormous impact on Starbucks North America as its president. He went on to become the first president of Starbucks International and led it to spectacular growth. At the time of his retirement, Starbucks had expanded to 15,000 stores across five continents. Behar was loved and respected throughout Starbucks for his heart and passion as well as his work ethic, open-mindedness, and judgment about the retail business.

In 2015, several years after Behar left the company, Starbucks partnered with *USA Today* on an initiative called Race Together. Howard Schultz was troubled by the racial injustice and growing division evidenced by the protests following the grand jury decision not to indict the white police officer who killed Michael Brown, an unarmed black man in Ferguson, Missouri. Schultz felt he could no longer remain silent. One day in December 2014, he called for an impromptu open forum on race at the Starbucks headquarters and 400 colleagues joined him. Executives shared that "the ensuing dialogue was unexpectedly rich and poignant." This then led to forums with Starbucks colleagues in other cities. Out of these experiences of giving people a voice, listening to each other, and engaging in dialogue, "Schultz wanted to do more with the idea—to take full advantage of Starbucks's massive platform and reach" (Carr 2015). Although intended to further cultural connection by engaging people in conversations related to race relations, the practice of writing "race together" on customers' Starbucks cups was controversial and promptly ended. Despite the criticism, Howard Schultz said other actions would go forward, including publishing special sections on racial issues in *USA Today*. Laurel Harper, a spokesperson for Starbucks, said the criticisms "have not dented Starbucks' determination. 'This is who we are,' she said. 'Our mission is to inspire and nurture the human spirit, one person, one cup, and one neighborhood at a time. We know that we don't have all the solutions and the answers, but for us, doing nothing makes us part of the problem'" (Somaiya 2015).

Finally, on a personal note, on one occasion when I was on a telephone call with Howard Behar, he casually asked how my wife, Katie, was doing. I shared with him that she had recently been diagnosed with a third type of cancer. After we discussed it for a while, he asked how I was doing in light of this news and whether I had anyone to talk with about it. Then he told me he wanted me to speak with his wife, Lynn, an expert on providing psychosocial support for people with cancer and co-editor of the *Handbook on Oncology Social Work*. I agreed. Over a series of calls, Lynn Behar was a caring and wise advisor who helped support me with guidance and encouragement. She also arranged for a world-renowned expert in breast cancer oncology social work at Memorial Sloan Kettering to stop in and spend a little time with us during one of Katie's chemotherapy treatments. Today, I look back at that time with gratitude for Howard and Lynn for the example they are of people who care about others and the difference they made to me during a difficult period.

Making It Personal

✓ Howard Behar explained how the widget-maker made a difference in the lives of others. How does the work you do serve others?

✓ Can you recall a time when a small thing you did for someone had a bigger effect on the recipient than you would have imagined? What is a small gesture you can do for a colleague or customer this week?

✓ Howard Behar liked to tell stories about others living up to Starbucks' values to shine the light on them and not bring attention to himself. Be on the lookout for colleagues who are living your organization's values and tell others about their example.

Healing Connections

The best culture in a healthcare organization is a connection culture. Patients and their families benefit from the feeling of connection among healthcare professionals that extends to them and it helps reduce the stress and anxiety that accompany illness.

Chapter 2 shared my family's experiences during my wife's battles with cancer. The healthcare workers we met were kind and compassionate and our whole family felt connected to everyone, from doctors and nurses to the environmental services staff and even the cafeteria workers. These connections helped us cope with the stress and anxiety surrounding Katie's uncertain future and are an important part of a healing healthcare culture.

The MD Anderson Cancer Center has a strong vision that is summarized in the phrase from its logo: "Making cancer history." In fiscal year 2018, MD Anderson invested more than $860 million in research and made progress in several areas, including inventing an immunotherapy treatment that resulted in the Nobel Prize being awarded to MD Anderson's chair of immunology, Jim Allison (MD Anderson Cancer Center 2019). Its vision to cure cancer is an enormous sense of pride to its employees.

When he was president and CEO of the not-for-profit New York–Presbyterian Hospital, Dr. Herbert Pardes was a great example of a leader who promoted vision and value. A well-respected psychiatrist and former director of the National Institute of Mental Health, Pardes (2014) described his vision of healthcare when he stated: "I anthropomorphize disease. I covert it to an evil enemy. I want to slay it before it hurts friends and family. But if anyone is ill—cancer, heart disease, depression, schizophrenia—what we want to do is bring everything we have, the very best, to fix the problem." Pardes always devoted time to making bedside visits to patients, something that other leaders might dismiss as inefficient, but he was passionate about providing humane healthcare and understood that connection made patients and their families feel better.

Pardes valued the people he was responsible for leading and put practices in place to ensure they were caring and engaged individuals. He advocated for personal and professional mentors, striving to help people balance their personal lives with professional growth. To extend the feeling of connection, he encouraged staff members to memorize and use the names of patients and their family members.

By combining a connection culture with sound management practices, Pardes and his team turned around the hospital system and New York–Presbyterian's revenue rose from $1.7 billion in 1999 to $3.7 billion in 2011. Whereas most hospitals find it difficult to attract and retain nurses, New York–Presbyterian's vacancy rate was less than a third of the national average. The *New York Times* observed that while "most urban hospitals have struggled, New York–Presbyterian has thrived" (Stodghill 2007).

The power of connection is also on full display at Mayo Clinic, America's top-ranked hospital and arguably the best hospital in the world. From the time of its founding in 1889, Mayo Clinic has been intentional about cultivating connection and community. Dr. Charlie Mayo, one of the earliest leaders, communicated an attitude that valued connection and warned about the dangers of isolation: "Our failures as a profession are the failures of individualism, the result of competitive medicine. It must be done by collective effort" (Burns et al. 2018).

One of the ways this is manifest is in Mayo Clinic's practice of compensating physicians through paying a salary rather than by an activity-based system. Not only does this promote collaboration for the good of the patient, it also alleviates the financial and time pressure of trying to see too many patients in a day, which often diminishes the physician-patient connection.

On its website, Mayo Clinic's stated mission and values point to the intent of its founders, the original Mayo physicians and Sisters of St. Francis. Mayo Clinic's mission is "To inspire hope and contribute to health and well-being by providing the best care to every patient through *integrated* clinical practice, education, and research" (italics mine). The language used to describe its values includes the following:

- "Compassion . . . [that treats] patients and family members with sensitivity and empathy"
- "Healing [that nurtures] the well-being of the whole person, respecting physical, emotional, and spiritual needs"
- "Teamwork [that values] the contributions of all, blending the skills of individual staff members in unsurpassed collaboration"
- "Innovation [that infuses and energizes] the organization, enhancing the lives of those we serve, through the creative ideas and unique talents of each employee"
- "Excellence [that delivers] the best outcomes and highest quality service through the dedicated effort of every team member."

Notice that words and phrases that reflect and enhance connection are woven throughout: sensitivity, empathy, treating the whole person (including emotional and spiritual needs), teamwork, blending skills of the team, unsurpassed collaboration, each employee, and every team member.

Mayo Clinic's belief in the importance of connection goes beyond attitudes and language to practical steps taken to see that connection is infused in the culture. Mayo Clinic's onboarding process for physicians and scientists includes extensive training in professionalism and communication, and assessments to help them develop emotional intelligence, which is instrumental to connecting with others. Physician leaders are selected, developed, and assessed based on their ability to connect, which includes listening to, engaging, developing, and leading other physicians. Informal opportunities for connection among colleagues are encouraged by providing dedicated meeting areas for physicians to gather.

Mayo Clinic's intentionality and commitment is evident in a program called COMPASS (Colleagues Meeting to Promote and Sustain Satisfaction). Under this initiative, self-formed groups of six to 10 physicians get together for about an hour every other week, usually over breakfast or lunch, with up to $20 provided to each participant to cover the meal cost. They begin by spending at least 15 minutes discussing assigned issues related to the physician experience. Two examples include "brainstorm ways to promote collegiality in your hallway or work unit" and "choose one stressor that you can control, come up with two concrete ways you can reduce it, and commit to trying one approach within the next week" (Berg 2018). Mayo Clinic's research has found that participants in COMPASS experience statistically significant improvements in well-being and satisfaction that can help reduce the risk of physician burnout and medical errors.

The COVID-19 pandemic placed a tremendous stress on individuals working in healthcare. Arriving in the United States in early 2020, the highly transmissible novel coronavirus sometimes spread undetected in communities for days and weeks before symptoms required patients to seek medical treatment. In the New York City area and other early COVID-19 hot spots, many hospitals experienced a surge of COVID-19 patients that threatened to surpass their capacity to provide intensive treatments, such as respiratory therapy requiring the use of ventilators. At times the onslaught was so great that patients were dying before they could be taken out of ambulances (Watkins et al. 2020).

The normal stress on individuals working in healthcare was magnified by demanding hours of intense work treating patients, the shortage of personal protective equipment, and the risk of contracting COVID-19 and passing it along to patients or colleagues. They also carried the weight of potentially bringing the virus home with them and infecting their loved ones. As a precautionary measure, some healthcare professionals even secured separate housing for a period of time, which added the potential of social isolation further increasing their stress level.

Recognizing the courage and selflessness of healthcare workers, people worldwide organized ways to express their appreciation. Appearing in front yards and on balconies, people clapped for healthcare workers at an appointed time in the evening. In some towns, police and firefighters ran emergency lights and sirens to show their appreciation, church bells rang, and people banged on pots and pans. The U.S. Air Force's Thunderbirds and U.S. Navy's Blue Angels jet fighters came together to do a joint fly-over across several cities in hard-hit areas to honor healthcare workers.

During this especially intense period, many individuals working in healthcare were inspired by their profession's healing mission; the camaraderie, caring, and kindness of their colleagues; and the appreciation expressed by their communities. At the same time, there is concern that the pandemic's physical and emotional demands on healthcare workers may contribute to higher rates of burnout (Haskell et al. 2020).

KP Mendoza, a 24-year-old ICU nurse in New York City dedicated to caring for the sick, poignantly articulated what it was like to be in the trenches of caring for critically ill COVID-19 patients. In a long post on social media, he wrote of the physical and psychological toll—some days he felt lucky if he ate or had more than one bathroom break during his 12-hour shift. It was a heavy emotional burden to be the one to tell a concerned relative over the phone that the loved one she could not be with in person was not doing well. Stretched to care for more patients at a time than normal, he felt guilt and shame for not being able to provide the attention to each one that he normally could. The lack of personal protective equipment (PPE) was especially troubling to him:

> In the last two weeks, I have seen more people die than most people see in their entire lives. Now, I am not so sure if death is something I am prepared to see anymore. Death is different now. Death could pick me. . . . I want people to know that this is beyond difficult. . . . I want the country to know that if I end up on the ICU bed it is because I was not given a hazmat suit or enough PPE to protect me. (Kane 2020)

In an interview on the PBS NewsHour, Mendoza observed that one of the few silver linings of the shared experience going through the pandemic was "that we realize how important it is to reach out to the people we love. . . that's the one beautiful part of this, it's going to make people feel connected" (Brangham 2020).

The COVID-19 pandemic may turn out to be an inflection point. In addition to greater use and acceptance of telemedicine and more remote work, it may also lead to post-traumatic growth that brings about a desire to increase connection in the cultures of healthcare organizations. I'm encouraged by the views of Dr. Robert McLean, past president of the American College of Physicians and a physician at Yale New Haven Health. He has stated that for the sake of the profession's future, healthcare leaders must explicitly address isolation, especially now that it has been made worse by the necessity of social distancing, quarantine, and the "emotional burden [from COVID-19] that will predictably develop over time."

In an address given in April 2020, McLean exhorted American College of Physicians' fellows to combat the isolation of their colleagues by making contact "via phone, video, or in person every day with at least one colleague to sincerely inquire about their personal well-being and personal life outside of a clinical context." He then noted, "Isolation is truly a significant challenge. As physicians, we understand that human connection is everything. . . . The emotional toll of this isolation on individuals will be large and with us for a long time. The little gestures and touches, even remotely, are so meaningful. We all know, but need reminders in these hectic days delivering care, to try to pause, [and] consider the emotional component of everything we do on ourselves and on those around us. That is what makes us healers in the truest sense of the word."

Making It Personal

✓ Mayo Clinic pays salaries to its physicians so that their behaviors are more likely to be aligned with Mayo Clinic's values of teamwork and integrated clinical practice. Is your organization's approach to compensation, recognition, and promotion aligned with its values? If not, how could they be changed to promote alignment?

✓ Mayo Clinic invests in getting physicians together in groups for meals as one way to boost connection and reduce the risk of physician burnout. One organization we know provides budget dollars to supervisors specifically to fund team-building activities outside of work. Can you invest in connecting people in your organization in ways that allow them to form groups that engage in meaningful conversations with their peers?

✓ Another deliberate step that Mayo Clinic took to provide opportunities for peers to be together and form supportive relationships was to bring back dedicated spaces for physicians, complete with free beverages and fruit, lunch tables, limited food for purchase, and computer stations. Does your workplace have spaces where colleagues can gather informally? Are they designed in a way that is welcoming, relaxing, and conducive to casual conversation?

✓ How do you cope during times of great stress? How does your organization help employees cope during times of adversity?

What Oprah Knows for Sure

The best leaders connect with the people they are responsible for leading by communicating and achieving an inspiring vision, valuing people, and giving people a voice. It should come as no surprise that Oprah Winfrey, one of the most influential, admired, and successful women in the world, meets that description. Harvard professor Nancy F. Koehn (2011), who has studied and written about Oprah, observed, "like all great leaders, [Oprah] connects—in meaningful, dignified ways—to people on an emotional level."

Early on, like other broadcast interview programs, Oprah's TV talk show included "sensational" guests. Over time, however, her vision became to lift up people by connecting them with ideas and stories that improved their physical and mental health, spirituality, and self-fulfillment. She began to require the producers who came up with guest ideas to present their vision for that episode and then she would decide if that was aligned with her vision.

Oprah also describes her vision as using her expanded platform to "connect people to themselves and a higher consciousness" (Winfrey 2014) and to "change the world" by being "a catalyst for transformation in people's lives" (Koehn 2011). When you listen closely to how Oprah articulates her vision in greater detail, you learn that she believes people need to get to know their calling and the values they believe in. "Know who you are and why you are here," she says. Doing so connects them with their "emotional GPS" that guides their actions and lives. She believes everyone has a calling. To help her discover her own calling and values, Oprah has reflected on her life experiences by writing in a personal journal since she was 15 years old.

Valuing people as human beings and not thinking of or treating them as means to an end is very much a part of Oprah's character. She does this in many ways. She believes that all people want validation and want to know: "Did you see me?" "Did you hear me?" and "Did what I say mean anything to you?" (Muller 2019). She has stated that she has taken the words of the Reverend Martin Luther King Jr. to heart to judge people not by externals such as the color of their skin or beauty but by the content of their character. Oprah has been described as being "unfailingly respectful to her colleagues" (Koehn 2011). Oprah gives the people she leads autonomy to do their work. She is grateful and expresses appreciation, stating "I could weep when I think about my team."

One can see other ways Oprah values people. Over many years now, she has focused on helping others through her substantial humanitarian and philanthropic efforts. A prime example is the generous donation she made to create and fund an academy for academically gifted girls in South Africa whose disadvantaged backgrounds might otherwise hinder them from receiving an excellent education. The Oprah Winfrey Leadership Academy opened in 2007 for grades seven and eight. The boarding school now serves grades eight through 12, and its vision is to "[create] a safe space to educate, to nurture, to empower, and, of course, to inspire this next generation of leaders for South Africa and for the world" (Winfrey 2017a).

Oprah gives people a voice by leading by example and being open to sharing her experiences in life. For instance, she has shared her struggles to lose weight. She's spoken about being raped by a teenage cousin and molested by one of her mother's boyfriends. Her vulnerability has given courage to others to speak out. She is confident while also being humble and open to new ideas.

Her passion for connecting with people and cultivating a connection culture has helped Oprah advance from being a local television reporter first in Nashville and then in Baltimore to founding and leading a phenomenally successful production company, Harpo, and then founding and leading the

Oprah Winfrey Network (OWN) in partnership with the Discovery Channel. Harpo, the production company Oprah started in 1986, was reported to have a low annual employee attrition rate of 10–15 percent, and the tenure among senior executives averaged 11 years (Koehn 2011). She wrapped up *The Oprah Winfrey Show* in 2011 after 25 seasons. Along the way, Oprah has acted in a number of movies, including *The Color Purple* (1985) and *A Wrinkle in Time* (2018), as well as authored several books. *O, The Oprah Magazine* carries forward her vision. The monthly magazine was launched in 2000 and now reaches more than 22 million readers across the magazine, website, and social media (*O* Media Kit 2020). Oprah is still going strong, and it will be exciting to see in the years ahead how this extraordinary leader continues to live out her calling.

Making It Personal

✓ Oprah Winfrey exhorts people to "know who you are and why you are here." In *The Path Made Clear: Discovering Your Life's Direction and Purpose*, she shared, "All humans have value and a voice. And I consider it my purpose here on earth to celebrate and validate both" (Winfrey 2019). What are the core values that define who you are and point to what is important to you? Do you have a sense of "calling" or purpose, and have you articulated it? If not, to help you hone in on your unique purpose, consider these questions: What matters most to me? If I knew that I only had nine months to live and I had unlimited resources, what would I want to do? What activities energize me? In articles, books, or movies that I have found to be really thought provoking, is there a common theme?

✓ Oprah believes that people want to know "Did you see me?" "Did you hear me?" and "Did what I say mean anything to you?" In your interactions with people, what do you do or say that validates them? What is a habit you have that might get in the way, such as interrupting the other person so you can insert your own view? According to Bob Tiede, author of *Now That's a Great Question*, after we've asked someone a question and there is silence before the person answers, many of us wait only two to three seconds before either rephrasing the question, answering it ourselves, or moving on. Pay attention to see if you have this tendency.

✓ Oprah has been open about her struggles. Think of a time when you were vulnerable about an issue or hardship you have faced. How did you see that affect your connection with the listener?

Main Street Connectors

The Kneaded Bread, a bakery on Main Street in Port Chester, New York, is renowned for its delicious baked goods, including up to 20 varieties of bread. The line that queues up just before the bakery opens its doors is a testament to its enduring popularity.

For more than two decades now, the bakery has been owned by Jeffrey Kohn, a Culinary Institute of America-trained chef, and his wife, Jennifer, who oversees operations. A few years ago, I was concerned when a celebrity chef opened a beautiful new bakery directly across the street. The new bakery has since closed its doors. I think there are several reasons why the Kneaded Bread outlived the celebrity chef's bakery. One reason is the quality of everything at the bakery reflects task excellence. The bread is baked fresh each day, the soup is made from scratch, and the turkey in their sandwiches is roasted by them. The second reason is relationship excellence, reflected in the bakery's connection culture. Task and relationship excellence together help the bakery achieve sustainable superior performance and provide it with a competitive edge.

The Kneaded Bread's connector-in-chief is its manager, Fernando Bastida. Whenever I ask people if they are aware of the Kneaded Bread, inevitably they bring up Fernando. Everyone knows Fernando.

Bastida, who came to the United States from Mexico, is beloved by the people who work at the bakery and by its customers. He's always quick with a smile and loves to engage in conversation. You can see by the way that people who work at the bakery interact with him that they feel connected to him. We feel connected to him too. Sometimes we visit the bakery just to say hi to Fernando, and we leave having purchased something to enjoy back home! Since he is a food and dining aficionado, we'll ask him for dining recommendations. On more than one occasion, he has joined us for dinner.

The Kneaded Bread has become a hub in the community, with people gathering throughout the day for coffee and a pastry. Jeffrey Kohn has said, "We never got too fancy. It's a feel-good place and it's been a feel-good place from the minute we opened our doors" (Muchnick 2018).

The Kneaded Bread has expanded twice over its 20-year life. In 2018 the Kohns purchased the building where the Kneaded Bread has been a tenant. There's talk that they may expand yet again. Given its popularity, I expect there will be more expansions in the future for this Main Street go-to.

Do you know people like Bastida in your local business community who connect with customers and make your community all the better for it? Several other community connectors come to mind.

Judy Gilmartin-Willsey, the owner of a framing shop in Armonk, New York, is often referred to as the unofficial mayor of her adopted town. Years ago, she rallied with others to put it on the map as the "birthplace of Frosty the Snowman," and now thousands come out for family-friendly activities and a parade down Main Street on the annual Frosty Day.

There's the team at Threads and Treads, an athletic apparel store in Greenwich, Connecticut, that was founded more than 30 years ago by Mickey Yardis. The store sponsors race events throughout the year, including the "Jingle Bell Jog," the "Cook Your Buns" run in the heat of the summer, and a triathlon. Threads and Treads has developed a community of runners (and bikers and swimmers) and their families who connect by participating in these runs; people stick around afterward to enjoy food, drink, and conversation.

When one of our daughters taught English in the small town of Guardo in northern Spain, she took exercise classes from Isabel Rojo Alvarez, who owns a gym with her husband. Our daughter admired how Isabel connected personally with each of her students and motivated them to work even harder. As Elizabeth adjusted to life in a new setting, Isabel's welcome was especially important. "Isabel really cared and took the time to get to know our goals in the gym and what was happening in our personal lives, which helped her not only be an excellent trainer but also a valued friend. People found community in the gym and missed fewer days because they wanted to see Isabel and the strong group of women she brought together in classes" (Stallard 2019).

Connectors who cultivate community make all our lives better. The moment of connection may appear small to a casual observer—a kind word, a listening ear, an explanation that brings clarity to a situation—but might have a significant effect in the recipient's life. The next time you encounter people who are a force of connection in your community, make sure you thank them for the positive impact they have.

Making It Personal

✓ Who comes to mind when you think of "Main Street" connectors you've encountered? What attitudes, language, or behaviors have you observed in that person that make a difference?

✓ Is there anything that holds you back from offering a moment of connection to a passerby or someone you recognize but don't really know? What is one thing you could do for a neighbor, store clerk, or waitress this week?

✓ It helps to have a few go-to questions that will start a conversation or draw out the other person. One of mine is "What do you like to do outside of work?" After listening, and resisting the natural temptation to jump in with your own story, ask follow-up questions about details shared, what the person felt, or what the person learned from the experience. What are a few open-ended questions that you might ask someone you are just getting to know?

Horned Frog Family

Texas Christian University (TCU), with more than 11,000 students, is located in Fort Worth, Texas. In recent years, TCU has been consistently recognized as a top 100 *U.S. News & World Report* college and in the top 20 list of up-and-coming national universities. TCU is listed number 2 of best-run colleges by the *Princeton Review.*

As word about TCU has spread across the country and around the world, applications have soared. Almost half of the students now hail from outside Texas and more than 85 countries are represented in the student body. Over the past five years, total applications received for the incoming freshman class have been steadily increasing, with a new record of 20,156 set in fall 2018. The fall 2018 entering class was the largest in university history at 2,194. Admission numbers tell the story of TCU's incredible momentum and its rise as a desirable learning laboratory and reputable academic community.

TCU's sports teams have put the university in the national spotlight too. Competing at the NCAA Division I level, the football team has appeared in 16 bowl games, including winning the Rose Bowl in 2011. TCU has hosted the live broadcast of ESPN's *College GameDay* on several occasions, its baseball team has traveled to the College World Series five times since 2010, and men's basketball had an NIT win and NCAA tournament appearances. In the 2017–2018 school year, 11 of TCU's 21 sports were ranked in the top 25. It's indeed an exciting time to be part of the Horned Frog family.

Seeing TCU up close allows you to appreciate that its true strength—indeed its competitive advantage—is more than just academics and sports. What really makes TCU stand out is its connection culture.

TCU's formal vision is "to be a world-class, values-centered university" and its mission is "to educate individuals to think and act as ethical leaders and responsible citizens in the global community." The university values "academic and personal achievement, intellectual inquiry and the creation of knowledge, artistic and creative expression, a heritage of service in pursuit of the greater good, personal freedom and integrity, the dignity of and respect for the individual, and an active appreciation for the array of human experience and the potential of every human being." Of note, the TCU mission and vision statements were affirmed by the board of trustees in April 2019, while the values statements were adjusted and approved by the board upon suggestions made through a task force comprising faculty, staff, and students.

Valuing people is a signature character strength of TCU's culture. The university's faculty members clearly value their students and, thanks to a student-teacher ratio of 13-to-1, they have time to get to know them. The enthusiasm of its faculty and staff members has helped raise TCU's status in the academic community. For nine consecutive years, TCU was named by the *Chronicle of Higher Education* as one of the "Great Colleges to Work For." Additionally, TCU received Honor Roll designations in several categories, an accolade reserved for institutions with the most recognitions across categories. This status demonstrates the united effort across all departments and divisions to make TCU a top-tier academic community.

TCU Chancellor Victor J. Boschini Jr. leads the culture in word and deed. In his 2018 University Convocation and Founders' Celebration address, in reference to the university's strategic plan as directed by the Board of Trustees, Vision in Action: Lead On, Chancellor Boschini said:

> Lead On is more than just a tagline, a color, a logo, or a campaign.
> It's about bringing the TCU essence to life from the inside out
> through the inspiring stories of our people, at all levels, taking the
> lead on making TCU a force for the greater good.

An advocate of servant leadership, Chancellor Boschini praises TCU's faculty and staff for continuing to "build the mentoring relationships that have long defined TCU." The university is intentional about hiring teacher-scholars who mentor students and who involve them in their research activities—in fact, approximately 25 percent of the student body, both undergraduate and graduate students, are involved in research projects.

Boschini's mantra is "listening," and he encourages others to stop and listen and be curious about what people think. He is outgoing, enthusiastic, and energetic, and when he engages in conversation, he is present and focused on the other person. To stay in touch with students, he teaches a freshman seminar in education. He not only knows every student's name in his class, but also what is going on in their lives. Whenever I walk with him across campus, invariably we stop to talk with a student or he engages with someone who has called out a friendly greeting. Through simple gestures of making eye contact, smiling, and greeting a passerby, Boschini communicates that he is interested in them.

TCU places a high priority on the importance of students making friends and establishing a support network. Recognizing the high level of stress felt by incoming college students and the negative impact of loneliness, TCU has myriad programs to help students make connections, even before the first day of class. Send-off parties occur around the United States to connect incoming students and their parents with others from their region before they leave home. Frog Camps—whether held in Fort Worth, the mountains of Colorado, or in an international location—introduce new students to each other and to TCU's history and traditions. Frogs First helps new students connect through activities during their first few weeks on campus, culminating with dinners hosted by faculty and staff members in their homes. A Connections program places students in small groups and encourages meetings led by upper classmen during the fall semester.

More than 200 student organizations offer opportunities to gather around a common cause or shared interest—from community engagement and religious life organizations to sororities and fraternities, multicultural resource groups, and campus recreation. The annual TCU Day of Service program connects student volunteers with opportunities to serve. Throughout the year, the university's student affairs department orchestrates initiatives and events "to endear students to TCU through irresistible events and experiential leadership opportunities." Concerts held on the commons unite the community, allowing students to make connections with other students on campus. Community-wide events like the Christmas tree lighting also attract alumni and neighbors to gather with faculty, staff, and students on campus to celebrate the holiday season.

To cultivate inclusion excellence, TCU established an Office of Diversity & Inclusion to promote campus conversations and advance goals and strategies as recommended by the Diversity, Equity, and Inclusion Committee. The DEI strategy focuses on four actions (attract, teach, reach, and embrace) to serve as the foundation on which academic units, administrative departments, and student groups may develop processes and plans to achieve desired goals within their respective areas. These actions are intended to enhance recruiting and retention of under-represented faculty, staff, and students; bolster curriculum and training; increase outreach and engagement with external communities; and promote a campus environment that is welcoming for all and free of bias.

In an effort to ensure that its students spend four years immersed in cultures of connection, the university established the TCU Center for Connection Culture. The purpose of the center is to "instill a lifelong commitment to connection, promote connection opportunities in the TCU community, promote the teacher-scholar model, and value diverse perspectives."

Fort Worth embraces TCU as its university and the students embrace the city in return. Merchants display posters of TCU's sports teams, many residents fly TCU flags, and local street signs are TCU purple with small white icons of the Horned Frog mascot.

My colleagues and I are encouraged to see that the education of rising healthcare professionals is beginning to include the importance of human connection and connection culture, and TCU is taking the lead. The new TCU and UNTHSC School of Medicine, a partnership with the University of North Texas Health Science Center, welcomed its inaugural class of 60 medical students in July 2019. The school is intentionally developing Empathetic Scholars using an "interdisciplinary curriculum designed to build skills in awareness, listening, inquiry, and engagement to foster exceptional connections between physicians and their patients, their teams, and their communities." Incorporated in the education is a physician development coaching program, which assigns a coach to student team members. The coaching relationship will "assist in the development of resiliency, collaboration, communication, and continuous improvement for personal and professional development" (TCU and UNTHSC School of Medicine 2019).

With all that it offers, it is no wonder that TCU has been ranked number 3 in the United States for student engagement by *Wall Street Journal* and *Times Higher Education*. As the university continues to educate and equip students to become intentional about connecting with others and influencing the cultures they are in, I am confident their students are destined to help change the world.

Making It Personal

✓ Do you know the stated vision, mission, and values of your organization? In what ways do you see the organization living out the vision and mission? Which of the values resonate with you the most, personally, and in your role at work? Is there a value that is more aspirational than actual, in your opinion? What can be done to put it into practice?

✓ Pick a day to smile and make eye contact with people you come into contact with at work or around your community. Note the results. How did people react to you? How did doing this make you feel?

✓ What does your organization do as part of the onboarding process for new employees that makes them feel connected? Are there other steps that could be taken to make new hires feel like part of the team?

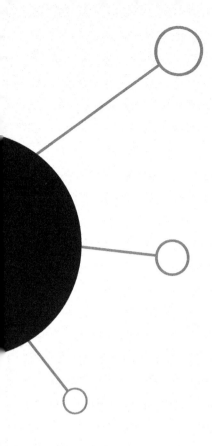

PART II
The Superpower of Connection and Dangers of Disconnection

Are you harnessing the power of connection in your work life? Are you aware of the harmful effects that disconnection can have? Thanks to breakthroughs in scientific research, we now have a better understanding about aspects of our environment that help people flourish.

In part II, you will learn why connection is a force referred to by a prominent neuroscientist as a "superpower" for individuals. This section includes a brief review of landmark research that shows connection helps individuals and organizations thrive and that a lack of connection is harmful. Part II concludes with additional profiles in connection.

PART II
The Superpower
of Connection
and Dangers of
Disconnection

4

Connection Helps Individuals Thrive

Connection is a "superpower," a turbocharger, that makes people "smarter, happier, and more productive." At least, that's how UCLA neuroscience professor Matthew Lieberman, author of *Social: Why Our Brains Are Wired to Connect*, has described it (Lieberman 2013a).

Most people don't yet recognize connection as a superpower that can protect them and propel them forward; therefore, they miss out on its benefits. In their defense, they may be living and working in cultures that have conditioned them not to see, feel, or experience connection as much as they should to live the most productive and enjoyable lives possible.

To truly understand why organizations with high connection and employee engagement outperform other organizations, one must begin by discovering what makes individuals thrive. It should be noted that describing all the research on connection that's been collected or conducted over the years would require multiple volumes. This chapter features carefully curated research and evidence that's especially relevant to illustrate the power connection has to improve individual health and performance.

Individual Wellness, Well-Being, and Performance

When John Bowlby studied homeless and orphaned children following World War II, he found that children who experienced little or no connection developed emotional and behavioral problems (Karen 1990). Describing connection as "attachment," Bowlby was the founder of a field of study called attachment theory, which he articulated in a three-volume work, *Attachment and Loss*, published in 1969, 1972, and 1980, respectively.

Mary Ainsworth, Bowlby's onetime student and eventual colleague, went on to conduct research on infants that identified patterns of connection that are formed in early childhood. The attachment patterns she identified were shown to affect the development of social skills, confidence, curiosity and exploratory behavior, enthusiasm, persistence in problem solving, and the ability to cope with ambiguity, change, and stress. Children with secure attachments developed well, whereas children with insecure attachments developed poorly (Karen 1990).

The environment in which a child is raised is not the sole determinant of human strengths or vulnerabilities; genetics also plays a role. Genes and the environment interact to affect emotions and behavior. In fact, scientists have come to believe that the environment in which people live alters gene expression. Because genes are inherited and environments affect gene expression, this means that your genes are shaped by the environments in which your mother and your father lived (Hurley 2013). Thus, the degree of connection your ancestors experienced is expressed in the genes that were passed on to you. With this in mind, putting yourself in healthy environments filled with positive connection not only benefits you in your lifetime but will also benefit your descendants.

What neuroscience and endocrinology have discovered about connection is illuminating. Neuroscience studies the brain and nervous system, while endocrinology studies hormones and the glands that secrete them. Research shows that feelings of connection affect neurotransmitters (chemical messengers in the brain, including serotonin, dopamine, and norepinephrine), hormones (chemical messengers that travel throughout the body, including adrenaline, cortisol, oxytocin, and vasopressin), and enzymes that affect chromosomes (such as telomerase). These biochemicals help us thrive and live longer. However, a lack of connection negatively affects them, and a sustained connection deficit can cause dysfunction and even increase the likelihood of premature death (Hallowell 1999a; Sapolsky 2008, 2010).

We've seen the importance of connection affirmed in research on wellness and well-being. In their book *Wellbeing: The Five Essential Elements*, Tom Rath and James Harter (2010) discuss a holistic view of what contributes to well-being during a lifetime. The following are just a few of the positive influences that connection has:

- Individuals who have the highest well-being get an average of six hours of social time (connection) each day through face-to-face, telephone, email, and Internet interactions.
- Self-control and goal accomplishment are positively correlated to connection, especially in regard to diet and exercise. A study showed that a 10-month intensive weight-loss program was maintained only 24 percent of the time when undertaken alone but had a success rate of 50 percent when undertaken with a group of three strangers and 66 percent when undertaken with three friends or colleagues.
- The single best predictor of employee engagement is who people are with (relational connection) rather than what they are doing (tasks).

When connection, wellness, and well-being are high, life span and achievement increase. The Harvard Grant Study, one of the longest-running studies of human flourishing, followed 268 male Harvard graduates beginning in 1938. It found that the warmth of relationships (connection) positively correlated with individual health, happiness, professional success, compensation, and longevity (Valliant 2012). In addition, a 20-year longitudinal study of 820 individuals showed that employees who experienced greater connection in the workplace had a 240 percent lower death rate. Researchers concluded that "only one main effect was found: the risk of mortality was significantly lower for those reporting peer social support" (Shirom et al. 2011).

Perhaps one of the most famous studies of the effect of connection within a community was the case of Roseto, Pennsylvania, which gave birth to the Roseto Effect. The predominantly Italian-American community, which Malcolm Gladwell wrote about in *Outliers: The Story of Success*, had half the risk of death from heart attacks versus the overall U.S. population. In addition, the community had no reported suicides, alcoholism, or drug addiction, and very little crime. After ruling out other factors, including diet and environment, researchers concluded that the Rosetans' health and longevity benefitted from the high degree of connection within the community. They visited one another, participated in community groups, and in many households several generations lived together (Gladwell 2008; Bruhn and Wolf 1979).

The opposite of connection is feeling unsupported, left out, or lonely. In numerous peer-reviewed journals and his book *Loneliness: Human Nature and the Need for Social Connection*, the late John T. Cacioppo, director of University of Chicago's Center for Cognitive and Social Neuroscience, reinforced these views by helping better explain the effects of disconnection. He made the important point that feeling connected is subjective—an individual may be surrounded by people throughout the day, yet still feel disconnected. According to Cacioppo, connection has three avenues: intimate connectedness with a soulmate, relational connectedness with family and friends, and collective connectedness with intermediate associations (groups we are not related to by blood, such as community, religious, or alumni organizations; Cacioppo and Patrick 2008). When one of these three avenues of connection declines, feelings of stability and security diminish, and are often replaced by a sense of loneliness, which is frequently coupled with depression, although they are distinct experiences.

The most extreme feelings of disconnection come when people feel left out (referred to as social exclusion). Think of a time when you felt socially excluded. Perhaps it was during middle school or in your first semester of college, or maybe it was at work when you weren't invited to a meeting that related to a project you were working on or a group of co-workers headed out to lunch together and didn't ask you to join them. This feeling is particularly destructive. Research on the effects of social exclusion has found that it makes people more aggressive not only toward those who excluded them, but also innocent bystanders; results in self-defeating behavior, including excessive risk taking, procrastination, and unhealthy diets; reduces intelligent thought, including logic and reasoning skills; and diminishes willpower to persevere in frustrating tasks (Twenge et al. 2001; Baumeister et al. 2002, 2005; Olds and Schwartz 2009). In addition, the 10-year MacArthur Foundation Study of Successful Aging, which included dozens of research projects, found that social exclusion is a "powerful risk factor for poor health," social support has "direct positive effects on health," and social support can reduce the health-related effects of aging (Rowe and Kahn 1998).

Clearly, an abundance of research has found that connection positively affects human wellness and well-being, including mental and physical health, performance, and longevity. Likewise, the evidence supports the conclusion that disconnection leads to dysfunction and, when sustained, even premature death.

The Current State of Connection

Much has been written over the years about the declining state of connection, including Robert Putnam's *Bowling Alone: The Collapse and Revival of American Community*, David Myers' *The American Paradox: Spiritual Hunger in an Age of Plenty*, Robert Lane's *The Loss of Happiness in Market Democracies*, and Jacqueline Olds and Richard Schwartz's *The Lonely American: Drifting Apart in the Twenty-First Century*. These works present compelling evidence that a broad decline in connection and community has been occurring since the post–World War II economic boom, which has contributed to a decline in both mental and physical health and life expectancy. The frequency of books published about loneliness and longing for connection has increased recently, including *The Crisis of Connection: Roots, Consequences, and Solutions* by Niobe Way, *Lost Connections: Uncovering the Real Causes of Depression* by Johann Hari, and *Together: The Healing Power of Human Connection in a Sometimes Lonely World* by Vivek Murthy.

Authors aren't the only ones who have their fingers on the pulse of culture. Increasingly, performance artists are producing works—including musicals, songs, and videos—that reflect the themes of loneliness and longing for connection. Here are three examples:

- The Tony Award-winning musical *Dear Evan Hansen* is about a teenager with social anxiety who desperately yearns for connection. Steven Levenson, who wrote the musical's book (script), explained, "At the heart of our story, in a world starving for connection, [is] a character utterly incapable of connecting." In the liner notes of the cast recording, Levenson (2017) shared what the show's creators wanted to convey as the setting: "a world fractured and broken, in which people no longer remember how to connect, where technology allows us to chat, any time and any place, with our thousands of 'friends' and yet not have a single person to whom we can actually speak."
- The hit song "Connection" by OneRepublic (2018) is about longing to connect but struggling to find others who will take time to connect. In the song's music video, lead singer Ryan Tedder walks through the World Trade Center's Oculus mall in New York City trying to connect with passersby who don't even acknowledge him, or

each other, because they are staring into their palms as if in a trance-like state glued to their smartphones. Tedder sings, "If there's so many people here, then why I am so lonely? Can I get a connection?"

- *Maniac* is a Netflix miniseries about a dystopian future world falling apart from loneliness and social isolation. In this world people rent friends, and some individuals are so incapable of coping with social interaction that they isolate themselves in containers that meet only their most basic biological needs (Leszkiewicz 2018).

What television shows or movies come to mind that explore this theme of loneliness and a longing to connect beyond the surface? Once you start looking for it, you'll spot it all over, even in corporate taglines.

The issue of declining social connection grabbed national media attention in 2017 when Julianne Holt-Lunstad, a professor of psychology and neuroscience at Brigham Young University, gave a presentation titled "Loneliness: A Growing Public Health Threat" at the annual convention of the American Psychological Association. Holt-Lunstad presented data from two research studies. The first aggregated 148 independent studies that collectively included more than 300,000 participants. The second study aggregated 70 independent studies of more than 3.4 million individuals from North America, Europe, Asia, and Australia. Holt-Lunstad reported that results of the two studies and other data suggested that:

- Greater social connection was associated with a 50 percent reduced risk of early death (Holt-Lunstad et al. 2010).
- Feeling lonely, being socially isolated (that is, not around people), or living alone each was associated with a risk of premature death that was equal to or greater than the risk of premature death from widely known risk factors including obesity and smoking up to 15 cigarettes per day (Holt-Lunstad et al. 2015).
- Several nations around the world are presently facing an "epidemic of loneliness" (Holt-Lunstad 2017).

Holt-Lunstad recommended that nations place a higher priority on research and resources to identify solutions to the public health threat from rising social disconnection. In response to research on the levels of loneliness in the United Kingdom, then–Prime Minister Theresa May appointed the first Minister for Loneliness in January 2018 to work on policies to address the issue and ramifications of loneliness. One new program called "Safe and Connected" has postal carriers from the Royal Mail check in on residents, ask them questions, and connect those who are at risk for loneliness to local resources in their community (Anderson 2018). Now many nations, including Australia, Canada, China, France, Germany, India, Japan, and Russia, are debating how to address the issue of rising loneliness and social isolation (Wahlquist 2018; Stroh 2019; Cai 2018; Whiting 2018; Noack 2018; Ali and Barnagarwala 2018; Hoffman 2018; Russia Beyond 2018). Responses include a program in Denmark that connects isolated individuals together for group meals (Global Health Aging 2016) and Japan's citizens' register that identifies isolated, older individuals who are then visited by volunteers (Wong 2019).

Holt-Lunstad's warning about the epidemic of loneliness was supported when in early 2018 the insurance company Cigna reported research that found chronic loneliness in America had reached epidemic levels. Cigna research in 2019 found a further rise in loneliness. Based on its 2019 survey of 10,400 U.S. adults age 18 and older, Cigna stated:

- Three in five Americans are lonely (61 percent), up from 54 percent in 2018.
- More than half of Americans report sometimes or always feeling left out (52 percent).
- Nearly half of Americans (47 percent) report their relationships with others are not meaningful.
- Generation Z (adults ages 18–22) is the loneliest generation (Cigna 2020).

About Cigna's research, David M. Cordani, president and chief executive officer of Cigna, commented, "we're seeing a lack of human connection, which ultimately leads to a lack of vitality" (Cigna 2018a).

Thanks to modern technology and the increased pace of the modern business world, prior to the COVID-19 pandemic many people had less time to connect at home because they were spending more time at their workplace or monitoring work from home via mobile devices. Longer commute times were also affecting the amount of time available for connecting.

When the COVID-19 pandemic occurred, many organizations quickly shifted employees to remote work. One survey of 200 companies across multiple industries found that 59 percent expected their work-from-home policies to remain in place after the pandemic ended (Willis Towers Watson 2020). The net effect of remote work on connection remains to be seen. While eliminating commute times theoretically frees up time to connect, remote workers miss out on the planned and organic social connection that occurs in the physical workplace.

What else is contributing to the rise in disconnection? Some families, nuclear or extended, have spread out geographically, which results in less time spent connecting. The increasing number of single-person households is another factor. In 1950, less than 10 percent of American households contained only one individual; by 2013 that number had nearly tripled, to 28 percent, the highest in U.S. history, where it has remained through 2019 (Marche 2012; Masnick 2015; U.S. Census Bureau 2019). I should point out that although living alone does not mean an individual is lonely, it has been shown to be associated with a risk of early death that is on par with the risk from loneliness and social isolation (Holt-Lunstad et al. 2015).

Other factors that may also contribute to declining connection include historically high divorce rates (which have recently been on the decline due to lower marriage rates); more two-parent working families; lower participation in community organizations, including faith-based communities; higher layoffs and employee turnover; and a productivity push in organizations that has squeezed out time for people to connect, whether they work from the office or remotely.

Recent research suggests that increased time in front of screens (television, computers, mobile devices, gaming) may be displacing time previously spent connecting face-to-face. Professor Jean Twenge of San Diego State University and author of *iGen: Why Today's Super-Connected Kids Are Growing Up Less Rebellious, More Tolerant, Less Happy—and Completely Unprepared for Adulthood—and What That Means for the Rest of Us* (2019) argues the shift in how adolescents spend their leisure time from face-to-face to digital communications may account for the decline in adolescent well-being after 2011. Research of parents has found they spend an average of more than nine hours a day with digital media. This may explain some of the decline in happiness among adults since 2000 (Common Sense Media 2016).

The Dangers of Disconnection

Disconnection has a ripple effect. When people feel disconnected, they are vulnerable to stress. And as the pace of change speeds up and competition increases in today's hyper-competitive global marketplace, stress levels will naturally rise too. In 2017, Gallup Research found that eight out of 10 Americans report they are afflicted by stress (Saad 2017). The combination of rising stress and declining psychological resources results in a volatile mix.

Short-term stress is manageable for most people, but a sustained period of stress is extremely unhealthy. During a state of stress response, the human body reallocates resources, including blood, glucose, and oxygen, to bodily systems that it expects to use for fight or flight, including the heart, lungs, and thighs, while reducing those same resources to the digestive system, immune system, reproductive system, and parts of the brain. If this denial of resources is sustained, it could result in feelings of ill health and even cause serious damage. For example, after just a few hours, the lack of nutrients to the brain begins to alter the structure of neurons in the hippocampus, which is involved in the learning and memory function (Sapolsky 2010).

The combination of stress and disconnection can also trigger unhealthy behaviors. In the workplace, you might see a rise in gossiping, overreacting and making false assumptions, incivility, bullying, or violence. When people feel unsupported, left out, or lonely, they often turn to coping mechanisms to feel better. These behaviors run the risk of becoming obsessive and addictive because when people try to stop, they experience unpleasant sensations of withdrawal, which may include anxiety, depression, feelings of emptiness, irritability, lethargy, or numbness. Furthermore, some addictions may require increased frequency and involvement to produce the desired pleasure, causing the addictive behavior to crowd out time spent on healthy activities. People who struggle with loneliness and addictive coping behaviors are also more likely to commit suicide. In fact, suicide is now the leading cause of injury-related death in America, outnumbering even car accidents (this is similar to findings for the European Union, Canada, and China; Rocket et al. 2012). Within the U.S. Department of Health and Human Services, the Centers for Disease Control and Prevention (CDC) recommends individual, family, and community connectedness to prevent suicidal behavior. (If you or someone you know is considering suicide, please call the National Suicide Prevention Lifeline at 800.273.8255.)

The lack of connection has been shown to contribute to substance and process addictions. In a review of 83 studies on addiction with at least 500 subjects, Sussman and others (2011) focused on the following potential substance and process addictions: cigarettes, alcohol, illicit drugs, binge eating, gambling, Internet, falling in love, sex, exercise, work, and shopping. They concluded that nearly half the adult U.S. population suffers from an addiction "with serious negative consequences." Substance addictions include eating disorders as well as behaviors that attempt to manipulate pleasure by ingesting products into the body, such as dependence on alcohol, tobacco, or mood-altering legal and illegal drugs. Process addictions are pathological behaviors that involve mood-altering events that produce feelings of pleasure. These addictions include dependence on busyness and work, exercise, shopping, gambling, gaming or social media, falling in love, sex, and pornography.

A lack of connection is a contributor to the alarming decline in the mental and physical health of Americans under 50. A 2013 National Research Council and National Academy of Medicine report titled *U.S. Health in International Perspective: Shorter Lives, Poorer Health* found that, in comparison to their peers in 16 wealthy nations, Americans under 50 now have the lowest average life expectancy. The report noted "when compared with the average for other high-income countries, the United States fares worse in nine health domains: adverse birth outcomes; injuries, accidents, and homicides; adolescent pregnancy and sexually transmitted infections; HIV and AIDS; drug-related mortality; obesity and diabetes; heart disease; chronic lung disease; and disability." Loneliness has been shown to contribute to many of these adverse health outcomes. Rising stress makes the problems worse (Woolf and Aron 2014).

Discrimination—whether it is based on gender, ethnicity, sexual orientation, age, political opinions, or other differences that affect how a person might view or treat another person—is a cause of disconnection and a source of stress. More women than men report that stress is on the rise and that they rely on social connection as a means to manage stress (American Psychological Association 2010). Research found that African Americans' use of social resources had a "significant stress-suppressing effect on race-related stress"

(Utsey et al. 2008). These research studies suggest that efforts that employ social connection to support individuals who are at risk for gender or race-related stress, including employee resource groups and mentoring, are having a positive effect.

Finally, practices that physically separate or isolate individuals for periods of time may increase disconnection and contribute to declining emotional health. As I noted in the introduction, at the time of writing this second edition the COVID-19 pandemic necessitated "social distancing." This public health strategy was implemented to reduce the risk of disease transmission until a vaccine could be developed. Social distancing measures include large-scale practices such as canceling group events and closing public spaces, and individual practices such as maintaining a six-foot distance from other individuals and wearing a face mask when physical distancing isn't possible. People suspected of having been exposed to the novel coronavirus were asked to quarantine for 14 days to see if they developed COVID-19. Individuals who tested positive for COVID-19 were physically isolated until they recovered.

Across the United States, governors and local authorities put a variety of "stay safe, stay home" policies in place. I live in a region that was hit hard by the virus in the early months of 2020. Unless you were an essential worker, you were asked not to leave your home except to buy food or medicine or to exercise outdoors while maintaining social distancing. In other countries, the restrictions were even tighter.

A review of studies on the psychological impact of quarantine reported negative outcomes including post-traumatic stress symptoms, confusion, and anger. The review noted that some researchers suggested the negative effects from quarantine could be long-lasting (Brooks et al. 2020).

Reasons for Optimism

Although research on the lack of connection today is troubling, there is cause for optimism and there is a path forward. My colleagues and I are encouraged to see rising awareness of the benefits of connection and the dangers of disconnection from the research and artistic works that we mentioned earlier in this chapter. Furthermore, we see more leading scientists who have concluded based on their areas of research expertise that cultures of connection are essential to promote human flourishing (Lieberman 2013a; Marmot and Sapolsky 2014; Wilson 2012).

We are encouraged that through the work we do with clients, we are witnessing more leaders come to the realization that cultures of connection provide both a performance and a competitive advantage, and they are taking intentional steps to boost connection. In a group that embraces a connection culture mindset, individuals understand that we all have universal human needs for respect, recognition, and belonging. They appreciate that each person has unique contributions to offer, given their experience and perspectives, and that the diversity that brings to the table is a good thing. They seek input and feed-back from others, and share their own opinions—all in a way that safeguards relational connections.

We also see it as a positive sign for the future that research shows younger generations place a high priority on connection. When the global market-ing firm McCann Worldgroup (2011) surveyed 7,000 young people (16- to 30-year-olds) around the world, they found that more than 90 percent rated "connection and community" as their greatest need. As the researchers put it, "to truly grasp the power of connection for [Millenials], we can look at how they wish to be remembered. It is not for their beauty, their power, or their influence, but simply for the quality of their human relationships and their ability to look after those around them." Younger generations long for greater connection, and leaders who engage them will create cultures that meet that need.

We know several young entrepreneurs who are tapping into the power of human connection and creating ways to bring people together. They've iden-tified market segments that could benefit from better connection and crafted a customer experience using products and services to meet that need. One is Riley Kiltz (2019), whom we met when he was a student at TCU and we were consulting for the TCU Center for Connection Culture. Following gradua-tion, Kiltz landed a position as an analyst at one of America's premier private equity firms. For the next three years, he often experienced little connection due to frequent travel and being away from a centralized team. "I was surprised by my need for connection because I tend to be socially reserved; it seemed like there was something deeper that I was longing for than simply being social," Kiltz said. He parlayed his own longing for connection into a vision for a workplace where he and others would experience a sense of community. The result was Craftwork Coffee, a co-working space and specialty coffee retailer with locations in Austin and Fort Worth, Texas. Craftwork was created to combat the isolation epidemic facing the next generation. "Work and coffee are some of the most common daily rhythms in our society, and we have the opportunity to create human-centered experiences around these rhythms that help our cities flourish."

Most people are familiar with post-traumatic stress but less familiar with the concept of post-traumatic growth. When times of adversity are followed by connection that heals the physical and psychological damage done from trauma, individuals can be transformed in positive ways, including becoming more grateful, humble, compassionate, and courageous. The experience of going through the COVID-19 pandemic—because of the physical and often social isolation—may make people value connection all the more. If it has the effect of increasing the desire to connect and underscoring the importance of connection, the pandemic could have a substantial positive ripple effect on human flourishing.

In summary, human connection matters to the health, happiness, and productivity of individuals. Disconnection sabotages human flourishing by increasing a host of negative outcomes including ill health, anxiety, depression, addiction, and suicide. For our own sake, and because of the impact we have on those around us, each of us needs to make sure we have sufficient connection in our lives. In later chapters, I'll provide actions you can take to boost connection in your personal life and at work.

Making It Personal

✓ What research presented in this chapter really jumped out at you? How is it relevant to your work and your life outside of work?

✓ What was your experience like during the "stay safe, stay home" period of the COVID-19 pandemic in 2020, when strict social distancing measures were in place? What happened to your stress levels and how did you manage that? Did you feel an increased desire for connection with others? If so, what did you do?

✓ Research clearly shows that connection is critical for our personal health and well-being. On a scale of 1 to 10 (with 10 being fully connected), how would you rate your current level of personal connection?

✓ Based on what you learned in this chapter about the importance of using connection to manage stress levels, write down two positive actions you can take the next time you feel overwhelmed at work. If you are a supervisor, write down two ways you can use connection to help your direct reports feel less stressed.

5

Connection Provides a Performance and Competitive Advantage to Organizations

To determine America's best large employer each year, Statista and *Forbes* survey 30,000 workers at U.S. organizations, asking them questions about their work experience. Costco, a multi-billion-dollar retailer with warehouse club operations in 11 countries, has consistently appeared in the top five. Clearly, Costco is doing something right.

In 2017 I attended Costco's Annual Managers' Conference, where I gave a keynote speech based on *Connection Culture*. Since that time, I've learned a lot about Costco. While the level of engaged employees in America is stuck at around one-third of employees and American-style capitalism has fallen out of favor with many younger Americans, I have come to believe that Costco's culture provides the solution to what ails American business. It provides a model corporate culture that all organizations should strive to emulate. I realize that's a bold claim.

Looking at Costco through the lens of the Vision + Value + Voice model, I see that task excellence plus relationship excellence is resulting in sustainable superior performance. I've met connected members and connected leaders. I believe the high degree of human connection in Costco's workplace culture helps explain why it is one of America's best employers. As Brenda Weber, vice president of human resources, told me, "Connection is at the heart of our culture at Costco."

Let's start with the connection culture element of vision, which is how employees connect to the organization's mission, values, and reputation. The vision of Costco is to help people make ends meet, help businesses be more efficient, serve customers better, and be a positive force in its communities.

Costco's values are summed up in the phrase "do the right thing." This is elaborated in its code of ethics:

- Obey the law.
- Take care of our members.
- Take care of our employees.
- Respect our suppliers.

The attitude at Costco is that if people throughout the organization live up to these standards, it will reward Costco's shareholders. Costco lives this out in the way it faithfully serves its members, the way it treats employees like family, and the positive things it does for local communities. It's reinforced in stories of Costco doing what's right even when it hurts.

Because Costco deliberately lives out these aspirations, its reputation is stellar. As a result, Costco employees trust that the company's leaders will treat them well. Costco members trust the company will provide quality goods and services at attractive prices. This extremely high level of trust and loyalty comes through in the data. Costco's annual employee turnover is around 5 percent, management turnover around 1 percent, and annual membership renewals are close to 90 percent in the United States and Canada. Such low levels of employee and management turnover combined with a high level of membership renewal rates (which encourages members to shop regularly at Costco) help the company maintain its selling, general, and administrative expenses (SG&A) under 10 percent versus competitors' SG&A rates, which are in the 18–23 percent range.

The connection culture element of value exists in a culture when people feel valued as human beings rather than being thought of and treated as means to an end. Compared to competitors, Costco provides generous compensation and benefits as well as career opportunities. At the local level, leaders at warehouses hold programs to help employees move up in responsibility, and they teach managers to connect. The fact that many of Costco's senior executives started out working on the warehouse front lines is a testament to upward career mobility. The job security Costco provides also shows that employees are valued as human beings.

Valuing people has been stress tested at Costco too. In 1993, when Costco merged with a competitor, Price Club, no jobs were cut. The times Wall Street analysts have criticized Costco for its generous compensation and benefits, Costco's leaders didn't cave in (Zimmerman 2004). Instead, they continued to do what was best for the long-term by giving raises to Costco's people. During difficult economic seasons, Costco tightened its belt, rolled up its sleeves, and worked harder and smarter so that its employees would continue getting raises.

In a conversation with Jim Sinegal, Costco's co-founder and CEO from 1983 to 2011, he emphasized to me that valuing people is the right thing to do, and it's a good business practice. Costco's low employee turnover is a case in point. Furthermore, longtime Costco employees develop friendships with each other—a factor which has been shown to boost employee engagement and performance. A word you will hear frequently at Costco is "family." The intentional attitudes, language, and behaviors at Costco make its people feel like valued members of the Costco family.

Giving people a voice to express their ideas and opinions, and then taking this input seriously, reflects the element of voice. While attending Costco's Annual Managers' Conference, I observed the company continuously tapping into the ideas and opinions of its employees to identify methods to improve its delivery of goods and services to members as well as improve efficiencies that could result in reducing costs. Video after video showed employee ideas that have been implemented, along with estimates of the economic benefits associated with each. In highlighting these stories at the conference, Costco leaders celebrated these improvements while at the same time disseminating practices that could be replicated across the company.

In his research on the character of CEOs, Fred Kiel, author of *Return on Character: The Real Reason Leaders and Their Companies Win*, ranked Jim Sinegal among the top (Kiel 2013). Ever humble, Sinegal made it clear to me he doesn't like to be singled out for credit that he feels should go to the entire Costco team. Craig Jelinek, Costco's current CEO, shared with me that he learned much over the years from reporting to and observing Sinegal.

It's this knowing who you are and what you believe, and sticking to those values that produce a connection culture—especially in times when you are being stress-tested—that makes Costco a truly great organization, in my view.

This was apparent in early 2020 following the COVID-19 outbreak when Costco experienced a surge of shoppers loading up on groceries and household supplies. Deemed an essential business that should remain open, Costco put practices "too numerous to list" in place to protect employees and members, including enhancing sanitation procedures, limiting the number of members in its stores at a given time, wiping down shopping carts as members entered the store, making hand sanitizer available throughout, requiring social distancing in the check-out area, and adding plexiglass shields between members and cashiers. It also established special shopping hours for individuals who were vulnerable to COVID-19 and provided priority access for healthcare workers and first responders (Costco 2020).

In April, Jelinek made the decision to go further in protecting people, requiring everyone in a Costco store to wear a mask to reduce the risk of virus transmission. Costco was criticized by some who argued this was an infringement on their liberty. However, given Costco's strong values of caring about members and employees, I was not surprised that Jelinek opted to go the extra mile to protect people from the highly contagious virus (Clarridge 2020).

Jelinek says the Costco leadership team is focused on leading for Costco's long-run success. As the organization prepares future generations of leaders in the ways of connection, Jelinek encourages their current leaders to be intentional about connecting. These efforts will help ensure that Costco continues to thrive for decades to come.

Six Benefits to Organizations That Have Connection Cultures

Unlike Costco, most organizations show a high degree of variation regarding employee engagement and connection (Fleming et al. 2005). These organizations contain a mixture of subcultures, some of which are connection cultures, but most of which are either cultures of control or cultures of indifference. This variation suggests that most leaders are not intentional about developing connection and connection cultures.

This is a great opportunity. By becoming more intentional about cultivating connection cultures across all levels and teams, organizations will benefit in six ways that my colleagues and I have identified:

1. **Superior employee health and cognitive advantage.** People who feel connected perform at the top of their game. They experience superior health, wellness, and well-being; are more enthusiastic, energetic, and optimistic; make better decisions; are more creative; and live longer.

2. **Higher employee engagement.** People who feel connected give their best efforts. They care about achieving results, so they exert additional effort and persevere. People who are disconnected and disengaged show up for the paycheck, giving the minimum level of effort required to keep their jobs.

3. **Tighter strategic alignment.** People who feel connected align their behavior with organizational goals. Research has shown over the last decade that nearly one in five individuals works against their organization's interests (Gallup 2017). Connected individuals, however, are more likely to work toward their supervisor's and organization's goals. Thus, organizations with greater connection experience a higher percentage of people who pull in the same direction.

4. **Superior decision making.** People who feel connected help improve the quality of decisions. Disconnected individuals are less likely to give decision makers the information they need to make optimal decisions. People who care about their organization's performance will speak up and share information, even if decision makers would rather not hear it.

5. **Higher level of innovation.** People who feel connected actively contribute to innovation. They look for ways to improve the organization and contribute to its marketplace of ideas, which is important because innovation frequently occurs when ideas from different domains are synthesized. As a result, new products, services, processes, and businesses will arise. This cognitive process has been described as integrative thinking, blending, and connecting the dots (Brooks 2011; Martin 2007; Stallard 2007).

6. **Greater agility and adaptability.** Organizations with higher levels of connection from connection cultures have people who communicate, collaborate, and cooperate more than organizations that lack connection. These connected individuals work together to identify and address external opportunities and threats. As the world becomes more complex and dynamic, agility and adaptability will become increasingly important for organizations to thrive and survive.

Absent connection, not only do organizations miss out on these six benefits, but they also run the risk of developing knowledge traps that sabotage performance. I think of knowledge traps like cholesterol building up in the human body until it clogs an artery and leads to a heart attack. Knowledge traps hinder the free flow of information or know-how, such as a critical piece of data or an insight into a competitor or feedback from a customer. Without it getting into the mix, a suboptimal decision might be made. If more and more knowledge traps build up throughout an organization and less-than-optimal decisions are made, a drag on organizational performance can occur, leading to managerial failure and eventually threatening an organization's survival.

FIGURE 5-1. KNOWLEDGE TRAPS

Be on the lookout for these types of knowledge traps that act as barriers, blocking information from getting to the person who may need it to make the best decision. Let's look at an example of each:

- **"Leader lacks humility" trap:** Richard, the head of a business unit, doesn't seek the ideas and opinions of others. The best thinking is trapped in the minds of the people who report to him, and they are getting frustrated that Richard thinks he knows what's best and won't consider their input. Some of his decisions don't reflect what they feel the unit is capable of doing and it's affecting morale.

- **"Internal rival" trap:** Amanda and Brian started at the company at the same time and went through new employee orientation together, becoming friends. They maintained their friendship as they rose through the ranks of their respective divisions, one in sales, the other in finance. They appreciated being able to have each other as an independent sounding board or a fresh perspective on an issue. Now that they are both in the running for the same senior position, Amanda has become more guarded and is withholding information that would help Brian, lest it diminish her own chances for receiving the coveted promotion.

- **"Fiefdom" trap:** Susan and Eduardo are managers of departments that are contributing work to an important project under development. They don't get along after Susan seemed indifferent to Eduardo, which he felt was condescending. He has been passive-aggressive toward her ever since. Now these managers no longer cooperate or share information that would help the other department to make the best decisions. Their teams know animosity exists between Susan and Eduardo, so out of loyalty or fear of repercussions, they too have pulled back from freely sharing information.

- **"Chain of command" trap:** Rashid expects everyone to follow the chain of command, including when it comes to communications. Natasha in customer service fielded a call from an upset customer about a defect in one of the company's new products. Natasha has been hearing similar complaints lately and is concerned that a pattern is emerging. She's filed the required paperwork with her supervisor, John, who is two levels below Rashid in the reporting structure. Natasha likes John, but she knows that he tends to drag his feet when it comes to sharing negative news on a product that is selling well. Meanwhile, Rashid needs to make an immediate decision about manufacturing a new batch of the product in order to keep up with demand. He sees strong early sales figures but the quality issues have not reached his desk yet.

- **"Out of sight, out of mind" trap:** Yu leads a hybrid team of people who work at the headquarters, in regional offices, and remotely. When the entire team meets for all-hands video conference calls, it's apparent that those who work at Yu's location have regular interactions with her and that she's relying more on their input. Anat worked closely with Yu before she transitioned to working remotely, so she is surprised that Yu didn't reach out to her on two different occasions when she made significant changes to a project Anat is working on. When Yu does connect with her it's mainly to check in on pressing deadlines. Anat knows Yu is well-intentioned, but she's discouraged that Yu isn't doing more to actively involve the people she doesn't see every day. Anat is becoming disengaged and less inclined to share her insights and perspectives.

- **"Isolationist culture" trap:** Giant Corporation has 70 percent market share and is so focused on internal matters that it fails to stay connected to its clients' changing needs. Meanwhile, a small competitor, FastX, has spent a lot of time with clients and used the knowledge it gained to develop a new technology that better meets customer needs. As a result of Giant's failure to remain aware of the changing environment, it is caught off guard when FastX launches its technology and Giant's customers flock to FastX. The loss of revenue threatens to put Giant out of business.

The Role of Connection in Engagement

In 2007 the Conference Board asked its employee engagement and commitment working group of 24 human resources and employee communications leaders to come up with a definition for employee engagement. The group offered the following definition, which is consistent with our findings on connection and connection culture:

> Employee engagement is a heightened emotional and intellectual connection that an employee has for his/her job, organization, manager, or coworkers that, in turn, influences him/her to apply additional discretionary effort to his/her work. (Gibbons 2007)

Unfortunately, since 2000, on average, more than two-thirds of people working in the United States have been disengaged with their jobs (Gallup 2017). To measure engagement, Gallup developed the Q12 survey. Like other employee engagement surveys, the Q12 asks questions to assess your level of connection with your organization's mission and purpose, as well as with your supervisor and colleagues, such as whether your supervisor or colleagues care about you as a person, make their expectations clear, encourage your development, and consider your opinion. It also assesses whether you feel connected to your work, by asking whether your job is a good fit with your strengths and if you are learning and growing. The Q12 even asks if you have a best friend at work—a question that certainly affects connection but is one that many leaders struggle with because they believe it isn't reasonable to hold a leader accountable for delivering best friends at work.

In 2016, Gallup performed a meta-analysis of 339 research studies comprising 82,248 business or work units and 1.8 million employees within 230 organizations across 73 countries. Their findings were highlighted in an earlier chapter and bear repeating. The research concluded that top quartile units with higher Q12 scores (in other words, higher connection) outperform bottom quartile units. The units with higher connection and engagement had:

- 20 percent higher sales levels
- 17 percent higher productivity
- 21 percent higher profitability
- 10 percent higher customer metrics
- 40 percent fewer quality defects
- 70 percent fewer employee safety incidents
- 24 percent lower employee turnover in higher-turnover organizations and 59 percent lower employee turnover in low-turnover organizations (low-turnover organizations were defined as those organizations with 40 percent or lower annualized turnover; Gallup 2017).

Skeptics argue that favorable organizational outcomes affect employee engagement more than employee engagement affects organizational outcomes. Gallup chief scientist James Harter teamed up with Frank Schmidt, the Gary C. Fethke chair in leadership and professor of management and organizations at the University of Iowa, to put this theory to the test. They and a group of researchers completed a meta-analysis on longitudinal research from 2,178 business units within 10 large organizations working in diverse industries. The research established causation by measuring across three time periods, finding conclusive evidence that engaged employees caused higher employee retention rates, better customer loyalty, and superior financial performance. The evidence for causality in the reverse direction—from performance to employee engagement—was, according to Schmidt, "pretty weak in comparison." The results of their study were presented in the article "Causal Impact of Employee Work Perceptions on the Bottom Line of Organizations" published in *Perspectives on Psychological Science* (Harter et al. 2010).

Many other studies confirm the positive effect connection has on organizational health and performance. Here is a small sampling of the largest and most robust studies:

- A global research study of 50,000 individuals found that employees who feel engaged and connected are 20 percent more productive than the average employee and 87 percent less likely to leave the organization (CLC 2004).
- The Hay Group (2010) studied more than 400 companies for more than seven years and found that companies with top quartile engagement and connection scores grew revenues by 2.5 to 4.5 times as much as companies with bottom quartile engagement and connection.
- A 2013 Temkin Group study of 2,400 workers in the United States found that when compared with disengaged employees, highly engaged employees are nearly six times more committed to helping their companies succeed, three times more likely to recommend improvements, and nearly five times more likely to recommend that someone apply for a job at their company.

In 1997 Arie de Geus published "The Living Company" in *Harvard Business Review*. He and his team studied 27 organizations that had been in business more than 100 years, are still important in their industries, and continue to have strong corporate identities. They concluded that those companies' leaders valued the people in their organizations more than the type of tasks they performed. The study found that each of the 27 companies had changed its business portfolio at least once—chemical company DuPont began as a maker of gunpowder, and Mitsui, which began as a drapery shop, also ventured into banking, mining, and manufacturing. As de Geus (1997) observed, the "case histories repeatedly show that a sense of community is essential for long-term survival."

Google has conducted two internal studies that underscore the importance of connection for their employees and teams to be successful. The first, Project Oxygen, was a multiyear study of its top-rated managers that was begun in 2005. Google's people analytics teams used data from performance reviews, feedback surveys, and nominations from top-manager awards to identify the factors that made the best managers. Google has since updated two of the original eight leadership behaviors and added two more to the list. Here are the Oxygen behaviors (Harrell and Barbato 2018):

1. Is a good coach
2. Empowers team and does not micromanage
3. Creates an inclusive team environment, showing concern for success and well-being
4. Is productive and results-oriented
5. Is a good communicator—listens and shares information
6. Supports career development and discusses performance
7. Has a clear vision/strategy for the team
8. Has key technical skills to help advise the team
9. Collaborates across Google
10. Is a strong decision maker.

Laszlo Bock, Google's vice president for people operations at the time of Project Oxygen, summed up the study by saying, "We'd always believed that to be a manager, particularly on the engineering side, you need to be as deep or deeper a technical expert than the people who work for you. It turns out that's absolutely the least important thing. It's important but pales in comparison. Much more important is just making that connection and being accessible" (Bryant 2011). Google took what it learned and incorporated it into training given to managers, resulting in an "improvement in management at Google and team outcomes like turnover, satisfaction, and performance over time" (Harrell and Barbato 2018).

The second was Project Aristotle, a two-year study launched in 2012 of 180 teams across the company with the goal of learning what the best teams had in common. The research identified five traits, listed here in order of importance:

- psychological safety
- dependability
- structure and clarity
- meaning
- impact (re:Work 2018).

They found that although issues like clear goals and dependability were necessary, most important was how people felt and whether they could be themselves and speak honestly while interacting with the group. Reporting on the study, author Charles Duhigg observed about Project Aristotle that, "Google's intense data collection and number crunching led it to the [conclusion] that . . . in the best teams, members listen to one another and show sensitivity to feelings and needs." He noted that members "seemed to know when someone was feeling upset or left out" and, "by the end of the day, everyone had spoken roughly the same amount" (Duhigg 2016). In a word, it's all about connection.

Todd Hall (2015), chief scientist at Connection Culture Group, has also written about psychological safety:

> There is more and more compelling evidence that safety and security are critical for effectiveness. A recent study published in the *International Journal of Stress Management* provides a great example of this. A research team from Australia predicted and confirmed that a "psychosocial safety climate" was associated with more learning opportunities, higher levels of engagement, and better performance. In addition, psychosocial safety predicted performance indirectly through learning opportunities and engagement. When [people at work] feel emotionally safe, they are more motivated to engage in their work and perform at a high level.

Diminished Health When Connection Is Lacking

An understanding of connection can be enhanced by integrating research from Abraham Maslow on the hierarchy of human needs, Mihaly Csikszentmihalyi on optimal experience (or flow), Victor Frankel on meaning, Edward L. Deci and Richard M. Ryan on autonomy, and Teresa Amabile and Steven Kramer on progress. Their works, along with our research, led to the conclusion that there are seven universal human needs necessary to thrive at work. As introduced in chapter 2, the seven needs are respect, recognition, belonging, autonomy, personal growth, meaning, and progress. Meeting these needs helps people feel connected to their work, their supervisor and colleagues, their organization's identity, and, in many cases, the people they serve (their customers, clients, or the beneficiaries of their work). The sense of connection helps them thrive. When these seven needs are not met, people don't feel connected and report feeling bored, lethargic, lonely, anxious, sad, or depressed. These emotions diminish their enthusiasm and energy, which undermines their ability to perform well.

When organizational cultures lack sufficient connection, people in the lower end of an organization's chain of command and status hierarchy suffer. The pioneering Whitehall studies of British civil servants found that government workers who were lower in the hierarchy experienced poorer cardiovascular health and lower life expectancies, even though they had the same access to healthcare services as their higher-level counterparts. The researchers found that "good levels of social support had a protective effect on mental health and reduced the risk of spells of sickness absence," whereas a lack of support and unclear or inconsistent information was associated with a twofold increased risk of poor general mental health (Ferrie 2004). A more recent study found that nonleaders showed higher levels of salivary cortisol and anxiety, which are physiological and psychological indicators of stress, respectively (Sherman et al. 2012). These studies suggest that people with less power, control, influence, and status are especially in need of connection to protect them from the biological damage caused by chronic stress and the additional damage caused by coping behaviors that may include smoking and alcohol and drug abuse.

In his excellent book *Dying for a Paycheck: How Modern Management Harms Employee and Company Performance—and What We Can Do About It*, Stanford Business School professor Jeffrey Pfeffer (2018) makes a compelling case with an abundance of evidence and examples that workplace cultures today are harmful and unsustainable. He addresses the harmful effect of layoffs, lack of health insurance, work-family conflict, long work hours, lack of job autonomy, and the choice of remaining in toxic work cultures.

Empirical Evidence Supporting Connection Culture

Research from the positive psychology field provides crucial insights into connection and how it works in organizations. In chapter 3, I shared 24 character strengths (or values) that provide a survival advantage to individuals and groups. The Character > Connection > Thrive Chain (Figure 3-1) ties all the pieces together by showing how individual character strengths promote the core elements of a connection culture, which in turn meet the seven universal human needs for individuals and organizations to thrive.

In 2018, a scholarly study conducted by Jon Rugg and supervised by our chief scientist Todd Hall, "The Connection Value Chain: Impact of Connection Culture and Employee Motivation on Perceived Team Performance," identified two interrelated ideas that are emerging in research, which support the positive impact of connection in organizations. First, organizations comprise a complex web of intricate relationships. Second, effective leaders who foster positive relationships and care about people possess "relational virtues." Connection is cited as a new general theory of leadership and organizational culture that integrates these broad ideas.

The research follows similar value chain logic based on the Character > Connection > Thrive Chain from my earlier books, *Fired Up or Burned Out* and the first edition of *Connection Culture*. The study modifies that chain into the Connection Value Chain (Figure 5-2; p. 106–107).

The study's rationale is based on this value chain logic:

1. Connected Leader Virtues (connection, compassionate love, wisdom, humility, and courage; these are reflected in a leader's character)
2. Connected Leader Practices (create unity around a shared vision, implement vision, establish security and trust, nurture development, stimulate creativity and innovation, and cultivate collaboration; these represent a leader's prosocial behaviors and create an environment of safety and connection)
3. Connection Culture (Vision, Value, and Voice; these attributes promote shared identity, empathy, and understanding)
4. Employee Motivation (intrinsic needs that, when met, produce high levels of employee engagement)
5. Team Effectiveness (quality, productivity, and performance)
6. Organizational Effectiveness (market share growth, revenue growth, and customer loyalty).

The Connection Value Chain study examined leader virtues and practices as inputs, organizational culture and employee motivation as mediating factors, and perceived team performance as an outcome. Ideally, three factors would be used to capture organizational effectiveness: market share growth, revenue growth, and customer loyalty and retention. Data was not collected on these variables in the study, although the variables were shown in the model for conceptual purposes and future research. The study's results supported this value chain model. In other words, leaders influence team performance through the mechanisms of employee motivation and organizational culture.

In addition, the study found that connected leader virtues and practices were positively associated with a connection culture and negatively associated with cultures of control and indifference. Similarly, the results revealed that a connection culture predicted more positive team performance, whereas a culture of indifference predicted more negative team performance and a culture of control showed no association with team performance.

Overall, the results suggest that a connection culture outperforms cultures of control and indifference. This finding is consistent with growing literature affirming that organizations that value their employees produce better performance outcomes and a greater sense of accomplishment. Additionally, the study provides empirical support for the value relationally oriented leaders bring to organizations.

Disconnection: A Hidden Systemic Risk to Organizations

In earlier chapters, I made the case that social connection is a primal human need. Its presence appears to improve the cardiovascular, endocrine, and immune systems' performance; it makes us happier, healthier, and more productive. Disconnection is associated with poorer cognitive performance, impaired executive control and self-regulation, and lower levels of self-rated health, as well as increased substance abuse, depressive symptoms, and suicidal ideation. I also noted that loneliness is on the rise and disconnection is widespread, with research conducted in 2019 showing three out of five American adults to be lonely. Researchers have also found an association between disconnection and poorer task, team role, and relational performance (Ozcelik and Barsade 2018). It should come as no surprise that when human beings are not thriving, neither do the teams and organizations they are in.

FIGURE 5-2. CONNECTION VALUE CHAIN

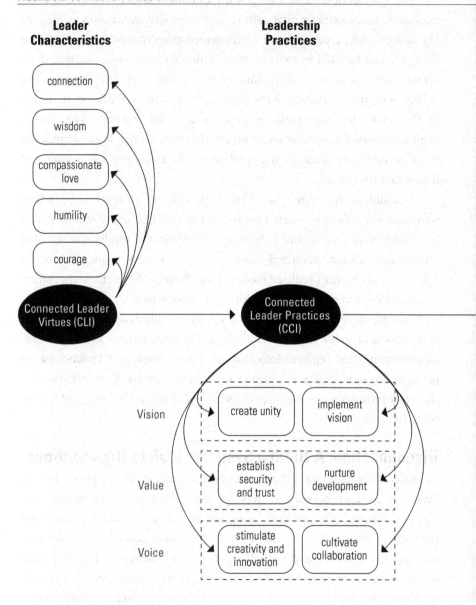

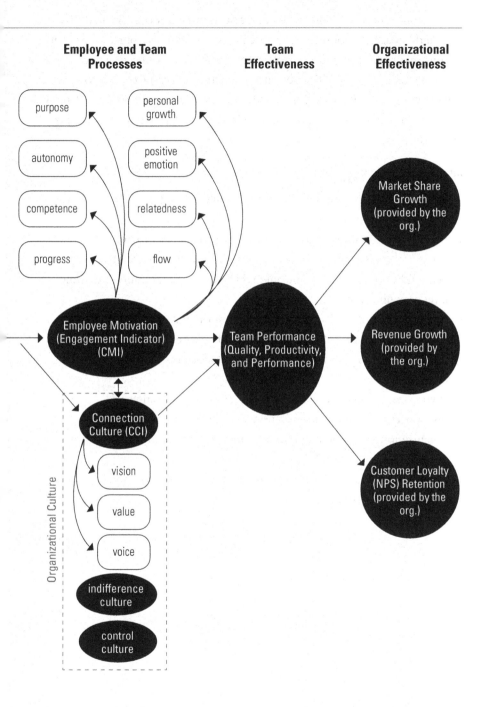

Disconnection is a hidden systemic risk to organizations (Stallard 2020). It should be taken seriously. The research on organizations from a wide variety of sources proves beyond any reasonable doubt that connection provides a performance and competitive advantage and that a lack of connection sabotages performance. Following a second set of profiles in connection, I'll show you how to operationalize connection culture so that you and your organization thrive.

Making It Personal

✓ What research presented in this chapter really jumped out at you? How is it relevant to your work?

✓ Research clearly shows that connection provides a performance and competitive advantage to organizations. On a scale of one to 10 (with 10 being fully connected), how would you rate your organization's current level of connection?

✓ Organizations often display two or more of the three types of cultures: connection culture, culture of control, and culture of indifference. Which culture describes your team? Which cultures are present throughout the organization?

✓ If your team lacks a connection culture, what are the causes of disconnection, in your view? Consider contacting a leader in your organization who is an intentional connector and ask for tips on turning your team's culture around.

✓ Read through the examples of knowledge traps. Have you observed these traps over your career?

Profiles in Connection

As people, we're curious. How do others go about sharing their vision, demonstrating value, and increasing knowledge flow as they give people a voice? Knowing their stories might shed some light on our situation, affirm what we're doing right, or give us new ideas of what to try. Stories are powerful. Here is another collection of inspiring leaders who are results driven and relationship minded.

One

> "We're one, but we're not the same. We get to carry each other . . . "
> —lyrics from "One" by U2

U2 began as a rock band that people booed and laughed at. That was then. Now, after receiving its 22nd Grammy Award, U2 has more Grammys than any band in history. It is the only band to win Album of the Year twice (1987, 2005). Its album *The Joshua Tree* was inducted into the Grammy Hall of Fame in 2014, a recognition bestowed to honor "recordings at least 25 years old that exhibit qualitative or historical significance" (Grammy 2013). U2 surpassed the Rolling Stones' record for the highest revenue-grossing concert tour ever and held that distinction from 2011 through August 2019. Critics rave over the band's music, and fans worldwide can't seem to get enough of their songs and concert appearances. All the signs indicate that U2 will be going strong for the foreseeable future. So how did this group rise to such lofty heights, and what can we learn from its success?

The way U2 functions is just as extraordinary as its music. The band's four members—lyricist and lead singer Bono, lead guitar player "the Edge," bass guitar player Adam Clayton, and drummer Larry Mullen Jr.—have known one another since they were teenagers in Dublin, Ireland, in the 1970s. Bono has described the band as more of an organism than an organization, and several of its attributes contribute to this unique culture. Members value continuous improvement to achieve their own potential, always maintaining the view that they can become even better.

U2's members share a vision of their mission and values. You might expect a band's mission to be achieving commercial success as measured by number 1 hits and concert attendance. However, U2's mission is to improve the world through its music and influence. Bono has described himself as a traveling salesman of ideas within songs, which address themes the band members believe are important to promote, including human rights, social justice, and matters of faith. Bono and his wife, Ali, help people experiencing poverty, particularly in Africa, through their philanthropy and the organizations they've created.

U2's members value one another as people and don't just think of one another as a means to an end. Bono has said that although he hears melodies in his head, he is unable to translate them into written music. Considering himself a terrible guitar and keyboard player, he relies on his fellow members to help him write the songs and praises them for their talents, which are integral to U2's success.

Bono has also had his band members' backs during times of trial. When Larry lost his mom in a car accident a short time after the band was formed, Bono was there to support him. Bono, who had already lost his mother, understood Larry's pain. When U2 was offered its first recording contract on the condition that it replace Larry with a more conventional drummer, Bono told the record company executive, "There's no deal without Larry." When the Edge went through divorce, his bandmates were there to support him. When Adam showed up to a concert so stoned he couldn't perform, the others could have thrown him overboard for letting them down. Instead, they had someone step in to cover for him and then went on to help Adam overcome his drug and alcohol addiction.

Bono's bandmates have his back too. One of the most vivid examples of this came when U2 campaigned during the 1980s for the observance of a Martin Luther King Jr. Day in the United States. Bono received a death threat that warned him not to sing "Pride (In the Name of Love)," a song about the Reverend Martin Luther King Jr., at an upcoming concert. The FBI considered it a credible threat. Bono described in an interview that he closed his eyes as he came to the lyrics in the song about the bullet that rang out in the Memphis sky that killed Dr. King. When he opened his eyes again at the end of the verse, he discovered that Adam was standing in front of him to shield him from potential harm. Years later, when U2 was inducted into the Rock and Roll Hall of Fame, Bono thanked Adam for being willing, literally, to take a bullet for him.

Unlike many bands in which one megastar gets most of the economic profits, U2 shares its profits equally among the four band members and their manager. This further shows the value Bono has for his band members and manager. (We're not saying that all organizations should split the company's economic profits equally; simply recognize that when leaders take too much, it works against engaging the people they lead.)

Each member has a voice in decisions, thanks to the band's participatory, consensus-oriented decision-making approach. If one person strongly opposes a particular action, the band won't do it, which encourages the flow of knowledge among band members, allowing the best ideas to come to light. Their passion for excellence is also reflected in relentless arguments over their music. Bono has stated that this approach can be slow and frustrating at times, but the members of U2 believe it is necessary to achieve excellence.

These factors of shared identity, empathy, and understanding create a culture of connection, community, and unity among the members of U2. Bono has described the band as a tight-knit family and community. Their commitment to support one another extends beyond the four members of the band to a larger community that includes their families, crew members, and collaborators—many of whom have known each other for decades.

The secret of U2's success is its leadership and culture. Bono connects as a leader among equals because he communicates an inspiring vision and lives it, he values people as individuals, and he gives them a voice in decision making. It is this culture of vision, value, and voice that has helped U2 achieve and sustain its superior performance.

Making It Personal

✓ What are some ways you could reach out to a colleague who is going through a personal difficulty that would show you care?

✓ Knowing that a colleague is for you (rather than against you) and wants to see you be able to do your best and succeed makes a difference, especially when you are working through a setback or receiving constructive feedback. How can you show the people you are responsible for leading that you have their back?

✓ Like U2, do you take the time to try to develop consensus among the people you are responsible for leading? Why would it be important to include people in decisions about their work? What decision do you need to make in the coming weeks that could benefit from bringing others into the conversation at this stage?

Miracle in Motor City

When Alan Mulally was introduced as the next CEO of Ford Motor Company in 2006, he stunned the audience by candidly answering the question "what kind of car do you drive" with the response, "a Lexus . . . the finest car in the world." The room fell silent. Mulally's tenure as CEO of Ford was also full of surprises, particularly the remarkable turnaround he orchestrated.

The year Mulally arrived at Ford, sales, market share, and profits were falling, and the automaker's culture comprised silo rivalries with leaders embroiled in turf wars. This culture drove Ford to the verge of bankruptcy. By the time Mulally announced his retirement in May 2014, he had led Ford to 19 consecutive profitable quarters and rising market share in North America. And unlike American rivals General Motors and Chrysler, Ford did not seek a U.S. government bailout following the financial crisis in 2008. At his retirement, rather than the stunned silence Mulally experienced when first introduced, Ford employees gave him a standing ovation.

Alan Mulally is an excellent example of a leader who created a connection culture. He used founder Henry Ford's original vision of "opening the highways for all mankind" to express how the company makes the world a better place by serving others. Mulally explained that Ford gives people freedom of mobility so they can access opportunities for growth. This united employees around the vision and focused them on a cause greater than self. The vision was also factored into decision-making processes, such as in evaluations of new product development. The newly designed F-150 pickup, for example, got an aluminum-based body that made it lighter, more fuel efficient, and more affordable.

Mulally also boosted value in the Ford culture. He frequently used the phrases "One Ford," "one team," "the power of teams," and "working together always works." He also distributed wallet-sized cards with Ford's business plan on one side and 16 expected behaviors (values) on the other, including "work together effectively as one team." In meetings, he acted as a facilitator and coach rather than a dictator, prohibiting humor at the expense of others. Rather than thinking of other individuals and organizations as competitors, Mulally employed a win-win approach to external relationships. This helped him forge an agreement with the United Auto Workers union to make the changes necessary for Ford to make a profit in return for bringing production back to the United States. It also helped him consolidate Ford's purchases to suppliers that were willing to partner with Ford to drive down costs in return for receiving a greater share of Ford's business.

Mulally expected leaders to openly share the obstacles they faced, and celebrated leaders who helped one another instead of focusing solely on problems in their domain. Another way he increased voice was through the weekly business plan review (BPR) meeting. Held at Ford's global headquarters in Dearborn, Michigan, the BPR was attended by the global leadership team and all business and functional leaders, either in person or by teleconference. At BPR meetings leaders gave updates on their goals, which were color-coded green for on-target, yellow for at-risk, and red for off-target. When problems were identified, follow-up meetings were scheduled to dig deeper and identify solutions. BPRs also addressed strategic topics, such as the economy, labor supply, and competitive developments. Feedback was encouraged during BPRs, which made it a safe environment for honest dialogue. This prompted people to move toward consensus, rather than forcing it, as well as helped decision makers identify optimal solutions, making alignment and excellence in execution more likely.

Making It Personal

✓ Alan Mulally did many different things to address the silo behavior and rivalries he found at Ford when he became CEO. One avenue he used was employing catch phrases that promoted collaboration and unity, such as "working together always works" and "One Ford." What are some of the words or phrases that your organization or team uses to encourage or celebrate good work? What are phrases that family members or teachers used when you were growing up that are ingrained in your memory and still guide you?

✓ The childhood rhyme "sticks and stones may break my bones, but words will never hurt me" doesn't ring true. Though we may hide or suppress our response, words can sting us emotionally. Humor has a place and can be effective at building team rapport and shared experiences. But when humor is at the expense of another person it should not be welcome. Have you observed or experienced how a sarcastic remark has broken connection? Is there anyone you have "wounded," even unintentionally, while going for a laugh from others? Consider apologizing to that person.

✓ Mulally's weekly business plan review meeting included leaders across functions who provided updates on their area of responsibility and were encouraged to participate in giving feedback on issues being raised. How open are you to input on a project from people who don't have a role or responsibility for it? Who might you ask to be a "sounding board" on a project?

Saving the Girl Scouts

There was a time in the countercultural 1960s and 1970s when the Girl Scouts, like other youth organizations, were viewed as increasingly irrelevant. As a result, the Girl Scouts experienced declining membership. Fortunately, Frances Hesselbein came to the rescue. Hesselbein began her association with the Girl Scouts in the 1960s when she agreed to temporarily lead a troop of 30 girls in Johnstown, Pennsylvania, whose leader had recently left. Although she had no daughters of her own, it wasn't long before her experience with Troop 17 developed into a lifelong commitment to Girl Scouting. In 1976, she became CEO of the national organization.

With membership falling and the organization in a state of serious decline, Hesselbein put sound management practices in place. During her tenure, Girl Scout membership quadrupled to nearly 3.5 million, diversity more than tripled, and the organization was transformed into what Peter Drucker described as "the best-managed organization around." She accomplished this amazing turnaround with 6,000 paid staff members and 730,000 volunteers. Her use of connection culture put the Girl Scouts on track for success.

Hesselbein stressed the importance of reaching out to scouts and educating them about the threats they face, such as drugs and teen pregnancy. She helped women to envision the Girl Scouts as a professional, well-managed organization that could carry out this important work.

Hesselbein's leadership style boosted the culture's value. She once wrote that effective leaders have a genuine "appreciation of their colleagues individually and the dignity of the work their colleagues do" (Hesselbein 2002). Hesselbein's leadership philosophy is "to serve is to live" and her words and actions embody human value. She built a conference center to train Girl Scout staff and invested in improving Girl Scout leaders' people skills. As a role model, she effectively increased human value in the Girl Scout culture and multiplied her actions as other leaders across the organization adopted her leadership style. She kept up with what was going on in the lives of the people around her and personally reached out to anyone when congratulations or consolation were in order.

Voice is key to innovation because it creates a marketplace of ideas that allows people to more easily spot new opportunities to improve the organization. Hesselbein increased this element of a connection culture by approaching communication in an inclusive way, expanding information in ever-larger circles across the organization. Rather than lecturing, her style was to ask insightful questions to draw out relevant issues. In planning and allocating the Girl Scouts' resources, she introduced a circular management process that involved nearly everyone within the organization.

Frances Hesselbein stressed that communication is circular—listening and responding to one another—and therefore listening must be valued. She wanted the Girls Scouts organization leaders to listen to Girl Scouts, to each other, and to those outside of the organization. When writing about the art of listening, Frances Hesselbein has given this advice: "Banish the 'but.'" This is especially important when you are giving feedback. According to Hesselbein, "'But' is nobody's friend—listener or speaker. 'And' provides the graceful transition, the nonthreatening bridge to mutual appreciation, the communication that builds effective relationships" (Hesselbein 2012).

The Girl Scouts' future was once again looking bright when Hesselbein passed the leadership torch to her successor in 1990. Of affecting change in a large and complex organization, she has written, "Inclusion is a powerful value: when we open up the organization, dispersing the leadership, including people from across the enterprise, there is a new energy, a new synergy" (McKinney 2011).

She was able to continue spreading her leadership legacy when Peter Drucker recruited her to be the head of the Drucker Foundation (which was renamed the Leader to Leader Institute, and then the Frances Hesselbein Leadership Institute in 2012). Through its activities, including publication of the award-winning *Leader to Leader* journal, the institute is dedicated to carrying out the passion that Drucker and Hesselbein shared for strengthening leadership in the social sector. That dedication was further recognized in 1998 when she was awarded the Presidential Medal of Freedom by President Bill Clinton for her work as "a pioneer for women, volunteerism, diversity, and opportunity."

Making It Personal

✓ Value exists in a culture when everyone understands the needs of people, appreciates their positive, unique contributions, and helps them achieve their potential. According to Frances Hesselbein, effective leaders have a genuine "appreciation of their colleagues individually and the dignity of the work their colleagues do." Think about the people you work the most closely with in your job or volunteer work, including those who may work in a different group or location. From your vantage point, what does each person do really well? What aspect of their character can you affirm? Whether in private or in front of your peers, take a moment to recognize that individual.

✓ Frances Hesselbein's leadership philosophy is "to serve is to live." Scientists have found that when we help others, we experience a "helper's high," a term for how we feel after the release of endorphins, a "feel good" chemical naturally made in our bodies that can boost our happiness and relieve pain (Berry 2018; Bourg Carter 2014). Serving someone else can shift our focus off ourselves, bring a sense of satisfaction for having done some good, and prompt feelings of gratitude for the blessings we have, however great or small. Have you had that experience of feeling more "alive" after serving others in some capacity?

✓ Do you recall a time when a supervisor was talking with you about your performance and all was going well until you heard the word "but"?

For many of us, any encouraging comment that was said before then will fall by the wayside; what sticks with us is what was said after the "but." Test out this advice from Frances Hesselbein to "banish the 'but'" from your vocabulary.

Coach K's Aha Moment

Mike Krzyzewski, Coach K, as he is better known, has led the Duke University men's basketball team to the Final Four of American college basketball twelve times. Consider what he's accomplished as he entered the 2019–2020 season:

- five national championships (1991, 1992, 2001, 2010, 2015)
- six Olympic gold medals as head coach of the U.S. men's national team
- 1,132 career wins (the most in NCAA history).

One look at his 21-page biography on the Duke website is all one needs to truly appreciate the magnitude of his accomplishments. Coach K's phenomenal success as a coach and leader raises the question: How does he do it?

The obvious reasons are that he's talented, disciplined, and works hard. But a lot of coaches fit that description, so there must be something else that separates Coach K from other coaches and provides his team with a sustainable competitive advantage.

Coach K grew up in a male-dominated culture. He attended an all-boys Catholic high school in Chicago and went on to play basketball at West Point under the driven, domineering, and perfectionist coach Bobby Knight. He also served in the U.S. Army.

His outlook took a major turn when he found himself outnumbered at home by his wife, Mickie, and their three daughters. Every night at dinner, Coach K observed how Mickie and the girls reconnected by sharing the details of their day, including what they had done and how they felt about it. Whereas guys often cut to the chase in conversations, his wife and daughters invested time each day to reconnect.

He also observed how attuned they were to how people felt—their intuition was like radar. Time and again Mickie could sense when something was bothering one of Coach K's players. She was nearly always right, so he learned that it was wise to follow up and ask the player if something was wrong. Sure enough, something was always amiss and talking about the problem made the player feel, and play, better. When he didn't follow up, the player often fell out of sync with the team and performance suffered.

Coach K's aha moment about the importance of connection and relationships transformed his coaching style. He began involving Mickie and his daughters in the Duke men's basketball program. The Krzyzewski women became, in military terms, a reconnaissance team to sense the state of relationships, emotions, connection, community, and unity among the team. The boys became extended members of their family. As Coach K became more intentional about developing the feeling of connection among the team, it produced superior results. He stressed the importance of knowing everyone's name and being courteous to fellow players: "You know what? 'Please' and 'Thank you' go a long way. You can be damn sure that every guy on my team says that. The best way to get better as a team is if everyone has ownership, and if you do these things they will" (Sokolove 2006).

If you study Coach K's approach, you'll see that he clearly articulates a connection culture in which shared identity, empathy, and understanding move primarily self-centered individuals toward group-centered membership. When speaking to potential recruits, Coach K tells them, "We're developing a relationship here, and if you are not interested, tell me sooner rather than later. . . . If you come here, for however long, you're going to unpack your suitcase. We're going to form a bond, and you're going to be part of this family" (Sokolove 2006).

On the surface, this sounds easy. But it's not. Human beings are complex. We are driven consciously and unconsciously by an infinite variety of past experiences, temperaments, perspectives, and thinking and learning styles. Coach K and his coaching staff, including the Krzyzewski women, have been developing ways to connect for years. Whereas many coaches and leaders remain clueless to the power of connection, the Krzyzewskis continue refining their methods while adding to Coach K's legacy and the remarkable record of success of Duke's men's basketball program.

Making It Personal

✓ Who on your team or in your organization is a natural connector? What are their "best practices" that you and others could adopt?

✓ Is there someone on your team who is "along the edges" and not very connected? What can you do that would make them feel more connected to the group?

✓ How are you at remembering names? Here are common tips to try: When you are first introduced, mentally commit to capturing the person's name. Use it right away if you can ("It's nice to meet you, Jane") and casually use it several more times over the course of your conversation. If you didn't quite catch it, ask the person to repeat the name. If it is not a common name to you, you might ask the person to spell it for you. Other recommendations include thinking of a rhyme or an association.

Designing Connection Into Culture

The Institute for Healthcare Improvement (IHI) is a not-for-profit independent healthcare organization headquartered in Boston, Massachusetts, with a mission to improve health and healthcare worldwide while reducing waste and cost. Since its founding in 1991, IHI has worked with healthcare providers and leaders throughout the world to achieve safe and effective healthcare. IHI's work has included motivating healthcare organizations to change, designing and testing new models of care in partnership with both patients and healthcare professionals, and ensuring the adoption of best practices and effective innovations.

IHI is a mission-driven organization that defines clear goals for its work. In 2004, for example, IHI set out to save 100,000 lives in 18 months through six best practices it identified and shared with healthcare organizations (Baehrend 2016). More than 3,000 hospitals in the United States joined the campaign, and they saved more than 120,000 lives (Bisognano 2018–2019). In addition to being task and results oriented, IHI has cultivated a culture of connection that achieves relationship excellence.

Maureen Bisognano was hired in 1995 to become chief operating officer and executive vice president. From 2010 to 2015, she served as president and CEO. Bisognano recounted to me that "when Don [IHI founder Donald M. Berwick, MD] and I got together, we were very intentional about the culture." They invested considerable time researching and discussing how to develop the best organizational culture, even meeting with seasoned corporate leaders to get their perspectives.

Speaking with Bisognano, I asked her to share specific ways that connection was infused in the culture through vision, value, and voice. She was looking at connection in all areas of IHI, starting with whether a potential new hire would fit in well with the culture. She mentioned that when candidates were interviewed to join the team, they met with staff at all levels at IHI. The interviewers would then get together and decide if there was a connection, and if so, a job offer was extended.

Even the physical space of the Boston office was evaluated as to whether it was conducive to connection. Office space was designed to be open and to encourage "accidental" conversations. No one had a private office, including Berwick and Bisognano, who shared an office with six other colleagues. Leaders were accessible and approachable. Bisognano was known to keep a bowl full of chocolate in the CEO's space to encourage people to stop by.

Berwick and Bisognano developed a set of values with input from IHI staff. To keep them in front of people, the values were printed on coffee cups and stenciled on the walls of IHI's office. Going deeper, an IHI citizenship guide was created to articulate the values. The *IHI Citizenship Guide* provided clear statements to help everyone across the organization understand how they were expected to conduct themselves and how they would like to be treated. Also expressed was "The Reputation," which described how IHI aspired to be viewed by people outside the organization. It included the following:

> IHI is a delight to work with. All the people . . . are intensely focused on their Mission above all. . . . The people of IHI are generous, honest, transparent, and experts on improvement. . . . They respond with breathtaking speed, and they are always respectful, dignified, and affirming. They share what they know. . . . They are one team, seamless. (Roth 2019)

In the first week of January, Berwick and Bisognano would roll out the strategic plan for the year. Then, on the first Friday of the year, every person at IHI would attend a day-long gathering that would go beyond discussing the upcoming year from an organization-wide standpoint. It would get personal. First, they would write down their own goals for the year and rate themselves on how they were currently doing. This included assessing themselves on personal growth, professional growth, family and loved ones, health, finances, and commitment to their community. Then they would write out where they wanted to go in the year ahead. They also created a personal asset map with their past accomplishments and skills. When the process was completed, decisions were made about job assignments for the year. Some people moved from answering phones to learning programs. Some moved from teaching patient safety to working in Africa to save the lives of mothers and babies. In other words, people had a voice in crafting their work and career path at IHI.

IHI was intentional about creating and maintaining feedback loops. A monthly pulse survey consisting of six questions provided Bisognano with feedback about how people were doing. At the coffee gatherings Bisognano held twice a month, she would share the results and what actions were being taken to address issues that had been raised. Bisognano described a profound lesson for her when a young male colleague shared that IHI's paternity policy was outdated. She responded that IHI was progressive and she was sure he was wrong. But when Bisognano checked on it, she was "horrified" to discover he was right. At the next coffee meeting, she announced IHI was changing the paternity policy so fathers had more time with their newborns and that IHI's maternity policy was also being changed to give new mothers additional time.

Between those coffee gatherings, an informal and whimsical method of gauging how things were going was on display for all to see. Placed at the door where people left the office each day were two bowls and a tin can containing white and blue beads. If they had a good day, they would pick up a white bead and drop it in the bowl that had a smiling face on it; if they had a bad day, a day of setbacks or frustrations, a blue bead was selected and placed in the other bowl. The ratio of white to blue beads was tallied each day and communicated at the next group gathering with Bisognano.

As another means of ensuring that lines of communication could flow smoothly, colleagues could "request mast," a term IHI borrowed from the U.S. Navy that meant individuals had the right to take an issue or concern to a leader who is more senior than their direct supervisor.

When it comes to the individuals a leader is responsible for leading, Bisognano told me she believes it is critical for leaders to understand the person's whole life. In addition to knowing employees' names, leaders should know what's going on with their families and lives outside work. IHI encourages everyone to "never worry alone," which communicated that their colleagues have their backs and they don't need to deal with difficult problems and issues on their own.

Bisognano believes it is important to build teams that are multi-generational, multicultural, and multi-professional. (At IHI, a multi-professional team would be one that includes physicians, nurses, and administrators, for example.) One means of promoting multi-generational connection was to encourage mentoring in which young people felt comfortable asking older colleagues to guide them as well as reverse mentoring that might pair an older colleague with a younger colleague to bring them up to speed in an area in which the younger colleague had more experience, such as using a new technology tool.

To help the mix of diverse individuals work well together, Bisognano asked staff from many cultures to speak at Lunch & Learn sessions. The sessions included foods from the speaker's culture and gave attendees an appreciation for the language, family values, and way people from that cultural background viewed work.

IHI's Ministry of Fun organized events to boost connection, including sports outings, in-office golf tournaments, and retreats. One event was the annual IHI Olympics held at Bisognano's home, with teams comprising people from different departments (so they would get to know one another) competing in games. Leading up to the IHI Olympics, teams met to prepare for the competition and make team T-shirts, learning more about each other, personally and professionally, along the way.

Bisognano began each Monday morning meeting with the senior executive team by asking the members to take one or two minutes and share one good thing, a practice that helped the leadership team get to know one another better. In these meetings, most of the good things were personal memories of the weekends with family and friends. Then, at 9:30 a.m., an hour-long all-staff meeting was facilitated by a staff member, with remote workers dialing in. Bisognano usually told a story of a patient who benefited from IHI's work to reinforce the meaning of the team's work. This was followed by a mix of agenda items that included describing project results, sharing ideas for new research, thanking people, and seeking opinions and ideas about work-related issues.

Meetings at IHI were conducted with the expectation that anyone could contribute great ideas. This mindset made it safe for even college interns to speak up and share their ideas and opinions. When a meeting was held, the rule was that if you were in the office and you were interested in the content being covered, you were free to join in.

In early 2016, Maureen Bisognano retired from a full-time role at IHI. As president emerita and senior fellow, she continues to speak at healthcare conferences and advise healthcare organizations.

Making It Personal

✓ For a group to have sustainable superior performance there needs to be both task excellence and relationship excellence. Therefore, it's not enough to base a hiring decision on a candidate's competence with the task side. If the candidate is not a good fit relationally, they will disrupt the connection that is in place. As part of its interview process, IHI has candidates meet with staff at all levels of the organization. What steps does your organization take to determine if a candidate will work well with the existing team and will be aligned with the vision, mission, and values of the group? What questions would you ask a candidate to draw out the person's ability to connect in your setting?

✓ As you read the profile, did you notice the range of opportunities that IHI offers for colleagues to have a voice and be in the loop? Which one most resonated with you—the company-wide review of the strategic plan for the coming year, the regular informal gatherings with the CEO, or the invitation to attend a meeting that interests you even if it is outside of your area of responsibility?

✓ What is the age diversity within your group and across the organization? In what ways can you encourage multi-generational connections? Are there topics that younger employees can "reverse mentor" older employees on?

Prescribing Connection

As a shy, young boy growing up in Miami, Florida, Vivek Murthy often was anxious when dropped off at school. It wasn't the academics that concerned him; it was the social aspect. Although he felt alone and had experienced racism, he didn't tell his parents because he did not want them to worry.

His parents had a profound influence on him. Originally from India, they first emigrated to England, where Murthy was born, and then moved first to Newfoundland in Canada, and then to Miami, Florida, when he was three years old. His father, Hallegere, is a primary care physician, and his mother, Myetriae, manages her husband's medical office. Murthy spent a fair amount of time at the family's medical office, helping out with simple tasks, greeting patients, and opening mail. Murthy witnessed how his parents approached medicine as more than diagnosing and treating sickness. They viewed patients as family and cultivated a powerful and healing bond of trust. "I was too young to understand the science, but what I did see was my parents building these extraordinary relationships with people," he recalls (ACGME 2019). Years later, not only did Murthy follow in their footsteps but so did his sister, Rashmi, who practices family medicine alongside her father.

When Murthy was seven years old, his parents woke him and his sister up in the middle of the night, loaded them into the car, and drove to a trailer park. En route, their mother explained they were going to see the widow of a patient named Gordon who had just died from a prolonged battle with cancer. They were concerned Ruth might be grieving alone. Murthy recalls seeing his mother climb the steps of the trailer, dressed in her traditional Indian sari, and knock on the front door. Murthy remembers seeing tears streaming down Ruth's face as she embraced his mother. How the Murthys cared for their patients and how they lived their lives serving others inspired him to become a physician.

As a teenager, Murthy observed how people connected and selflessly pulled together to help each other following the damage caused by Hurricane Andrew in August 1992.

After graduating magna cum laude from Harvard University, Murthy went on to Yale University where he earned MD and MBA degrees. His residency in internal medicine was completed at Boston's Brigham and Women's Hospital, and he joined Harvard Medical School as an instructor.

Over the next years, Murthy co-founded and led several not-for-profit and for-profit organizations to serve others. One is TrialNetworks, a software company that improves research collaboration in clinical trials and was subsequently acquired by DrugDev. Another is Doctors for America, a nonprofit that in 2019 numbered more than 18,000 physicians and medical student members committed to bringing high-quality, affordable healthcare to all.

On December 15, 2014, the U.S. Senate confirmed Vivek Murthy's nomination as America's 19th surgeon general, the youngest in U.S. history. During his ensuing 28-month tenure, Murthy made many contributions, including leading initiatives to reduce addiction, reduce e-cigarette use on the part of youth, promote walking and walkable communities, and encourage vaccination. With the rank of vice admiral in the U.S. Public Health Service Commissioned Corps, Murthy led the uniformed service of more than 6,500 public health officers who worked to protect the country from outbreaks of the Ebola and Zika viruses, and to respond to major hurricanes and healthcare shortages occurring in rural communities.

Murthy's experience as a physician, combined with his listening tour of America after he became surgeon general, convinced him that the root of many health problems is chronic loneliness and stress. In hearing people share their stories of substance use or obesity or mental illness, for example, he felt the story behind the story was usually one of deeper emotional pain. He pointed to several causes for those feelings of loneliness, including more people moving away from home, additional time spent interacting with technology, and the nature of work crowding out time for relationships. "The topic is personal to me," he said in an interview, "because I was lonely for many years as a young child, but I felt too ashamed to admit it to my family or teachers" (Schwabel 2017).

Murthy is a fellow advocate for greater connection in society. Since leaving his post as surgeon general in 2017, Murthy has expressed his desire to help foster a society for his own children and all children that values them for who they are—compassionate, kind, and generous, for example—and not for their material possessions, financial worth, or whether they are wearing the latest fashions. He is the author of *Together: The Healing Power of Human Connection in a Sometimes Lonely World* (2020).

Murthy strongly believes that organizations need to make boosting connections in their cultures a strategic priority. He recommends that organizations measure loneliness and that everyone in the workplace freely give and receive help, take the time to get to know each other, and protect personal time with family and friends. He likes to share examples from when he was surgeon general of practices he and his colleagues developed to boost connection. For example, "Inside Scoop" helps colleagues get to know each other on a deeper level without cutting into personal time or requiring a lot of planning, preparation, and resources. As part of the weekly all-hands meeting, one individual would have five minutes to show a few photos related to their life and tell the others about them. Over time, each participant took a turn.

"In listening, in just five minutes, we got to see whole other dimensions of people we had not understood in working together for a year," Murthy said. "People started treating each other differently, stepping out of their lanes and helping each other more. They felt they had been seen. It's powerful as institutions to create simple opportunities like that to see each other clearly for who they are" (ACGME 2019).

As a result of "Inside Scoop," Murthy observed that people felt more valued when their colleagues learned about them on a more personal level, introverted individuals began speaking up more and taking more responsibility, people seemed less stressed, and they commented that they felt more connected.

In a 2019 keynote interview in front of a physician-led organization that establishes and monitors the professional educational standards for residency and fellowship programs for physician training, Murthy reinforced the critical role of connection, stressing that if we are going to tackle and address big issues facing our society, we need to be able to dialogue with one another, and that is hard to do when we are increasingly disconnected. He said, "I have come to believe that the foundation on which we build everything else in our life, whether it's our political system, our healthcare system, or the workplace, is our connection with each other. And if that connection is weak, then we are building a house on a weak foundation and it is going to crumble easily. . . . We have to go back to rebuilding our foundation and we do that by focusing on connection in our lives, in our institutions, in society more broadly, and, ultimately, by trying to create more connected lives for ourselves and the people around us" (ACGME 2019).

Making It Personal

✓ As you consider the people you work with, do you see signs of loneliness in anyone in particular? What might you do to come alongside them.

✓ If you were to bring the "Inside Scoop" exercise into a regular meeting you have with your group, what photos would you choose to share with your colleagues and what do they represent about you?

✓ Dr. Murthy has said that if we are going to tackle big issues facing our society, we need to be able to dialogue with one another, and that is hard to do when we are increasingly disconnected. In your organization, how has connection enabled people to be more cooperative and aligned when addressing a big issue, whether it is a competitive threat to prepare for or a market opportunity to pursue?

Called to Connect

Because of the way our brains work, we need to interact with a variety of people or we are more likely to feel threatened when we encounter people who are different than us. Ralph and Rich Brandt understand this from their experience growing up as identical twins. Because they primarily interacted with each other, being exposed to people who were different made them feel anxious. For example, as boys, when they watched the old Westerns of "cowboys and Indians" on TV, they were terrified.

Twins, as Ralph shared with me, can become so attached that they shut others out. Ralph and Rich were so close that they went to the same college then attended the same theological seminary and worked for the same church. Being in full-time ministry was not, as it turns out, their calling.

Over time, as their circle of friends and acquaintances expanded, Ralph and Rich grew comfortable with people who were different than them. They even began to enjoy many of the differences they encountered as they got to know people. The twins discovered that helping people connect despite their differences is their calling.

Today, Ralph, Rich, and their colleagues at RDR Group based in suburban Chicago train people in organizations to increase inclusion by practicing it—not just discussing it—because it's about cultivating connection. As it turns out, the Brandts (who are older white males) serve a client base that is mostly younger, women, and people of color. This means connecting with those who are different is a regular practice and a needed business skill. But for both of them, it is also part of their private lives—and now that Ralph has a son-in-law who is African American, diversity is more than a vocational calling, it's intensely personal.

When the Brandts are brought in to work with a group to increase diversity and inclusion, their approach begins by defining diversity as "any difference that makes a difference" and inclusion as "getting people fully engaged" (not just present, but involved). Differences might be anything from gender, race, age, appearance, interests, personality type, communication style, sexual orientation, or even family status (single, married, divorced). Participants are then asked to consider how connection and disconnection affects their organization internally and externally. Inevitably, this exercise makes the case for connection with all people and not just some. Participants talk about how it holds them back from performing their best work when people feel disconnected because of differences and how making everyone feel connected helps the entire team perform to its highest potential.

After people see the positive impact connection makes and the negative impact of disconnection, the Brandts share five human tendencies that create these "disconnects" and the corresponding competencies to help people connect better despite their differences. Then they offer follow-up practices to actually make inclusion happen. Here's a broad overview:

- **Replace flocking with networking.** You've probably heard the old saying, "Birds of a feather flock together." Our natural tendency is to "flock" with people with whom we have more in common. Flocking, while comfortable and familiar, is not bad, but it can be exclusionary in the workplace because it separates people. Instead of defaulting to flocking, each of us should be more intentional about networking with people who are different than us. This is one of the inclusive practices, and it involves spending time with, delegating projects to, or just affirming someone of a different age, race, gender, and so on—and in the process expanding our circle of connections.

- **Replace cultural naivete with sensitivity.** Most of us don't know what we don't know (especially when it comes to people who are different than us), so it's easy to say or do something that gets misunderstood and creates a "disconnect." We may inadvertently communicate indifference without ever intending to because of our own ignorance. The only way to correct this tendency is through sensitivity or raising our awareness and increasing our understanding of other perspectives. Employers can promote sensitivity by sponsoring forums at work where members of various identity groups can educate colleagues about their backgrounds and points of view. Sensitivity is another inclusive practice and on a personal level it can be as simple as inquiring about someone's experiences and just listening.

- **Replace monoculturalism with calibration.** Expecting everyone to conform to a particular set of cultural norms reflects monoculturalism and projects indifference because it implies we are all the same. This creates a distinct disadvantage for those who do things differently and limits their unique contributions. Adjusting for differences, on the other hand, reflects calibration. This is the inclusive practice of getting to know someone else's tendencies, strengths, preferred language of appreciation, and communication style, then being willing to adapt accordingly to improve the connection.

- **Replace pejorative behavior with advocacy.** Showing or tolerating overt disrespect toward people who are different is pejorative behavior. This is when people disconnect on purpose (they are exclusionary), which would include discrimination, derogatory or disrespectful comments, and the like. It reflects profound indifference. Those who are truly caring have to take a stand against inappropriate behavior aimed at others. The inclusive practice in this case— advocacy—is when we help others feel connected by supporting them and doing what is right.

- **Replace unconscious filtering with positive expectancy.** "Unconscious filtering" is that habit we all have of making false assumptions based on stereotypes that always limit who people are and what they can do. In contrast, "positive expectancy" is assuming the best of others and acting on it—which in a work context might be the most essential connecting competency of all. In this inclusive practice we not only believe in someone's capabilities but include them by giving them opportunities and encouraging their success.

The Brandts advocate that only when these inclusive practices are implemented can biases be changed and workplaces transformed.

Fostering a connection culture for everyone is the right and smart thing to do. Connecting despite our differences seems more important than ever when we are surrounded by abuses of power, growing incivility, a deeply divided society, and hate crimes everywhere we turn. Connecting with everyone creates greater fairness, unity, civility, and an environment where people can maximize their contributions, irrespective of differences.

Making It Personal

✓ On your team, what are the "differences that make a difference"? Have you noticed a particular difference that is negatively affecting the ability of team members to work well together? What might you do to address the issue and encourage connection?

✓ Consider how connection and disconnection affect your organization internally and externally by jotting down words and phrases for the combinations below. You might think in terms of engagement, sales, reputation, trust, employee turnover, productivity, safety issues, innovation, and so forth.

  ○ What would it look like if we had high levels of connection within the organization?
  ○ What would it look like if we had high levels of connection with our customers?
  ○ What would it look like if we had low levels of connection within the organization?
  ○ What would it look like if we had low levels of connection with our customers?

✓ As you read the five human tendencies that hinder connection and the inclusive practices that would help people better connect despite their differences, was there one that stood out to you? Why did you choose that one?

Claiming Culture as the Advantage

"My biggest role is to create a great culture of trust at Progressive," says Tricia Griffith of Progressive Corporation, America's third-largest auto insurer with more than 20 million policyholders and more than 38,000 employees (Illinois State University staff 2019). Progressive, well-known for its popular series of television commercials that feature dependable and enthusiastic spokesperson Flo in her signature headband and white apron, has been growing faster than Apple in recent years.

Griffith started at Progressive more than 30 years ago after answering a classified advertisement to be an entry-level claims representative. While heading human resources from 2002 to 2008, Griffith launched Progressive's first diversity and inclusion program. She then gained broad experience as the president of the claims group, president of customer operations, and chief operating officer of the personal lines branch. When Glenn Renwick retired as CEO, Griffith stepped into the top role.

For successfully leading Progressive as president and CEO since 2016, Griffith was named *Fortune* magazine's Businessperson of the Year in 2018. Adding to the public accolades, Progressive was named to *Fortune*'s Best Workplaces list in 2018 and 2019.

Progressive's vision is "to reduce the human trauma and economic costs associated with automobile accidents." Griffith leads with Progressive's five core values that "enable the company to grow profitably and in the right way." They were described in a profile with her college alma mater, Illinois State University, as "maintain integrity, follow the Golden Rule, work from clear objectives, and stay committed to excellence while making a reasonable profit."

Griffith connects with the people she is responsible for leading, saying that it's important to her to be approachable. She attends new employee orientation so she can personally greet new colleagues. Most Fridays, she'll get lunch in the corporate cafeteria in Progressive's headquarters near Cleveland, Ohio, and join a table of people she hasn't met. "It's really fun to get to know people, and I have four or five new friends every Friday," she's said (Shookman 2019). She practices open communications, sharing both the good and the bad, and encourages healthy debate. People at Progressive are comfortable connecting with their CEO. Walking the halls with Griffith, you'll hear people greet her with "Hi, Tricia" and a smile. Her long-time colleagues rave about her ability to foster teamwork and connect with people who work throughout the company.

Progressive encourages creativity and innovation by holding hackathons and maintaining an "innovation garage," an employee-run internal think tank. These and other efforts have helped Progressive develop a widely known reputation for its analytics. In 2017 it rolled out a mobile phone app for customers that allows it to collect data on an individual driver's driving style and use an algorithm it developed to assess the risk of distracted driving.

In a 2019 presentation to Wall Street analysts and investors titled "Our Culture Is Our Foundation," Griffith made the case that Progressive's people and culture of "togetherness" provides the most powerful source of competitive advantage. Some of the factors she cited include that 90 percent of open positions at Progressive are filled internally, Progressive invests heavily in developing people, and Progressive welcomes disagreement, encourages debate, and values differing opinions. She argued that Progressive's culture and people strategies produced outstanding results. Those watching were already well acquainted with Progressive's stellar operational and financial results and stock performance. To connect Progressive's culture to its results, Griffith presented data from Gallup that showed:

- 68 percent of Progressive employees were engaged (versus 33 percent of the U.S. working population)
- 28 percent of Progressive employees were not engaged (versus 51 percent of the U.S. working population)
- 4 percent of Progressive employees were actively disengaged (versus 16 percent of the U.S. working population).

Griffith knows how important culture and connection are for Progressive to sustain its success, and she's not shy about saying this to an audience that is heavily numbers and data-driven. The leader who ascended from claims rep to CEO, Griffith is leading the way in claiming and cultivating a culture of connection that provides sustainable superior performance and a competitive advantage by bringing out the best in people, individually and collectively.

Making It Personal

✓ How would you describe the role of trust in whether you feel connected? Are you naturally a more trusting or distrusting person? What do you need to trust another person?

✓ How approachable are the leaders in your organization? If you are responsible for leading others, what steps can you take to make yourself available, such as deliberately putting space in your daily schedule to chat with people and build rapport? Are you someone whom a person at any level of the organization would be comfortable speaking to? Would others agree with that assessment?

✓ Are there vehicles in your organization to capture ideas, however raw and untested they may be? How do leaders feel about disagreement and debate? A consequence of having a culture of control is that ideas and information that are relevant or important but will be perceived by the leader as bad news may not come to the surface. How can you create an environment in which people will safeguard relational connections and have a dialogue?

Connecting During a Time of Change

This final profile will be a bit different from the others. For starters, this is Katie writing. At my request, Mike kindly passed me the pen.

What do leaders need to keep in mind when communicating during a time of crisis, great change, or prolonged uncertainty? With the onset of the COVID-19 pandemic in the first part of 2020, suddenly there were layers of leaders around the world talking about the same topic at the same time. In the U.S., it seemed that federal, state, and local leaders in all 50 states and Washington, D.C., were speaking every day. Leaders in business, education, entertainment, and nonprofits were also actively communicating. The messaging about the virus and what should be done about it varied, and so did the delivery of those messages.

When watching the news, reading articles online, and making my way through emails, I couldn't help but view these communications through the lens of connection and culture. Were the attitudes, words, and behaviors of our leaders serving to connect people or disconnect them? Were the elements of vision, value, and voice being employed in these communications? What could I tell about a leader's understanding that people have the need for respect, recognition, belonging, autonomy, personal growth, meaning, and progress? And finally, I thought about what lessons could be learned and applied in other contexts, such as merging two companies together or implementing a major software program involving multiple stakeholders across locations.

In an April 2020 interview, Dov Seidman, founder and chairman of an ethics and compliance company and an organization promoting values-based leadership, was asked what the best leaders have in common. He focused on three areas: trust, hope, and humility. "Great leaders trust people with the truth. And they make hard decisions guided by values and principles, not just politics, popularity, or short-term profits," Seidman explained. "Whenever there is more trust in a company, country, or community, good things happen." He then went on to distinguish between hope and optimism, saying that "the true antidote to fear is hope, not optimism. Hope comes from seeing your leader lead in a way that brings out the best in people by inspiring collaboration, common purpose, and future possibilities. It takes hope to overcome great fear and meet great challenges. People do, of course, appreciate good news and optimism from their leaders, but only if it's grounded in reality, facts, and data" (Friedman 2020).

It may seem natural for leaders to think they have to project power, authority, and unwavering confidence when guiding people through uncharted territory. They may be reluctant to show uncertainty about data in an evolving situation, concerned that it will negatively impact how they are perceived. Seidman's view is that people value leaders who have the humility to say that while they don't have the answer today, they are working with experts to learn more. A study published in March 2020 suggests that "being transparent about uncertainty does not harm the public's trust in the facts or in the source." This finding was supported by comments from the director general of the U.K.'s Office for Statistics Regulation, who said that "being trustworthy depends not on conveying an aura of infallibility, but on honesty and transparency" (Roberts 2020).

A number of leaders caught my eye this spring, for a variety of reasons, and I'd like to highlight a few positive examples. One of the first to go on my list was Dr. Anthony Fauci, the nation's leading expert on infectious diseases and director of the National Institute of Allergy and Infectious Diseases since 1984. A sought-after guest on news programs, Fauci was a member of the White House Coronavirus Task Force and frequently spoke at press briefings. Dov Seidman pointed to him as a model of humility: "The more I hear Dr. Fauci say that he does not know something, the more closely I listen to him discuss what he is sure of."

———◯———

Another medical expert who drew national attention and praise was Dr. Amy Acton, now-former director of the Ohio Department of Health, a multi-faceted role that also involved advising the governor and leading the department's ongoing work on a broad array of public health issues. How many state public health officials do you know who have a fan club and have inspired citizens to create merchandise using phrases they've said in a daily press briefing?

Under Acton's leadership, Ohio took bold, early action—declaring a state of emergency when Ohio only had three confirmed COVID-19 cases; becoming the first state to shut down schools; and implementing a stay at home order when the death toll stood at three people. At the time of this writing in mid-July 2020, Ohio continued to have the lowest infection ratio among the 12 most populated states (Hancock 2020). Normally, the person behind such strict measures would not be a "fan favorite," but Acton was able to connect with her fellow Ohioans as an empathetic expert.

In daily briefings alongside the governor, Acton calmly explained what was going on in a way that was relatable and understandable. She was honest about what was known and unknown, and regularly acknowledged how tough the situation was. "People at home, you are moving mountains. You are saving lives," she said in a press briefing on April 6. "Again, I get emotional talking about this because this is no small thing that we are doing together. It is so incredibly hard to have shut down our lives the way we have. I am absolutely certain you will look back and know that you helped save each other in this state, the impact is profound. Please, at home, don't stop" (Dosani and Westbrook 2020).

She also understood the importance of acknowledging that everyone was feeling the stress, including herself. "Every day I go through stages of grief," she shared on April 16. "I go through denial, I go through a little anger, I go through a little bargaining [with myself]. . . . I get a little down" (Dosani and Westbrook 2020).

Acton affirmed Ohioans over and over. Early on, she put in front of them the image of being heroes: "There are everyday heroes everywhere. We know that not all heroes wear capes," she said during the March 19 press briefing. A few days later she affirmed "You're heroic when you stay at home and watch your neighbor who is a nurse's child." During the April 17 briefing, Acton said it again: "I know you're all donning those capes in big ways and small ways." It was the phrase "not all heroes wear capes" that captured the public's imagination and reinforced that each person had a part to play in slowing down virus transmission (Dosani and Westbrook 2020).

Admired by many citizens and highly commended by peers in the medical community, Acton was also the subject of harsh criticism and opposition for her orders that resulted in tight restrictions. In addition to lawsuits and efforts by the Ohio state legislature to restrict her authority, protesters appeared outside Acton's home in early May, some carrying guns (Witte 2020). On June 11 she resigned as director of the Ohio Department of Health. Running the department, handling the pandemic, and advising the governor were three jobs, she said during the press briefing, and she wanted to devote her efforts to one area. She also wants to spend more time with her family. Acton will continue to serve Ohio as the governor's chief health advisor, focusing on the COVID-19 pandemic. Interestingly, Acton's not the only one to leave office during this crisis—more than 25 state and local health leaders across 13 states left their posts between April and mid-June (Weber et al. 2020). Ken DeBurgh, executive director of the Health Officers Association of California, commented, "It's disheartening to see people who disagree with the order go from attacking the order to attacking the officer to questioning their motivation, expertise, and patriotism. That's not something that should ever happen" (Borchardt and Balmert 2020). Ohio Gov. Mike DeWine expressed his deep appreciation for Acton's "selfless and tireless service to the people of Ohio" when he announced her decision to step down as director. He added, "No one is more passionate about public health than Dr. Amy Acton" (Mosby 2020).

New York was a hot spot in the early months of the pandemic, and had specific challenges because of the density of New York City. Similar to Acton, New York Gov. Andrew Cuomo was also getting quite a bit of out-of-state attention for his daily press briefings. Intrigued, I tuned in to a few to see what they were like.

One of the things I noticed right away was his use of phrases to remind the people of New York who they are. It made me think about self-fulfilling prophecy and psychology's Pygmalion Effect—what we say to others about our expectations of them affects how they view themselves and the effort they put in. When Governor Cuomo told his fellow citizens, "We are New York tough—which means tough, smart, united, disciplined, and loving," he was calling them higher and inspiring them. In his briefing on April 3, Cuomo spoke of the aspirational nature of the state motto, "excelsior" (which is Latin for ever higher), reminding listeners that "we can be better, we can lift ourselves." Later, he brought it back to the U.S. motto, "E pluribus unum": "How many times have we seen a disaster across this country and how many Americans just show up to help? I mean, it's in the American DNA to say, 'We're here to help one another.' It is E pluribus unum," Cuomo said. "Out of many, one—we're community, we're Americans, we're a family, we're brothers and sisters. There's a commonality" (Cuomo 2020b).

Known for speaking bluntly, Cuomo also kept the "why" in front of people, while being honest and empathetic about what people were feeling. "New Yorkers have been so supportive of each other. You can feel it. There's a spirit of community and mutuality," he said in a May 1 briefing. "You look at the way people have complied with these rules, as annoying as they are, masks, six feet, this, that's out of respect one for the other." Cuomo went on to share his thanks to those who were wearing masks. "The mask does not protect me. I wear the mask to protect you. What a beautiful sign of caring, of mutuality. . . . That's the spirit, even in this terrible time of difficulty" (Cuomo 2020a).

Earlier in his May 1 briefing, Cuomo also spent a lot of time addressing the mental health issues the pandemic had caused or exacerbated in the general population. He assured New Yorkers that they were not alone and that help was out there. "People shouldn't be shy in any way or have any second thoughts about calling [the New York State Emotional Support Hotline] for help," he said, perhaps with the shared identity of "New York tough" in mind. "There is no shame in reaching out and saying, 'I need help.'"

He also acknowledged that the pandemic has been a very difficult situation for everyone, but "when life knocks you on your rear . . . learn, grow, and get back up." It had also exposed a whole host of issues that need to be addressed by the state, and Cuomo assured New Yorkers that leaders "will learn [these hard lessons], and we will be better for it" (Cuomo 2020a).

An excellent example of a political leader on a national level is New Zealand Prime Minister Jacinda Ardern. In addition to holding formal press conferences and hosting online Q&A sessions with experts to educate and keep people informed, Ardern made herself accessible to citizens through informal live video chats on her Facebook page. While streaming the chats from home, Ardern comfortably mixed important information and comments about her personal life, often including humorous anecdotes about being a mom. Her calm demeanor and relaxed delivery made it feel more like a conversation with a trusted and caring friend than a politician. Ardern excelled at relating news to practical, everyday situations and then expanding on the topic by answering questions viewers posted during the session. I appreciated that she even used the viewer's first name when restating their question and starting her reply.

The evening before New Zealanders began a four-week lockdown in March, Ardern appeared on Facebook Live wearing an oversized green sweatshirt, apologizing for her informality and explaining that putting a toddler to bed could be messy. Then she went on to explain why the lockdown was necessary, answer scores of questions, and ask people to check on their elderly neighbors. "Stay at home, break the chain, and you will save lives," she said in closing. "It's as simple as that. That's everyone's job for the next four [weeks]" (Ardern 2020b).

Ardern often talked about "our team of 5 million" and "winning the fight against COVID-19," reminding people that this was a mission to be accomplished together (Cave 2020). When she hosted Q&A sessions with experts, she showed genuine interest by first asking how things were going in their self-isolation "bubbles" (Ardern 2020a).

New Zealanders rallied behind their prime minister and her call to "please be strong, be kind and united against COVID-19" (Editorial Board 2020). As of June 8, the country of nearly 5 million people had no active cases of COVID-19 and at just 22 deaths, one of the lowest infection and death rates in the world. In her Facebook Live post that day, Ardern confessed to doing a little happy dance when she found out that the Cabinet had agreed to move to Level 1, which meant no more limits on gatherings or physical distancing; a near return to normal for the country (Neuman 2020).

And, finally, here is an example from outside government life. The Aspen Music Festival and School is a classical music festival known for its eight-week summer season that draws 100,000 audience members to the beautiful mountain setting of Aspen, Colorado. I've attended concerts and programs there for over several decades now, and it is a glorious abundance of riches featuring performances by world-renowned artists alongside talented young-adult students who are there for training. What would social distancing and stay at home orders mean for this event that people look forward to and brings so many guests to this ski town?

On May 4, 2020, Festival president Alan Fletcher conveyed news that no one wanted to hear. I found his message so beautifully written that I am sharing it in its entirety. Notice his use of pronouns, how he shares that many voices and opinions were considered in making the decision, how he acknowledges emotions, and how he proclaims hope.

Dear Festival Friends,

For every day of the past two months, we have been analyzing the potential impact of the COVID-19 pandemic, in consultation with public health experts, hospital leadership, civic and county officials, and many others. In recent days, the collective data began to coalesce, and we have reached the conclusion, together with our board and faculty leadership, that we must cancel the full season.

We take this action in solidarity with our musical community, our Aspen community, and indeed the world community, as we commit first and foremost to keeping each other safe at this historic moment.

We will come together around music again, in fact sooner rather than later. We are already working on not only the 2021 season— which will be nothing less than an explosion of musical joy—but also on virtual ways the AMFS community can come together to enjoy music and each other. The medium may be different, but we can and will still share the essence of the Aspen experience. We are already fully engaged in this re-imagining and will be in touch with more about it.

This extraordinary time brings loss and profound change, but also carries important lessons. It asks us to reaffirm our deepest values, and understand it is in connection and in community we are most alive. We will emerge together, stronger, deeper, and more grateful, on the other side. I am already looking to that day.

Yours,
Alan Fletcher
President and CEO, Aspen Music Festival and School

Connection is all about "we." And these leaders showed that in their communications by employing the connection culture elements of vision, value, and voice. Through my observations of them and many others, I've come away with a few thoughts on what should factor into communicating in a time of big change:

- Engage, don't retreat or go silent.
- Keep vision in front of people. On a regular basis, remind them that "this is who we are and this is why we are taking this action." Relate each action to the big picture. Make it clear what their role is and why it's valuable.
- Be open about your own feelings (at an appropriate level, of course). Doing so and being vulnerable actually draws people in and helps them feel like you're all in this together.
- Recognize people for the good they are doing, their perseverance, and their positive attitude.
- Share the spotlight with your collaborators and be sure they are getting the credit they are due.

- Believe that people can handle the truth. Share what you are able to and let people know you will share updates as more information becomes known.
- Have your communications be a dialogue whenever possible. Ask people how they are doing and really listen to what they say.
- Balance the hard news with hope. Share any silver linings of the challenge that you and others are spotting as well as what you believe it will be like on the other side.

Shared identity, empathy, and understanding make a rocky path more manageable to navigate and traverse together.

Making It Personal

✓ Which leaders do you believe successfully communicated in the early months of the COVID-19 pandemic in ways that connected people? Why? How about the opposite?

✓ Think of your work experience and a time when your group or organization went through a major challenge or change. From your perspective, what did leaders do well and what did they do poorly when it came to communicating during that period?

✓ How willing are you to be open with others at work about your feelings, concerns, or what you don't know about a project? Can you think of a situation in which doing so would strengthen connection with your colleagues?

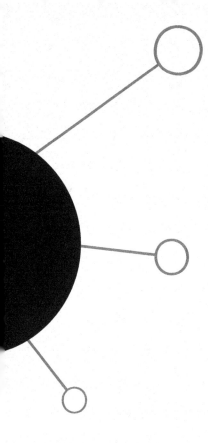

PART III
Operationalizing Connection Culture

Now that you've read about the who, what, where, and why, it's time for the how. How do you make a connection culture actionable and operational?

In part III, you will be equipped with 15 actionable building blocks you can implement to strengthen your culture. Adding any of the building blocks to your culture will increase connection. You will also learn a five-step process to operationalize connection culture. In the final chapter, I address issues that are relevant to cultivating connection culture, and I will help you be a more effective catalyst for positive culture change.

6

Taking Action:
Connecting Through
Vision, Value, and Voice

There is a broad range of practices that help create a connection culture. The pages that follow describe 15 building blocks, a collection of actions for building and maintaining a connection culture—five each for the three connection culture elements of vision, value, and voice. After that, you will find a five-step process to operationalize a connection culture.

Vision: Inspiring Identity That Produces Shared Identity

This element is present when everyone is motivated by the mission, united by the values, and proud of the reputation.

Develop an Inspirational Identity Phrase That Connects

Research shows that people who experience a sense of well-being from meaningful work exhibit gene-expression profiles that are associated with a lower risk of cancer, diabetes, and cardiovascular disease (Fredrickson et al. 2013). Connecting employees to your organization's vision, mission, or values of serving others and making a difference (practices also referred to as being prosocial) boosts employee productivity and protects people from burnout. To increase connection, I recommend leaders take an additional step beyond articulating the vision, mission, and values and develop a brief, memorable, and inspirational identity phrase that unites people and makes them feel proud.

An identity phrase could be based on vision or mission. Examples include Charles Schwab's "to provide the most useful and ethical financial products in the world," MD Anderson Cancer Center's "making cancer history," NASA's mission during the Apollo program "to put a man on the moon by the end of the decade," and Yale New Haven Health's "healthier together." Google's mission is summed up here: "to organize the world's information and make it universally accessible and useful." You might also consider an inspirational identity phrase based on core values, which are discussed in more detail later in this chapter. To generate ideas, read through the 24 character strengths in appendix I for a list of values that inspire people. Costco's "do the right thing" and Tata Capital's "we only do what's right for you" reflect caring, honesty, and courage; Lexus's "the relentless pursuit of perfection" reflects excellence and perseverance; and Apple's "think different" and General Electric's "imagination at work" reflect creativity and innovation.

If your organization does not have an identity phrase, or it's time to refresh or rethink it, you could spread engagement by involving your colleagues. Hold a contest in which people submit inspiring identity phrases for consideration, and then have employees vote on their favorites. You'll be able to see which ones are most inspiring and make employees feel proud.

Set the Top Five Annual Priorities

Both individually and as a team, set no more than five challenging but achievable annual priorities that are aligned with your organization's mission. If you go beyond five, it will diminish connection, focus, and effective execution by overwhelming those responsible for implementation. Take time to regularly review your weekly plans to make sure they are aligned with your top five priorities.

As much as possible, let your direct reports establish their own top five annual priorities. Talk through the team's top five priorities with each employee to find shared priorities that will advance the organization's mission and employee's interests. It may not be possible to find a perfect set of priorities for each person, but if you make the effort you will be rewarded with people who feel more connected and execute their tasks with greater enthusiasm, energy, and effort.

Identify and Establish Core Values That Connect

If you asked your fellow employees what the organization's core values are, could they tell you? Most cannot. To create a connection culture, employees need to be able to articulate the organization's core values.

To identify core values that create connection, leaders should begin by taking time to reflect on the values they believe in and want to promote in their organization. Start by reflecting on your most memorable experiences, including those at and away from work, and write down any lessons you've learned from them. Then use the 24 character strengths in appendix I to reflect on what strengths are most important to you and your organization's ability to achieve its mission.

Read what other leaders have written about their core values. Howard Schultz's book *Pour Your Heart Into It: How Starbucks Built a Company One Cup at a Time* provides an excellent example. Schultz, former chairman and CEO of Starbucks, articulates his experiences in life, how those experiences shaped his values, and how they became the values at Starbucks. In *Fired Up or Burned Out*, I included one of the best examples I've seen of a leader concisely articulating his core values. In the Montpelier Command Philosophy, the commander of USS *Montpelier*, a nuclear submarine in the U.S. Navy, describes the values he strives to meet, which ones he expects sailors under his command to follow, and why each value is important.

After you've completed these steps, organize your thoughts in a manner similar to the Montpelier Command Philosophy—name the value then explain why it's important and what it looks like in your work context. Ask trusted friends to read the values and provide feedback about what's right, wrong, or missing. Once your draft is in good shape, share it with your direct reports and ask them to provide feedback. Consider the feedback, make the changes that you believe improve it, then circulate the revised version to your direct reports. Have them go through the feedback process with their direct reports. Continue this process until everyone on the team has had an opportunity to voice their opinions and ideas. This process creates commitment and alignment with core values.

Finally, take your direct reports through the final core values you decide upon. Discuss and identify which values are most important to your team's success, which values your team is strong in, which values it needs to develop, and what can be done to develop and live by each value. Follow up with a written summary of your plan to live out the core values. It should include action items, responsibilities, and due dates.

Continuously Reconnect People to the Inspiring Identity

Connection to an organization's identity diminishes over time, so look for ways to keep people connected to the vision, mission, and values. This is important for all employees, and especially those who telecommute. Consider taking employees to visit customers or bring customers in to talk with employees about how they use and benefit from your products and services. Make videos of these conversations so that people who work remotely and future employees can view them. Internally circulate any press materials about your organization that reinforce your mission, values, and reputation.

Hold "continuous improvement" meetings three or four times a year to identify innovative ways to improve and achieve your mission. These meetings could be focused on ways to increase revenue, reduce costs, improve quality, or improve efficiency. You might also look at the frustration level of people who work on the front lines of your organization to identify ways that any issues can be addressed. List the ideas, prioritize them, select a manageable set to focus on, assign responsibilities, and track their completion. Make this information available to the entire group. Such meetings get people thinking proactively about how to improve.

Meet periodically with your direct reports to review and revise your plan to live out the core values; ask your direct reports to do the same with their direct reports. Consider having the core values printed on a small card that can fit in a wallet, like Alan Mulally did when he was CEO at Ford. When researching and writing *Fired Up or Burned Out,* I learned that each Ritz-Carlton Hotels & Resorts employee received a card with the organization's core values (then called Ritz Basics) printed on the front and back. When teams met briefly every day they would review one of the Ritz Basics, and each week the company highlighted a Ritz-Carlton employee who lived out a value (Stallard 2007). In recent years it has expanded to three times a week that a "WOW" story is shared of an employee who went "above and beyond to delight a guest, in a way that directly aligns with the ... values" (Harris 2015).

Don't forget to celebrate your successes. When your team accomplishes a major goal that helps achieve your mission, celebrate with a party, meal, or outing. Ask people for suggestions about how to celebrate, and if you can afford it, invite them to bring a significant other to join in. And don't forget to include employees who telecommute. For instance, if you are celebrating with a team meal, pay for remote workers to get take-out delivered to their home so they can join in virtually.

Celebrate culture carriers who embody your culture because they contribute to achieving your mission while behaving in ways that are consistent with your organization's values. You might create a blog or book to share stories about these people and their practices; see the annual Zappos *Culture Book* or *Smile Guide: Employee Perspectives on Culture, Loyalty, and Profit* from Beryl Companies for examples. Reading these stories will encourage others to become culture carriers and give them some ideas to try.

Hire, Develop, and Promote for Competence and Connection Skills

Most managers hire and promote for competence but are not as intentional about assessing connection skills. Involve many individuals in your organization's hiring and promotion processes. Have them compare notes by taking into consideration your organization's values and the 24 character strengths listed in appendix I before making hiring and promotion recommendations.

New employee orientation and new leader training must also address connection. Creating a connection culture requires developing a certain mindset, especially in leaders. Education is essential. In order to gain the support of your leaders, they must understand what a connection culture is, why it's important, and how they can contribute to creating and sustaining it. This information must be communicated to all current leaders during leadership training sessions and incorporated into new leader orientation.

People need to be encouraged to think of themselves as connected members and connected leaders. To do this, leadership training should include stories that celebrate connected members and connected leaders and describe how they contribute to a connection culture. This will spur people to develop their own character strengths. The inspiring stories presented in the Profiles in Connection sections in this book are excellent examples.

When training people on connection, remember to teach new terminology, including the definitions and descriptions of connection, connection culture, cultures of control, cultures of indifference, vision, value, voice, connected members, and connected leaders. Employees also need to learn about important frameworks that help them develop mental models and guide behavior, such as the Connection Culture model (Figure 3-2) and the Character > Connection > Thrive Chain (Figure 3-1). Presenting leaders with applicable research studies is another way to support a rational argument. Finally, creating a successful connection culture depends on whether practices that connect are acted upon by every individual. The practices must be taught, serving to both educate people and help them become intentional.

Providing a good variety of content in training makes it easier to reach people regardless of their learning style. Some people will be most receptive to research and hard data, whereas others will be more drawn to visual diagrams, stories, and case studies.

Value: Human Value That Produces Shared Empathy

This element is present when everyone understands the needs of people, appreciates their positive unique contributions, and helps them achieve their potential.

Make and Encourage Connections That Are Personal

Organizational behavior professor Ashley E. Hardin (2018) has found that greater personal knowledge leads to a more human perception of a colleague, which results in increased responsiveness and decreased social undermining. Take time to connect with people on a personal level and resist the inclination to skip time spent in conversation getting to know the people you are responsible for leading. This is an important step.

If you work at the same location, meet with employees over a meal or coffee. When team members who work in a different location or telecommute are on-site, be sure to set aside time with them for this purpose. For those who work entirely remotely, let that person decide whether to use a telephone or video call, because introverts can be overstimulated and uncomfortable with video (Grant 2020). Be open and share from your life outside work. Ask questions that are unrelated to work, such as "Where were you born?" "What are your interests outside work?" or "What are you looking forward to in the future?" Psychologist James Pennebaker (1997) has found that when you get people to talk, they feel more connected to you, like you more, and believe they learn more from you.

Leaders should schedule regular social time for people to connect. Genentech has a weekly Friday afternoon social time where they serve drinks and snacks. I know a manager who orders pizza and salad for his team every other Friday. During the warm summer months, organize an ice cream social to bring your team together for conversation. Consider helping serve those in attendance and make sure to say hello to everyone. Avoid talking about work; instead ask people about their interests or what they are looking forward to during the remainder of the year. If your team includes people who work remotely, plan a social hour via videoconferencing to encourage face-to-face interactions.

In chapter 4, we explained how discrimination—whether it is based on gender, ethnicity, sexual orientation, age, political opinions, or other differences that affect how a person might view or treat another person—is a cause of disconnection and a source of stress. We noted how many women report stress is on the rise and that they rely on social connection as a way to manage stress (APA 2010). Furthermore, we noted that research found many people of color use social resources to reduce race-related stress (Utsey et al. 2008). In your organization, establish and support employee resource groups and mentoring to connect with and protect individuals who are at risk for discrimination-related stress.

Finally, like Pfizer Corporation, communicate and enforce a "no jerks" policy (Stallard 2015). People who are consistently disrespectful to others undermine connection. Also, when people passively stand by and allow jerks to act out, it communicates indifference. Stanford University management professor Robert Sutton's research has found that the behavior of jerks harms not only their victims but also others in the environment, the organization's performance, and themselves (Sutton 2007).

Get People in the Right Roles

Most leaders identify the roles and responsibilities of people who can help achieve their organization's mission. To increase connection, leaders must help the people they lead get into roles that fit their interests and strengths and provide the right degree of challenge. If leaders can't get people in the ideal role, they should at least try to assign them responsibilities or projects that fit them well. Both hiring and promotion decisions should incorporate alignment with employee competence, connection skills, and the requirements of a particular job.

To learn about the interests of the people you are responsible for leading, take time to get to know them. Ask questions like these to learn about their lives and what's important to them:

- "Where did you grow up?"
- "What are your interests outside work?"
- "What people in your life have inspired you and why?"
- "What did you like and dislike about prior work experiences?"
- "What are your career aspirations?"

These questions provide insight into how employees are wired, including what they value.

You might consider using the core motivations inventory (MCORE for short), a tool our chief scientist, Todd Hall, helped to develop. MCORE asks people to write brief success stories and answer questions about the stories. It then provides a report that lists what motivates you as an individual. For example, my top three core motivations are explore, make an impact, and improve.

As you learn more about the individuals you are responsible for leading, write down what you learn and identify specific actions you can take to get them in the right roles and help them make progress toward their aspirations.

Create Personal Development Plans

People are more engaged and feel more connected when they are learning, growing, and experiencing a sense of progress. Work with your direct reports to create personal development plans addressing areas that require growth in order to achieve their potential. Help them make wise goals to advance their careers and put steps in place to help them achieve these goals. To evaluate progress and provide feedback, establish objective, quantifiable benchmarks whenever possible. Doing so will boost their effectiveness and connection to you.

When providing feedback to help someone improve, communicate in private whenever possible, be respectful in your tone of voice and volume, and consider beginning with three positive traits you like about that person's work or character. After sharing the three positives, you might say, "I believe you would be even more effective if . . . [insert what you want the person to do or stop doing]." Kindness matters and the approach you take will affect how the person receives the feedback.

Provide Training and Mentors to Support Personal Development

Do you ever wonder why all world-class athletes have coaches? It's because no one becomes great at anything that requires skill unless they undergo training and have coaches or mentors who help them grow. We need coaches and mentors to help us develop competence and excellence in the tasks that we undertake. Additionally, we all have blind spots—things we say or do that are disconnecting—and we need coaches and mentors to help us see them and then advise, encourage, and hold us accountable so that we grow to become connected members and connected leaders.

To support personal development, provide people with training and mentors or coaches. It would be beneficial to provide mentor training to all supervisors. Make peer mentors available for any direct reports who want to improve in a specific area of competence or character, and select a mentor who is strong in the given area. One way to match mentors and mentees is to use a flash mentoring format, which asks participants to commit to meeting once to see if both parties connect, and if the mentor has the knowledge, expertise, and time available to meet the mentee's needs and expectations. If both parties agree to continue, they should set a finite number of additional meetings, rather than leave the term open ended. Unless both mentor and mentee agree to the arrangement, there is no commitment to meet again (Derrick and Wooley 2009).

Larger organizations should implement integrated leader training and development. For example, Yale New Haven Health (YNHH) develops leaders using a combination of high-quality classroom instruction delivered by the Yale School of Management faculty, as well as coaching, action learning through critical strategic projects, and mentoring from senior leadership. YNHH creates cohorts of high-potential directors and vice presidents from across its system of hospitals (nurses, physicians, and administrators) who complete the eight-month program together. The program uses the Center for Creative Leadership's 70-20-10 learning guidelines: 70 percent of the learning comes from using the strategic projects and working in teams to identify recommendations, 20 percent comes from coaching and mentoring, and 10 percent comes from classroom instruction. It also includes feedback from Korn Ferry's Lominger 360 and the Hartman Value Profile. The program's objectives focus on strategic thinking, interpersonal relationships, interdepartmental relationships, dealing with ambiguity, developing others, and breaking down organizational and departmental silos. Participants are selected through management succession. The program is offered every two years, and of the 92 participants who have attended so far, 36 have been promoted at least one level and eight are currently at the senior vice president level (Morris 2020).

Help People Develop Connection Skills

Everyone in your organization needs to develop connection skills, especially leaders. Managers lead from authority, whereas leaders lead from a combination of authority and connection. It is not unusual for managers who are good at organizing tasks to require help developing the personal leadership skills necessary to better form and maintain a connection with people. Weak connection skills hold many managers back from becoming leaders who people want to follow. Here are some attitudes, language, and behaviors that will help facilitate connection.

Recognize varying connection needs. People have different predispositions when it comes to their sensitivity to connection or lack thereof. People also respond differently to actions; one action might make one person feel more connected while it leaves another person cold. Learn about the people you are responsible for leading, and tailor your behaviors to connect based on what you've learned about each individual.

Be present in conversations. It has been said that attention is oxygen for relationships. When meeting with people, whether in person, by phone, or over a video call, get in the habit of being present by giving them your full attention. Show that you are engaged and interested by asking questions, then asking follow-up questions to clarify. Listen carefully, observing facial expressions and body language. Don't break the connection by checking your phone, looking around the room, or letting your mind wander.

Develop the ability to empathize. Mutual empathy is a powerful connector that is made possible by mirror neurons in our brains. Mirror neurons act like an emotional Wi-Fi system (Goleman 2006). When we attune to the emotions of others, it makes them feel connected to us. When we attune to their positive emotion, it enhances the positive emotion they feel. When we attune to their pain, it diminishes the pain they feel. If someone expresses emotion, it's OK, and natural, for you to feel it too. Because it is easier to attune to another's emotions when we see their facial expressions, video calls are generally preferable when interacting with individuals who are working remotely and are comfortable using video.

Develop the habit of emphasizing positives. Psychologist John Gottman (1994) first observed that marriages were less likely to survive when the positive-to-negative ratio of interactions dipped below five-to-one (or five positive interactions to every negative interaction). Psychologist Barbara Fredrickson found that a positivity ratio also applied in the workplace (Fredrickson and Joiner 2002). When it comes to positives, small things can make a difference. For example, maintaining appropriate eye contact, periodically using people's first names during conversations, and connecting with people on a personal level in conversations before bringing up business tasks and issues all count as positive interactions in the five-to-one ratio. People need affirmation and recognition, so get in the habit of looking for ways to affirm and serve others. Do this by looking for task strengths and character strengths, which reflect the excellence of their work and the way they go about their work, respectively. For example, you might affirm a colleague by saying, "That was an outstanding website you created. The navigation design was easy to use, the writing was easy to understand, and the color scheme was beautiful." You might affirm their character strengths by saying, "I appreciate the way you persevered to make our new website happen. You showed wisdom in seeking the ideas of others and applying the best ideas to the design of our new website. Very nicely done."

Control your tone of voice. Recognize that people will instinctively react to the delivery of your message before they hear its content. They may put up a wall and become defensive or feel threatened if your tone of voice is booming, shrill, or strident.

Negotiate with the mindset to solve a problem rather than to win. You can build connections with people during negotiations if you adopt and maintain the right mindset. Thinking of the people you are negotiating with as competitors leads to disconnection and distrust. Instead, think of them as holding knowledge that you need in order to identify a win-win solution. Negotiating requires probing, patience, and perseverance to understand other people's objectives, perceptions, and sensitivities.

Provide autonomy in execution. Monitor progress and be available to help your direct reports but refrain from micromanaging. Favor guidelines rather than rules and controls, and let people know that you are available if they have questions or would like you to act as a sounding board. This meets the human need for autonomy and allows people to experience personal growth.

Learn and apply the five languages of appreciation. According to Gary Chapman and Paul White in *The 5 Love Languages of Appreciation in the Workplace: Empowering Organizations by Encouraging People*, the languages of appreciation are words of affirmation, quality time, acts of service, gifts, and physical touch. (Note that physical touch is not a primary language of appreciation in the workplace and should generally be avoided.) Ask your direct reports about the times they remember receiving recognition at work to find out what their primary and secondary languages of appreciation are.

Apologize when you make a mistake. We all make mistakes but not everyone says they're sorry. Apologizing is an important step that will help rebuild connection.

Develop social skills and relationship skills and recognize the difference between them. Many individuals develop social skills, which make them excellent networkers who impress and connect with others in casual interactions. However, in addition to social skills, it is essential to develop relationship skills, which help create deeper connections with a few people who have your back. Consider the skills you use when meeting someone for the first time versus nurturing your relationship with a best friend. Relationship skills—regularly spending time with an individual, being open to sharing your struggles, sharing someone's joy and pain, being there in times of need, and so on—help develop the deeper connections that are necessary for individuals to thrive in life and achieve sustainable superior performance.

Encourage remote workers to get the connection they need to thrive. Because they don't have the formal and informal interactions that happen when working with colleagues in the same location, remote workers are more prone to loneliness. For the people you are responsible for leading who telecommute, let them know that you care about them and want to be sure they are getting sufficient connection in order to thrive. Encourage them to get out of their home office to have lunch or a coffee break with a friend. If it's not disruptive to your organization, let them know it's OK to engage in other types of connecting activities during normal work hours, such as volunteering in their community or taking an exercise class, and that you trust them to get their work done.

Voice: Knowledge Flow That Produces Shared Understanding

This element is present when everyone seeks the ideas of others, shares their ideas and opinions honestly, and safeguards relational connections.

Create Forums for Organization-Wide Communication

Hold meetings periodically that bring everyone you lead together to discuss how the group is making progress toward achieving the mission. In addition, communicate the opportunities and challenges your organization is facing and how you plan to address them. The meetings should address progress in quantitative, measurable terms, while also connecting the mission to how it serves others and brings greater beauty, goodness, or truth to the world. Include stories that show how your organization is achieving its mission.

Make time for questions and answers at the meeting, or in separate meetings, to give people a voice. You can have people anonymously submit questions ahead of time or simply ask them during the meeting. Howard Behar, former president of Starbucks North America and Starbucks International, called the sessions he held Open Forums. Jim Goodnight, CEO of SAS Institute, holds Java With Jim sessions. Vineet Nayar, CEO of HCL Technologies, has people email questions, which he answers on his blog so everyone can see the question and his response. The founders of Google also do this at each Friday's TGIF meeting.

During meetings, be sure to listen actively. Jane Dutton (2003), professor of business administration and psychology at the University of Michigan, has several suggestions. For example, you might paraphrase by expressing what you heard in your own words ("Let me make sure I'm hearing you correctly. You are saying . . . ") or summarize what you heard ("Let me summarize your points to see if I fully understand. I hear you saying . . . "). A third approach is to clarify by asking questions ("Tell me if I'm hearing you correctly. Do you mean. . . ?").

Hold Knowledge Flow Sessions for Decision Input and Idea Development

Holding knowledge flow sessions is a practice that promotes connection through open communications—listening to others' opinions and ideas then considering them before making decisions. Team knowledge flow sessions should occur regularly to keep the team aligned and accountable (one organization I know calls their weekly operational knowledge flow session the Sweat the Details meeting).

Begin meetings with positive comments. This boosts energy and creativity. Share your vision—your thoughts about what actions need to be done, by whom, and when each action needs to be completed.

Make sure to ask people who are quiet to share what they think. Listen and consider the ideas put forth and implement good ideas, giving credit where it's due. This practice reflects the character strengths of integrity, humility, curiosity, and open-mindedness.

The Knowledge Flow Process
1. **Frame the discussion.** "Here's what I'm thinking." This is where you are putting your cards on the table by presenting what you believe to be true. It must be grounded in reality, and supported by facts, data, and analysis.
2. **Grant permission for knowledge flow.** "No one has a monopoly on good ideas so tell me what's right, what's wrong, and what's missing from my thinking." This step reflects humility.

3. **Share ground rules.** "Let's share actionable ideas and avoid personal attacks."
4. **Follow up.** Affirm in writing the people who gave useful ideas, what you heard, and the actions you plan to take.
5. **Appreciate the truth teller.** Be sure to personally thank people who had the courage to speak up and share a differing point of view.

In addition to group knowledge flow sessions, you can hold one-to-one knowledge flow sessions. Begin by making a list of the people you interact with in order to perform your work well. When meeting with individuals, share your vision for what relevant actions need to be taken in your work, whom you see as responsible for each action, and when the action needs to be completed. Ask them to tell you what's right, what's wrong, and what's missing from your thinking, and consider their ideas and opinions to learn from them and show that you value them. You may also want to hold a skip-level knowledge flow session periodically, in which you meet with a direct report and their direct reports.

After each group or individual knowledge flow session, follow up in writing to summarize what you heard, what actions are necessary, who is responsible for each action, and when each action should be completed.

Conduct Knowledge Flow Sessions to Evaluate Events and Activities

Every completed event provides an opportunity for learning and improvement. Post-event knowledge flow evaluation sessions give people an opportunity to identify what went right, what went wrong, and what was missing. This practice gives people a voice and helps them make continuous improvements.

Another type of knowledge flow session is the start-stop-continue meeting to evaluate and review your team's activities. Identify any activities your team should start that they are not presently doing, current activities they should stop doing, and activities they should continue doing.

Provide Training to Safeguard Relational Connections

Communicate that "creative friction" is desirable. People will often have differences of opinion, and leaders should assure them that this is healthy. With this understanding, holding and voicing opposing views shouldn't lead to combat. The key to maintaining healthy creative friction is to make sure you are trying to "get it right" to promote task excellence, rather than "be right" for the purpose of personal pride. Furthermore, civility should be encouraged, especially as individuals work through their differences.

Remind people to safeguard relational connections and avoid attacking individuals who disagree with them. If you disagree with someone, say so, but do it in a respectful manner. You could begin your response with, "I may be wrong, but is it possible that . . . ?" or "It's just one person's opinion, but I believe that . . . " If you offended or hurt someone's feelings, apologize. If people apologize to you, give them the benefit of the doubt and forgive them.

Author and executive coach Marshall Goldsmith (2007) recommends that when someone offers an idea, suggestion, opinion, or plan, you should take the time to reflect before offering a suggestion to improve it. Many people are in the habit of quickly adding their better idea by saying "but" or "however." Habitually doing this undermines connection, commitment, and engagement. People implement their own ideas with greater enthusiasm and energy, so consider whether your enhancement really matters before offering it.

Maintain Staff Connection and Development

Strong relationships are maintained by staying in touch. British prime minister Winston Churchill understood this. Historians have found more than 1,700 letters, notes, and telegrams that Churchill wrote to his wife so that they would remain connected (Soames 1999). Take a page from Churchill's playbook. Stay connected with your direct reports by meeting weekly with them in person, if at all possible. If you cannot meet weekly, use check-ins—phone calls, emails, and text messages—to help you stay connected. For people who work remotely, regularly call them; do a video call if possible. Remote work can be lonely, and people should believe that you are on their team and want to help them achieve their potential. In addition to work issues, ask about how they are doing personally. There is much truth to the old saying that people don't care what you know until they know you care.

The deepest connections are formed when you are open to communicate who you really are, what you really believe, and your struggles in life. Consider sharing lessons you've learned from past mistakes if it will help another person.

This openness communicates humility and promotes connection and trust. If you are uncertain about when it is appropriate to be open in a particular context, seek the advice of trusted friends.

Encourage other people to tell their stories too. Have you ever asked how someone's day went only to hear the standard reply, "fine"? If you really want to connect, try saying, "Tell me a story about your day." This practice also works well with children, spouses, and friends. Another way to bring people's stories forward is to hold Lunch & Learn sessions like they do at IHI (see the "Designing Connection Into Culture" profile). If the organization is providing the food for those who are gathering on-site, be sure to cover the cost of lunch for remote workers participating via videoconferencing.

You might also consider having your team periodically read a relevant book together. Meet to discuss and identify themes or ideas that could be applied to your work. Once you select the book, consider reaching out to the book's author to see if they would be willing to do a Q&A call or video meeting with your team. I've enjoyed the exchanges I've had with groups that have read this book.

Whether you're able to eventually implement all 15 building blocks or only a handful, the most important thing is to do what you can. Don't worry if you can't do all of them immediately—it's perfectly fine to start small and work up from there. With each effort you and your team make, you gain momentum.

Five-Step Process to Operationalize a Connection Culture

Developing a connection culture involves changing from cultures of control or indifference. Effecting lasting change takes effort and consistency. Here are five essential steps to developing and maintaining a connection culture:

Step 1. Develop a "connection mindset" among the members of your group.

The first step is to help people understand what connection is; why connection is important to help them personally, and their group, thrive; the consequences of failing to develop a connection culture; and how to go about developing and maintaining a connection culture.

You might recommend that colleagues read this book or have an event on connection culture (see appendix III: Additional Resources). Other materials consistent with connection culture should also be considered, such as content on appreciative inquiry, dealing with conflict, emotional intelligence, diversity and inclusion, psychological safety, resilience, and servant leadership.

During this first step, it's important for people to share their experiences and concerns. If we fail to engage people as they are developing a connection mindset and going through the process of embracing a culture of connection, fear may cause them to oppose change and work against it. By taking time to develop a connection mindset, you will be building a strong foundation for lasting change; however, forcing change is like building a foundation on sand that will make maintaining change less likely, especially during challenging seasons.

Step 2. Cultivate vision, value, and voice by intentionally developing habits of attitude, language, and behavior that connect.

This is the step in which you introduce and incorporate practices that increase vision, value, and voice. Why not model being a connected leader by asking members of your team to read the 15 building blocks presented in this chapter then discuss and identify which ones would have the greatest positive impact on your culture and which would be the easiest to implement? Select a manageable number of building blocks to start with and, over time, add more building blocks to strengthen connection in your group's culture.

Step 2 also requires eliminating attitudes, language, and behaviors that are counter to a connection culture. For example, humor that puts another person down is a behavior that is disconnecting and should not be tolerated.

One of the goals of this step is to repeat attitudes, uses of language, and behaviors with sufficient frequency that they become habits. This process of forming good habits—in other words, good character—is supported by what neuroscientists refer to as Hebb's Law, which states that "neurons that fire together, wire together." This means that if you repeatedly think, say, or act in the same way, the neurons in your brain form connections that are strengthened and in time become habit.

Step 3. Measure connection in each subculture to identify connected leaders, connected members, and individuals who need help connecting.

Most leaders are mistaken in their assessment of the engagement and connection levels of people they lead. As a result, they don't recognize a problem until they feel the pain from underperformance in the form of poor operating and financial results, incidents of managerial failure (including accidents and product failures), low employee engagement, or high employee turnover.

Implement a culture survey to provide accountability. The culture survey should ask all employees how their team, department, and organization are doing when it comes to acting in ways that are consistent with your organization's values. In the culture survey our firm has developed for the use of clients, which we refer to as the Connection Culture Inventory (CCI), we identify the extent of connection, control, and indifference in each subculture we assess.

Surveys can be designed to pinpoint where the organization's values are being met and where connection cultures, cultures of control, and cultures of indifference are found within an organization. It is typical to have a mix of subculture types when organizations do not intentionally develop culture. While some outstanding senior leaders are able to rely on interactions with people (rather than surveys) to identify pockets of disconnection throughout the organization, it is rare to find a leader who has the time to do this well. Conducting culture surveys on an annual basis is a best practice that provides a systematic way to assess connection and hold leaders responsible for creating connection cultures. Issues that arise from a culture survey must be addressed or else employees will feel that their feedback has not been taken seriously and they will grow cynical.

The vast majority of leaders who don't take the time to connect with the people they are responsible for leading do so because they don't see a clear link between behaviors that connect and superior performance results. One way to demonstrate that link is to integrate culture survey data with operational and financial metrics to establish, with empirical evidence, that greater connection leads to superior performance and results. This hard data gets the attention of critics and encourages them to improve connection by creating connection cultures.

Assessing connection both within and between organizational units—where interconnection, interaction, and cooperation are critical to achieve results—is highly recommended. For example, connections should be assessed between sales and marketing departments, between sales and customer service departments, and between support functions and the departments they support. When interdepartmental connections are broken, it affects employee engagement as well as results.

Finally, surveys hold leaders accountable so that connection cultures are maintained. They recognize leaders who are good at creating connection cultures and provide an important early warning system to help identify leaders and units that have drifted away from connection cultures. In time, a decision may need to be made concerning whether a leader is capable of working within a connection culture or should be replaced. Before replacing a leader too hastily, give them an opportunity to change by providing the support described in the next step.

Step 4. Mentor and coach individuals to become connected members and connected leaders.

Culture survey results from step 3 will help identify connected leaders and connected members who can become peer mentors to those who are struggling. One CEO client of ours selected a highly regarded, connected leader in the organization to become vice chair of the global organization and made him responsible for mentoring leaders who needed help developing healthy workplace cultures.

You have likely noticed throughout this book that I frequently write about mentoring. In interviews my colleagues and I have done with connected leaders and connected members, we've learned that they have been primarily influenced to become better connectors by mentors who connected with them.

Step 5. Celebrate and disseminate acts of connection (both stories and practices).

As mentioned in one of the building blocks under vision, celebrate people who embody your culture—"culture carriers." Culture survey results from step 3 will help identify connected leaders and connected members to be emulated. Celebrate these individuals through organizational communications such as the company intranet, social media, and print publications. This sends a powerful message and promotes best practices. This is particularly important because research has shown that standard practices within a culture have a higher probability of adoption (Dorsey 2000).

To make an intentional commitment to creating and maintaining your connection culture, you might want to establish a culture committee, office, or center to promote a connection culture across interdependent groups (such as groups within an organization that are dependent on each other to perform well). As I wrote in chapter 3, Southwest Airlines established a culture services department for the express purpose of "championing a culture through which every employee knows he or she matters," and its Companywide Culture Committee, comprising employees from across the company, works to "recognize, celebrate, and appreciate" all employees.

Making It Personal

✓ An important point made in this chapter is that connection occurs within groups of people in a subculture. The group might be a committee, a team, or a department. Connection also happens between subcultures, such as two departments. Which departments or people are most critical for you to have strong relationships with? What is the current state of those relationships?

✓ This chapter gives many practical tips for implementing a connection culture within your organization. Which three actions do you believe are most important for your team at this point?

✓ Connection is not just for the workplace. It's critical in all relationships, including community organizations, religious groups, families, and friends. What actions will you personally take to build connection in groups outside work?

7

Whom Will You Choose to Become?

For individuals and organizations to thrive from the benefits of connection, the leader of the future needs to look much different than the stereotypical leader of the present. There are three types of people when it comes to connection. Which are you?

The first type is the intentional disconnector. Psychologists describe these individuals as members of the Dark Triad: psychopaths, narcissists, and Machiavellians. They lack empathy and, as a result, are unable to attune to the emotions of others. They are focused on themselves and don't value others. Although they often learn how to manipulate others for a while and can appear smooth and charming, over time people see through them and discover that they are unable to connect.

The second type is the unintentional disconnector. This represents most of us. We have blind spots that hold us back in our ability to consistently connect with others. There are many types of blind spots, including being a know-it-all, argumentative, or a people pleaser who doesn't speak honestly when the truth is uncomfortable. If we don't become intentional about dealing with habits that hinder connection, they will become deeply ingrained in our character.

If, however, we are intentional about seeking the feedback of others and working to develop new and better habits of connection, we can join the ranks of the third type of person: the intentional connector. The individuals we praise in this book are intentional connectors. Their influence has enhanced the performance of their organizations and the lives of the people they've served, including their colleagues and customers.

In this final chapter, I cover a few additional issues that are important for you to know to have maximum positive impact on the cultures you influence.

You Can't Give What You Don't Have

Years ago, a friend who works in leadership development asked me to take the Hartman Value Profile (now called the Judgment Index). The results made me aware of a blind spot: I didn't take care of myself. My typical pattern was go-go-go until I collapsed from exhaustion, took time to recover, then repeated that pattern over and over in a continuous loop. My friend, who regularly uses the Judgment Index in coaching leaders, reviewed my results and gave me a stern warning that if I didn't change by taking better care of myself, I was going to burn out. Practically speaking, I needed to be more intentional about boosting connection in my life and boosting resilience practices. In our desire to get things done and do our best work, this "go until you drop" pattern is an easy trap to fall into.

Over time I came to see that I was an "achieve-aholic" who was addicted to busyness and achievement. As soon as I accomplished something, I immediately focused on the next task or problem to solve on my to-do list. This made it difficult to be present with and focused on interacting with others. If this describes you, you may have or be developing an addiction that's tied to dopamine, a type of neurotransmitter in your brain.

We tend to think of addictions as ingesting a substance that temporarily makes an individual feel better or more relaxed (being addicted to alcohol or drugs, for example), but it's broader than that . . . and sometimes less obvious when it's a behavior that has crossed over into addiction. As I pointed out in chapter 4, a review of 83 studies on addiction led by Steve Sussman and others concluded that nearly half the U.S. population suffers from one or more addictions that have "serious negative consequences" (Sussman et al. 2011). While the list of addictions studied included substance addictions (alcohol, eating disorders, mood-altering legal and illegal drugs, and tobacco), it also included process addictions (dependence upon busyness and work, exercise, gambling, online gaming or social media, shopping, falling in love, and sex).

So, what is dopamine and what role does it play in how we act? To put it simply, neurotransmitters are molecules that behave as chemical messengers in the brain. Dopamine is associated with the pleasure and reward pathways, and the positive emotion that makes us desire what we don't have and moti- vates us to go after the things we desire. In their book *The Molecule of More: How a Single Chemical in Your Brain Drives Love, Sex, and Creativity—and Will Determine the Fate of the Human Race*, authors Daniel Z. Lieberman and Michael E. Long (2018) give this interesting insight: "Dopamine has no standard for good, and seeks no finish line. The dopamine circuits in the brain can be stimulated only by the possibility of whatever is shiny and new, never mind how perfect things are at the moment. The dopamine motto is 'More.'" Another aspect of dopamine to be mindful of is that, like certain addictive substances, a person needs more dopamine to produce the same positive emotion over time.

While it is a good and useful thing to have an internal spark to pursue a goal and persevere on your quest to attain it, too much dopamine is a cause for concern. In organizations, leaders who have dopaminergic personalities are never satisfied. They continuously push people to achieve unrealistic goals in pursuit of boosting their own personal wealth, power, or status. This obsessive pursuit can overwhelm people working for dopaminergic leaders and create high levels of anxiety, incivility, stress, declining employee engage- ment, and rising burnout (and may push them toward an addiction of their own as they try to cope). Failing to feed the dopamine habit triggers pains of withdrawal. An individual who is overly reliant on dopamine may be headed for a crash.

The best leaders don't drink from the dopamine fire hydrant. In addi- tion to drawing on normal levels of dopamine, they benefit from other sources of positive emotion in the brain that make them more stable and more effective leaders who are in touch with the people they lead. Lieberman and Long (2018) contrast the "future-oriented dopamine" with "present- oriented chemicals, a collection of neurotransmitters we call the Here and Now molecules . . . [which] include serotonin and oxytocin, endorphins and endocannabinoids. . . . As opposed to the pleasure of anticipation via dopamine, these chemicals give us pleasure from sensation and emotion." Describing the interplay of these neurotransmitters, the authors explain that "though dopamine and [Here and Now] ('H&N') circuits can work together, under most circumstances they counter each other. When H&N circuits are activated, we are prompted to experience the real world around us, and dopamine is suppressed; when dopamine circuits are activated, we move into a future of possibilities and H&Ns are suppressed."

In his book *The Hacking of the American Mind: The Science Behind the Corporate Takeover of Our Bodies and Brains*, Robert H. Lustig (2017) sets out the differences between reward (driven by dopamine) and contentment (driven by serotonin). In Table 7-1, I've summarized his observations.

TABLE 7-1. REWARD VS. CONTENTMENT

Reward (Driven by Dopamine)	Contentment (Driven by Serotonin)
Reward is fleeting. It lasts about an hour.	Contentment lasts much longer. It can last for weeks, months, or years.
Reward is excitatory. It increases your heart rate and blood pressure.	Contentment is calming. It makes your heart rate slow and your blood pressure decline.
Reward can occur from engaging in addictive behaviors or ingesting addictive substances.	Contentment usually comes from achieving deeds.
Reward comes from taking.	Contentment comes from giving.
Reward pleases self.	Contentment has a positive impact on others and can affect society at large.

Lustig (2017) writes, "Reward, when unchecked, can lead us into misery, like addiction. Too much substance use (food, drugs, nicotine, alcohol) or compulsive behaviors (gambling, shopping, surfing the Internet, sex) will overload the reward pathway and lead not just to dejection, destitution, and disease but not uncommonly death as well."

Serotonin and the other Here and Now sources of positive emotion primarily come from healthy relationships at home and work. That's good news for people who have an abundance of connection in their lives. According to Lieberman and Long (2018), "We need H&N empathy to understand what's going on in other people's minds, an essential skill for social interaction." But here's a big issue affecting workplaces: Research published in *Harvard Business Review* found that half of CEOs reported feeling lonely and 61 percent of them believed it hindered their performance. Management expert and psychoanalyst Manfred F.R. Kets de Vries observed that many senior leaders struggle to maintain relationships and balance in their lives. In contrast, "healthy leaders . . . have the capacity to establish and maintain relationships (including satisfactory sexual relationships). Their lives are in balance, and they can play. They are creative and inventive and have the capacity to be nonconformist. These are the things that are fundamental" (Coutu 2004).

Here's the bottom line: You can't give what you don't have. Each of us needs connection in our lives in order to connect well with others. If you work in a culture that is disconnecting, one of the most important initial actions you can take is to find like-minded people who value connection and will support and encourage each other. We also need to take care of ourselves by attending to resilience practices. Here are several practices that help me cope with the stress that comes from living a full life.

- **Connect.** Spend time connecting with family and friends and in your community. I'm involved in a local faith community and volunteer to serve others. I spend time daily with my wife, Katie, talking over a meal, taking a coffee break, or going for a walk together.

- **Never worry alone.** When something is bothering me, I've learned to process it in conversation with Katie or a friend. This helps engage the rational part of my brain and quiet the part of my brain that makes me feel anxious.

- **Stay active.** Exercise often. Exercising several days a week energizes me and helps reset and calm my nervous system.

- **Rest.** Get adequate sleep and include quiet time each day. I rest each day, including time for prayer, pleasure reading, and listening to music (for you, it may include meditation or mindfulness practices). I'm committed to taking at least one day off each week to do things that rejuvenate me. When possible, I take a vacation during the year.

- **Avoid multitasking.** Try to focus on one task at a time. I've found that it helps me from an emotional health standpoint to create daily checklists of tasks I'd like to complete that day and check them off as I finish them.

- **Eat healthy.** Maintain a balanced diet. Watch sugar and refined carbohydrates. I weigh myself daily, and if my weight creeps up, I cut back on calories. Drink sufficient amounts of water. If you experience frequent headaches, you may be dehydrated.

- **Have an annual physical exam.** Get checked regularly. Every fall I go to my primary care physician for a complete physical. I find it helpful to track my medical records online.

- **Get out in nature.** Go for a walk, take a hike, read at the beach. These are ways I relax and refresh my nervous system.
- **Do something creative.** Sometimes our family will get out blank canvases and acrylic paints and have our own painting party, complete with snacks. I've never thought of myself as an artist and so it surprised me how absorbing and relaxing it can be to draw and paint. Whether you sing, dance, play an instrument, sew, take photos, cook, or bake a new recipe, find a creative outlet that will get your mind off your work or worries.
- **Organize your physical environment**, including your office. Research shows that clutter can make us feel overwhelmed.
- **Replace negative behaviors with neutral or healthy behaviors.** For example, if you are reaching for sugar or refined carbohydrates to get an energy boost in the afternoon, replace them with fruit or vegetables that will not trigger a crash (George 2013).

These and other resilience practices help give us energy and good health so we have the capacity to connect with others. Absent the energy and good health needed to connect, we are more likely to slip into attitudes, language, and behaviors that are disconnecting, especially if we have higher levels of stress in our lives. To learn more about resilience practices, read *The Resilience Workbook: Essential Skills to Recover from Stress, Trauma and Adversity* by Glenn Schiraldi (2017) and *The Waterwheel: Practical Wisdom for 64 Common Concerns* by Jill Woolworth (2018).

Be Aware of Trauma

Group culture is shaped by individuals who are driven by their past experiences, current situations, and genetic makeup. It may be helpful for you to understand how trauma affects a person's ability to connect.

Trauma may cause painful emotions, relationship problems, and physical pain. While these responses to trauma are normal, some people become stuck in a traumatized state that they cannot overcome alone. Trauma makes people more vulnerable to stress and feeling threatened.

People who are traumatized may suffer damage to part of the brain that can lead to extreme reactions, as described in Ted George's insightful book, *Untangling the Mind: Why We Behave the Way We Do* (2013).

George, a neuroscientist and psychiatrist, shared with me two helpful analogies. Humans resemble the Slinky, that popular childhood toy made of coiled wire or plastic. Our brains are like metal springs that can be stretched by the stresses of everyday life and under most circumstances return to their usual shape. However, if stretched beyond a limit, the Slinky stays bent. Traumatized people are like that too. Once afflicted by a trauma, their lives can be forever changed.

Connections between two parts of the brain, the cortex and the amygdala, typically regulate our response to stressors (threats) in a controlled fashion. Put simply, the cortex is responsible for higher thought processes such as language and decision making. The amygdala is part of the limbic system which controls emotions and is on guard for threats. The amygdala can be likened to radar that is programmed to detect enemy aircraft, serving as an early warning system to promote survival.

Exposure to terrible events such as domestic violence, sexual abuse, or other situations evoking extreme horror or helplessness can affect these connections in the human brain. In the workplace, being bullied or abused can also trigger trauma. The COVID-19 pandemic in 2020 traumatized many individuals, and will affect their emotional health for years following the pandemic's end, so understanding trauma today is especially relevant.

The affected connections are like the Slinky that gets bent. Returning to the analogy of the radar, without the self-control that comes from the cortex in our brains, the amygdala reacts to birds and mosquitoes as if they too were enemy aircraft.

People who have experienced trauma often overreact to perceived slights or threats. The uninhibited amygdala activates hardwired neurons located in a tiny structure within the midbrain called the periaqueductal gray (PAG), which gives rise to emotions such as fear, anger, or depression. Under such circumstances, these emotional reactions are troublesome and out of proportion to the actual environmental stimuli.

Here are other reactions:

- Thought processes become programmed for survival. Black-and-white thinking overtakes rational thinking.

- Vulnerability is minimized. The ability to trust and to either love or receive love is impaired. Feeling numb or detached from others becomes the norm.
- The future becomes darkened. Preoccupation with the past serves as a constant reminder that the threatening circumstances could return. One must be vigilant and ready! Healthy relationships seem out of reach.
- Experiencing extreme emotions and associated behaviors is exhausting. Not understanding how they arise is troubling. The need to reach out for help is perceived as an exercise in futility.
- Drugs and alcohol often are used to dampen emotional pain.

George explained that honesty with self and others is the first step in moving from a fear of connecting to a sense of personal freedom to connect.

The effects of trauma also factor into burnout, which progresses from emotional exhaustion to depersonalization to a diminished sense of personal accomplishment (Maslach and Leiter 2016). In his book *Finding Heart in Art: A Surgeon's Renaissance Approach to Healing Modern Medical Burnout* (2017), Dr. Shawn C. Jones shares how trauma experienced in his medical training and practice as an otolaryngologist, along with increased disconnection, led him to become extremely desensitized—to experience alexithymia. He described the condition as "completely unable to identify or feel anything in the way of happiness or sadness, anger, or calm. I felt no connection to anything—myself, my family, my associates, my patients. I felt completely disconnected from the world around me." Fortunately for Jones, he didn't merely carry on in that state of "emotional numbness." He sought professional help, recovered, and returned to practicing medicine. Jones went on to become president of the Kentucky Medical Association and in 2016 was honored with the association's Distinguished Service Award.

If you believe you or someone you know has been traumatized, I encourage you to seek help from a licensed professional and don't try to tough it out on your own. Ask friends in your community or your primary care physician for recommendations. Most of us will experience trauma at some point in our lifetime. Seeking help is wise and it is not something to be ashamed of.

The Changing Workplace and Future of Work

Today's workplace is undergoing accelerated change in ways that make connection more important.

Rise of Remote Work, the Gig Economy, and Side Hustles

Remote work, also referred to as telecommuting, is on the rise. Research by the Society for Human Resource Management (2016) found that the number of organizations offering remote work benefits increased from 20 percent in 1996 to 60 percent in 2016. Reasons cited for the shift included technological advances that make remote work possible and increased desire on the part of employees for more flexible work schedules and to reduce time spent commuting.

Research from Global Workplace Analytics for 2017 (the latest figures available prior to the COVID-19 pandemic) found that 4.7 million people (3.4 percent of the U.S. workforce) telecommute at least half-time while 40 percent work remotely at some frequency and 80–90 percent of the workforce would like to telecommute at least part time.

It should be noted that there are limits to the rise of remote work. Certain jobs require the physical presence of employees—a salesperson in a retail store, a machine operator in a manufacturing plant, or an airline flight attendant, for example. The U.S. Bureau of Labor Statistics (2019) reported that only 29 percent of Americans had jobs that could be done from home.

And then there is the question of whether employers are willing to allow off-site work. The reluctance to embrace the option of remote work may stem from a concern that jobs requiring greater collaboration to boost creativity and innovation are best located on-site. Apple founder Steve Jobs wanted employees on-site because he believed creativity and innovation often came from serendipitous interactions in the physical workplace. It mattered so much to him that he was involved in the design of workplaces to encourage such interactions. IBM was an early adopter of having a portion of its workforce working remotely, going back to 1979. By 2009, 40 percent of IBM's 386,000 employees worldwide did remote work. Then in 2017 the company changed course and moved 5,000 people back on-site. Aetna, BestBuy, and Yahoo have also made similar moves to have remote workers return to the office (Useem 2017).

Supporting a move to more remote work is empirical evidence that tele-commuters are more productive (Bloom et al. 2015). It may be that organizations end up allowing telecommuting for jobs that predominantly require focus time and less interaction with colleagues, such as a financial planner or data analyst, but keep jobs on-site that are more collaborative and cooperative in nature (Useem 2017; Waber 2017).

The COVID-19 pandemic represented an inflection point in the rise and acceptance of remote work as many organizations had to quickly pivot their way of doing business and move large numbers of employees off-site to reduce the risk of virus transmission. Leaders who may have previously been averse to offering the opportunity for doing some or all work remotely now found themselves working from home and leading entirely remote teams.

It is believed that many jobs that moved off-site in spring 2020 will remain there following the pandemic. As I mentioned in chapter 4, a 2020 survey by Willis Towers Watson of 200 U.S. companies across multiple industry sectors found that 59 percent expected work-from-home policies to continue after the pandemic ended. A Gallup Research poll conducted in late March 2020 found that 62 percent of employed Americans worked from home during the pandemic, and three in five indicated they would prefer to continue working remotely as much as possible once public health restrictions are lifted (Brenan 2020).

From the organization's perspective, there are several advantages to remote work. A survey by Gartner of 317 chief financial officers found that 74 percent expected to move previously on-site employees to work remotely post-COVID-19. The desire to reduce commercial real estate costs was cited as one motivation (Dignan 2020). Another advantage is an improved ability to attract, engage, and retain talented employees who desire flexible work schedules with the option of remote work. Gallup data found that remote work was also appealing to workers who value the environment-friendly aspect of being able to reduce or eliminate carbon dioxide emissions related to commuting (Hickman and Robison 2020). Staggered work schedules that mix on-site and remote work days, and reconfigured office space that allows for fewer employees per square foot are likely to become the norm.

As leaders navigate the way forward with a higher percentage of the workforce working remotely, it raises the question of how working remotely affects connection and employee engagement. Gallup Research has investigated the issue of engagement and the amount of time spent working remotely for years. Results in 2012 showed the optimal engagement boost occurred when workers spent less than 20 percent of their time off-site. Five years later the percentage had risen significantly. Gallup's 2017 report indicated that connection and employee engagement were optimized when employees worked remotely 60–80 percent of the time, which is equivalent to three to four days in a five-day workweek (Hickman and Robison 2020). This finding suggests that once restrictions related to social distancing ease and non-essential businesses reopen, organizations could offer people a combination of on-site and remote work that reduces the risk of viral transmission while boosting connection and engagement.

Gigs—jobs that last a defined period of time—comprise any form of contingent work, including independent contractors, temporary agency workers, directly sourced temporary workers, statement-of-work consultants, and human cloud workers (where work is arranged and completed entirely online; SIA n.d.). Digital nomads, people who can work remotely given telecommunications technologies while living a nomadic lifestyle, are part of the gig economy. An estimated 48 million people did gig work in the United States in 2017, which represents 31 percent of all U.S. workers. Spending in the U.S. gig economy was estimated to be $864 billion of the total global gig economy, which was estimated to be $3.7 trillion (SIA 2018).

If you are working as an independent freelancer and not as an employee of an organization, you likely have an even greater need for connection because you may experience added stress from three sources:

- There may be constant pressure to sell and generate revenue or secure your next assignment.
- You may experience greater stress from increased competition of "telemigrants"—that is, people who work remotely from outside your home country and can afford to price their services at a lower cost (Baldwin 2019).
- Without the benefits provided as part of your compensation package, you may feel added stress from having lesser health insurance coverage and no paid time off, sick days, or vacation days.

There are positive aspects of working remotely if you are an employee or part of the gig economy, but a downside is that it can be isolating. Gallup Research found in 2016 that people working remotely were working at various times of the day outside the typical 8 a.m. to 5 p.m. workday, and they were interacting more online and less face-to-face. As I've noted earlier, if you are working apart from the rest of the team, don't neglect your need for meaningful connection that energizes you. Schedule time into your week to connect with family, friends, and your community outside work, such as going out to lunch with someone on a workday or engaging in group exercise. If your on-the-clock hours are flexible, consider doing some volunteer work with a local nonprofit during traditional business hours when others may not be available and there is a shortage of help.

Does your home double as your office? Depending on the kind of work you do, it might benefit you to rent co-working space so you can be around people during at least some of your time spent working. Have you noticed how some coffee shops are designed to encourage customers to open up their laptops and linger over a latte? Some hotels are even setting up their lobbies to welcome locals and make it an inviting space for guests to get some work done rather than sit alone in their rooms.

Are you responsible for leading people who work remotely, whether they are employed by your organization or are independent contractors with you for a short-term assignment? Keep in mind that they are at a higher risk of experiencing disconnection. They need connection to be healthy and perform well just as much, or even more so, than the colleagues around you in the office. In the busyness of your own schedule, guard against the attitude of "out of sight, out of mind."

An important point to remember about being responsible for leading remote workers is that the effective leadership of people, whether they work on-site or remotely, has more to do with observing good leadership practices than where individuals are located. The best leaders cultivate a connection culture by communicating an inspiring vision, valuing people, and giving them a voice. As pointed out in chapter 6, practices that boost vision, value, and voice will differ in some ways depending upon whether an employee is on-site or remote. Make an extra effort to be proactive about reaching out to them so that they feel included in a connection culture.

Lastly, a "side hustle" differs in that it is often driven by something the person enjoys doing and can do to make extra money to supplement another job (or jobs). As the name implies, it's a little something you have going on the side. It could be a creative outlet (doing lettering or illustrations that you sell online through a website), baking and selling your incredible chocolate chip cookies, dog walking for elderly neighbors, or offering proofreading services, for example. Here are a few statistics that show how widespread side hustles are becoming (Side Hustle Nation 2019):

- According to a 2017 Bankrate study, 44 million Americans have a side hustle. Younger Millennials (ages 18–26) are the most likely age group to have a side hustle as a means of earning extra cash, coming in at 28 percent (Berger 2017).
- The average person spends 11 hours a week on their side hustle and earns $12,609 per year (an average of about $25 per hour; Crockett 2018).
- The same study reported that while 76 percent of respondents loved their side hustle, only half loved their primary job (Crockett 2018).

What does this mean for you as a leader? Consider that some of the people you are responsible for leading may be doing work on the side beyond the work they do for your organization. A person who works multiple jobs, whether out of financial necessity or to gain more experience to open up future possibilities, or whose heart is really in the side hustle, is likely to not have the physical or emotional bandwidth to give their best for a sustained period of time.

Workforce Spanning Generations

In early 2019 it was reported that 20 percent of Americans ages 65 and older were working or looking for work, representing a 57-year high in that metric (Plews 2019). The Bureau of Labor Statistics expects the numbers to increase in the near term and it estimated that 13 million Americans over the age of 65 will be in the labor force by 2024 (Toossi and Torpey 2017). What is behind this upward trend? For some, the decision to remain in the workforce beyond the standard retirement age is driven by financial need. For others, though, the motivation may be tied to the intellectual challenge or the satisfaction of doing work that has meaning, or a desire to interact with others on a routine basis.

So, what if you lead a team or organization that is multi-generational? Left unaddressed, age and differing generational viewpoints may be a source of friction. I recommend openly recognizing age as a type of diversity to be acknowledged and explored as a strength. Embrace the opportunity to learn from each other. Older individuals have a lifetime of experiences to draw upon, and there is research showing with age often comes wisdom (the practical application of knowledge; Reistad-Long 2008). Younger individuals often bring a fresh perspective and an awareness of and experience using new technology tools.

Artificial Intelligence

Artificial intelligence (AI) is another factor that is likely to make connection more important in the years and decades ahead. AI will create new jobs and career opportunities that we can only imagine today. It will also, at least in the near term, cause stress to rise for many individuals from fears of job displacement and wage decline as more jobs in the global economy become automated and therefore obsolete.

As in the past, when the predominant economy moved from agrarian to industrial and then from industrial to services, many individuals will lose their jobs and not have the skills necessary to fill newly created jobs as a result of innovation (Baldwin 2019). Connection cultures in workplaces, homes, and communities will help people and society cope with the stress that these changes bring about and help make it more likely that people will avoid panicking and making rash decisions that may do more harm than good.

Another concern related to AI has been expressed by Professor Nicholas Christakis of Yale University. He argues that as a result of more time spent interacting with machines and less time connecting face-to-face, AI may have unintended disruptive social effects that diminish humans' ability to connect, including "how loving, friendly and kind we are in interactions with each other." As an example, Christakis cites a concern of MIT professor Sherry Turkle that children growing up relating to AI instead of individuals may not acquire "the equipment for empathic connection" (Christakis 2019).

I'm encouraged to see that there are signs that the demand for connection skills is on the rise and will continue to be in the future. LinkedIn Learning's *2019 Workplace Learning Report* observed, "The rise of AI is making soft skills increasingly important, as they are precisely the skills that can't be automated."

Richard Baldwin, author of *The Globotics Upheaval: Globalization, Robotics, and the Future of Work*, predicts demand for connection-related skills will continue as he sees work becoming more human and requiring greater skills in adaptability, empathy, ethical decision making, innovating, inspiring, teaching, and leading people.

As I look at these factors affecting the changing workplace and future of work—artificial intelligence, digital nomads, side hustles, the gig economy, the rise of remote work—I see people spending more time in front of screens and therefore there will be a higher risk of isolation and greater need for connection.

How all of these changes play out is difficult to predict, yet one thing is certain: Given all that we know about the positive effects of connection and dangers of disconnection, we need to be intentional about fostering connection in our own lives and fostering connection in the cultures we influence. Drifting toward greater disconnection as a result of the effects of new technologies and political, social, or economic change is unacceptable.

Must a Connection Culture Start at the Top?

Does connection culture have to come from the top of the organization? That would be the ideal situation, but if you are not a leader at the top of your organization and those who are more senior are not intentional about creating a connection culture, there is still hope.

As I have previously noted, organizations comprise many subcultures. Some subcultures are primarily connection cultures, some are primarily cultures of control, and some are primarily cultures of indifference. Although the macro-culture of your organization will influence your local subculture, it does not determine it. The primary determinants of connection for you are the predominant attitudes, uses of language, and behaviors of those in your local subculture. For that reason, you can have an influence on your local subculture—whether you are the leader, a supervisor, or informally lead others through your influence. In the work my colleagues and I do, we frequently see people change their local subculture for the better.

Several years ago, one of our clients, a global organization, hired a leader to manage its New Zealand unit, which had approximately 60 employees and was lagging in the marketplace. The new leader boosted vision by expanding the local leadership team and asking them to work together to create the culture they always wanted to work in. He boosted value by being approachable and getting to know all the people in the unit. When the global financial and economic crisis of 2008 affected the unit shortly after he arrived, rather than laying people off and imposing compulsory salary reductions on frontline staff like his competitors had done, he challenged the leadership team to make its top priority to save as many jobs as possible. He asked the executive team leaders to join him in taking a 10 percent pay cut, which they did. He boosted voice by putting an annual employee engagement survey in place and acting on the employees' feedback. He also shared financials with employees and asked them to help find ways to reduce costs in order to save jobs. The empowered employees found ways to cut costs and, as a result, they didn't have to cut any jobs.

Pulling through tough times brought the unit together. It won global recognition for its work, grew to almost four times its original size, and was recognized as one of the best places to work and the best in its area of expertise. The CEO of the global organization made the leader of the New Zealand unit a vice chairman of the global organization to help mentor leaders around the world on how to develop the best workplace cultures. The culture change that began locally in New Zealand is now spreading throughout the entire organization.

Connection Begins With You

A word of caution is in order. The number 1 obstacle to creating a connection culture is the knowing-doing gap, a term coined by Stanford professors Jeffrey Pfeffer and Robert Sutton in their excellent book of the same name. The knowing-doing gap recognizes many leaders fail to turn knowledge into actions that produce measurable results. Pfeffer and Sutton found common sense is uncommon in practice. They found that great organizations got outstanding performance from ordinary people by:

- valuing common sense and avoiding management fads
- valuing simple and easy-to-understand language
- investing the time to make sure people understood the philosophy and rationale supporting strategy and actions
- measuring to make sure critical actions get done.

In the context of promoting the need for connection in the workplace and how to create and maintain a connection culture, I've witnessed how the knowing-doing gap has held organizations back as leaders have fallen for one or more of the following fallacies (I've given each a label to make them easier to remember):

- **"Common Sense" fallacy.** Because actions that boost connection reflect common sense, they are assumed to be occurring in the organization (when in fact they are not).

- **"Seduced by a Management Fad" fallacy.** Leaders are seduced by sophisticated-sounding management fads, so there is an utter failure to implement simple, commonsense actions that boost connection and have the greatest effect on results.

- **"Only Give Me the Practical" fallacy.** Leaders want to get straight to the practical and actionable in training. Without helping people understand why connection is important and how it works, actions that boost connection don't take root. (Note: This is why we've made developing a connection mindset the first step in operationalizing connection culture, as described in the previous chapter).

- **"Failure to Measure" fallacy.** Leaders see connection as so obvious they fail to measure it, which signals to employees that connection is unimportant, and, as a result, they don't follow through on actions that boost connection.

Don't let the knowing-doing gap become your story. Like the great organizations, be intentional and action-oriented about developing a connection mindset, connection skills, and connection character—the habits of attitude, language, and behavior that connect—and work to develop a connection culture in your organization. Start local and see how it grows from there.

Throughout this book, I've given you tools and guidance to take action. I hope you've taken time to reflect on your past and current experiences, made some "try this" mental notes, and even started using some of the building blocks in chapter 6 for yourself.

Begin meeting individually with the people you are responsible for leading and use the knowledge flow process described in chapter 6 to communicate your vision for a connection culture, show you value them, and give them a voice. Follow these steps:

During the meetings:
- **Communicate your vision.** Share that your desire is to help each person on the team and the team as a whole to cultivate an environment where everyone can do their best work. Convey that you would like to hear their thoughts on some issues related to that topic.
- **Show you value people and give them a voice.** Ask the questions listed below, listen closely to the responses, take written notes, and do not challenge the individual but merely say "thank you" for sharing their point of view.
  - What have you enjoyed the most about working over your career? Are there any specific examples you can share?
  - What have you not liked about work over your career?
  - What work environment has helped you do your best work?
  - What has prevented you from doing your best work?
  - What are your hopes for the future as far as your work and career are concerned?
  - Is there anything else you'd like to share?

After the meetings:
- **Review your notes.** Identify actions you can take to show every individual you considered what they shared.
- **Acknowledge commitments.** Write the individual a note or email that summarizes what you heard and what you are committing to do.

By going through these steps, you will be getting off to a great start and boosting connection through vision, value, and voice.

As you become an intentional connector at work, look at how the level of connection in your personal life changes. Keep the formula Vision + Value + Voice = Connection in mind and consider how it applies to your family, your neighborhood, the community organizations you are involved in, and other areas of your life, and then take steps to increase connection in those spheres as well.

Mark this day—begin connecting and watch what happens. I promise that over time, you will see that connection affects much more than the bottom line. As you experience greater peace, hope, and joy that comes from having an abundance of connection in your life, you will discover wealth of even greater value.

Making It Personal

✓ Can you identify specific individuals you've known who fall into each of the categories of intentional disconnector, unintentional disconnector, and intentional connector?

✓ Consider asking a few of those close to you to honestly share which of your habits or behaviors they find disconnecting. Doing so will help you to become aware of your connection blind spots.

✓ Of the factors mentioned in "The Changing Workplace and Future of Work" section of this chapter, which do you expect might have the most relevance to you over the next three years? What other potential issues do you see on the horizon?

✓ What are your spheres of influence? What steps can you take to build connection in those local cultures?

Acknowledgments

I grew up in a family of boys living in a neighborhood of boys. Our lives revolved around the rhythm of three seasons: baseball, basketball, and football. Like many boys, we were not all that emotionally or socially intelligent. What I learned about connection and the emotions that increase connection, such as love and affection, came primarily from my devoted mother, Dorothy Hufstedler. Mom, for your loving influence and example, I am immensely grateful.

As an adult, I got caught up in the pursuit of money, power, and status, and that drive increasingly crowded out relationships. It was only later in life that I learned (the hard way) that we are hardwired to connect. I thank God, my family, and friends for saving me from myself.

To Katie Stallard, my best friend, wife, and colleague, and our daughters, Sarah and Elizabeth, each of you has had a profound effect on me when it comes to experiencing and understanding connection and healing from the damage of disconnection. I am so blessed and grateful that we are a family and that our extended family is deeply connected. I'm also grateful to our son-in-law, Jeremie Fagnan, and for how welcoming the Fagnan family has been to us. During the writing of this second edition, our first grandchild, Peyton Elizabeth, was born to Sarah and Jeremie.

To God and my church family, thank you for being and modeling connection. To my men's Bible study, I'm so thankful that we are connected by going through life together and being there for one another during the joys and challenges.

Finally, thank you to the many individuals who have helped make *Connection Culture* possible or contributed their talents to making it better. At E Pluribus Partners and Connection Culture Group, thank you Katie Stallard, Todd Hall, Jason Pankau, and Katie Russell. Katie Stallard is an exemplar of connection and character. She is my sounding board, editor, and encourager. Todd has taken our work to a new level with his wisdom, insight, research, and vision for sharing our work online. Jason and I have been friends working together for more than 15 years. He is a source of wisdom and someone I can always count on. Katie Russell contributed to the manuscript while ably leading our communications and social media efforts. Along with Jason, Carolyn Dewing-Hommes was instrumental in the early days of putting language around the core elements of a connection culture.

At the Association for Talent Development, I would especially like to thank Ryan Changcoco, who leads ATD's Management Community of Practice and has been an advocate for *Connection Culture*. Melissa Jones, our editor at ATD Press for both editions; Kathryn Stafford, the developmental editor for this edition; and Hannah Sternberg, the copy editor for this edition, went above and beyond to make the book even better. I would also like to thank others at ATD who've supported our work, including Kristen Fyfe-Mills, Tim Ito, and Lisa Spinelli.

Many people at TCU have supported and contributed to our work, including Victor Boschini, Ellen Broom, Yohna Chambers, Dee Dodson, Johny Garner, Angela Kaufman, Suzy Lockwood, Mariam MacGregor, Dianna McFarland, Sheri Miller, Jean Mrasek, Ron Pitcock, the late Karyn Purvis, Jim Riddlesperger, Chris Sawyer, Dana Sweatman, Tracy Syler-Jones, Dan Williams, Paul Witt, and Linda Wolszon.

Robin Wolfson of the Robin Wolfson Agency, our agent for speaking engagements, is the best, and we're grateful for her.

Finally, thank you to the many family, friends, and others who contributed ideas, feedback, or other support for *Connection Culture*, including Erika Andersen, Kare Anderson, Mary Jo Asmus, Howard and Lynn Behar, Jeff Benner, Ty Bennett, Hillary Bercovici, Jim Blasingame, Wally Bock, Jeff Boss, Ralph Brandt, Rich Brandt, Jim and Martha Brangenberg, David Brinkerhoff, Rob and Beth Bull, David Burkus, Kathy Caprino, Karen Christensen, Vernon and Connie Clark, Peter Clayton, Tom Cole, Randy Conley, Jack Covert, Bryan Crawford, Ian Cron, Mike and Jeannie Cunnion, Holly Dahlman, Steve Daniel, James daSilva, Joe and Lucille D'Auria, Robbie de Villiers, Craig Diamond, Mitch Dickey, Nowell Donovan, Michael Ebaugh, Kevin Eikenberry, Brian Ellis, Homer Erekson, Rosanna Fahy, George Faller, Pat Farnack, Kyle Farris, Lorri Freifeld, Stewart Friedman, D. Theodore George, Phil Gerbyshak, Seth Godin, Marshall Goldsmith, Charles Good, Denise Griffitts, Lisa Haneberg, John and Bunny Harrison, Nathan Hart, Mary Held, Doug Hensch, Frances Hesselbein, Trevor Hightower, William J. Holstein, Russ

Hufstedler, Matt Hultquist, Prakash Idnani, Nathan Ives, Justine Jannucci, Liz Kanoy, Guy Kawasaki, Rod Keffer, David Kelly, Angela Killian, Riley Kiltz, Alexander Kjerulf, Raj Kottamasu, Jeremie Kubicek, Jennifer Labin, Paul LaRue, Terry and Leslie Laughren, Jim Lemler, Kate Levine, Chip Lewis, Mark Linsz, Chad Littlefield, Thomas Loarie, Ann Louden, Katherine Love, Lucille Maddalena, Chris Mader, Drew Marshall, Roger Martin, Rob and Tammy Mathes, Dan McCarthy, Shawn McEvoy, Michael McKinney, Denise McMahan, Dwayne Melancon, Paul and Lisa Michalski, Morgan Mitchell, Blake Morgan, Cecile Morgan, Jay Morris, Robert Morris, Amanda Nickerson, Ryan Niemiec, Don Pape, Joon and Ann Park, John Pearson, Colton Perry, Gordon Peters, Katherine McIntire Peters, Jon Peters, Karla Peters-Van Havel, Becky Powell-Schwartz, Henry and Barbara Price, Kelsey Rogers, Francis Rose, Bruce Rosenstein, Jon Rugg, David Russell, George Ryerson, Zane Safrit, Robbie Samuels, Tim Sanders, John Saunders, Roy Saunderson, Rosa Say, Beth Schelske, Aaron Schleicher, Dylan Schleicher, Glenn Schiraldi, Tara Seager, Terrence Seamon, Rajesh Setty, Ken Shelton, Joshua Simpson, Andrzej and Karolina Skiba, Joe Stallard, Susan Stamm, Michael Bungay Stanier, Dave Summers, Greg Sumpter, Rich Tanaka, Greg Thomas, Mark Thompson, Bob Tiede, Michelle Tillis-Lederman, Khiem and Vicki Ting, Roger Trapp, Linda Tucker, Wayne Turmel, Joe Tye, Katy Tynan, Brenda Vallieu, Tony Vlahos, Jim Ware, Jenny Watkins, Randal Weidenaar, Alana Weiss, Paul White, Charlie Whitney, Drew Williams, Chris Winters, Guy Wisinski, Sean Witty, Stephen Woessner, Tom Woeste, Kitty Wooley, Heather Wright, Janis Yadiny, Don Yaeger, John Young, Susan Zeidman, and David Zinger.

Appendix I
VIA Institute Classification of Character Strengths

The following are descriptions of the 24 character strengths. Based on the findings of positive psychology, the character strengths were developed by the VIA Institute on Character, a not-for-profit organization focused on advancing both the science and practice of character strengths. (Note that here the 24 character strengths are organized into six virtue categories rather than into vision, value, and voice, as we organized them to show how they support a connection culture.)

The Classification of Character Strengths

1. **Wisdom and Knowledge:** Cognitive strengths that entail the acquisition and use of knowledge.
   - **Creativity** (originality, ingenuity): Thinking of novel and productive ways to conceptualize and do things; includes artistic achievement but is not limited to it.
   - **Curiosity** (interest, novelty-seeking, openness to experience): Taking an interest in ongoing experience for its own sake; finding subjects and topics fascinating; exploring and discovering.
   - **Judgment** (open-mindedness; critical thinking): Thinking things through and examining them from all sides; not jumping to conclusions; being able to change one's mind in light of evidence; weighing all evidence fairly.
   - **Love of Learning:** Mastering new skills, topics, and bodies of knowledge, whether on one's own or formally; related to the strength of curiosity but goes beyond it to describe the tendency to add systematically to what one knows.

- **Perspective** (wisdom): Being able to provide wise counsel to others; having ways of looking at the world that make sense to oneself or others.

2. **Courage:** Emotional strengths that involve the exercise of will to accomplish goals in the face of external or internal opposition.
   - **Bravery** (valor): Not shrinking from threat, challenge, difficulty, or pain; speaking up for what's right even if there's opposition; acting on convictions even if unpopular; includes physical bravery but is not limited to it.
   - **Perseverance** (persistence, industriousness): Finishing what one starts; persevering in a course of action in spite of obstacles; "getting it out the door"; taking pleasure in completing tasks.
   - **Honesty** (authenticity, integrity): Speaking the truth, but more broadly presenting oneself in a genuine way and acting in a sincere way; being without pretense; taking responsibility for one's feelings and actions.
   - **Zest** (vitality, enthusiasm, vigor, energy): Approaching life with excitement and energy; not doing things halfway or halfheartedly; living life as an adventure; feeling alive and activated.

3. **Humanity:** Interpersonal strengths that involve tending and befriending others.
   - **Love** (capacity to love and be loved): Valuing close relations with others, in particular those in which sharing and caring are reciprocated; being close to people.
   - **Kindness** (generosity, nurturance, care, compassion, altruistic love, niceness): Doing favors and good deeds for others; helping them; taking care of them.
   - **Social Intelligence** (emotional intelligence, personal intelligence): Being aware of the motives and feelings of others and oneself; knowing what to do to fit into different social situations; knowing what makes other people tick.

4. **Justice:** Civic strengths that underlie healthy community life.
   - **Teamwork** (citizenship, social responsibility, loyalty): Working well as a member of a group or team; being loyal to the group; doing one's share.
   - **Fairness:** Treating all people the same according to notions of fairness and justice; not letting feelings bias decisions about others; giving everyone a fair chance.
   - **Leadership:** Encouraging a group of which one is a member to get things done and at the same time maintain good relations within the group; organizing group activities and seeing that they happen.

5. **Temperance:** Strengths that protect against excess.
   - **Forgiveness** (mercy): Forgiving those who have done wrong; accepting others' shortcomings; giving people a second chance; not being vengeful.
   - **Humility** (modesty): Letting one's accomplishments speak for themselves; not regarding oneself as more special than one is.
   - **Prudence**: Being careful about one's choices; not taking undue risks; not saying or doing things that might later be regretted.
   - **Self-Regulation** (self-control): Regulating what one feels and does; being disciplined; controlling one's appetites and emotions.

6. **Transcendence:** Strengths that forge connections to the universe and provide meaning.
   - **Appreciation of Beauty and Excellence** (awe, wonder, elevation): Noticing and appreciating beauty, excellence, or skilled performance in various domains of life, from nature to art to mathematics to science to everyday experience.
   - **Gratitude:** Being aware of and thankful for the good things that happen; taking time to express thanks.
   - **Hope** (optimism, future-mindedness, future orientation): Expecting the best in the future and working to achieve it; believing that a good future is something that can be brought about.

- ○ **Humor** (playfulness): Liking to laugh and tease; bringing smiles to other people; seeing the light side; making (not necessarily telling) jokes.
- ○ **Spirituality** (religiousness, faith, purpose): Having coherent beliefs about the higher purpose and meaning of the universe; knowing where one fits within the larger scheme; having beliefs about the meaning of life that shape conduct and provide comfort.

Appendix II
Study Questions
for Book Groups

Chapter 1

- Reflect on a time when you were energized by your work. What factors were present that contributed to your energy?
- Reflect on a time when your work felt draining. What factors were present that contributed to your fatigue?

Chapter 2

- Describe a time when you truly connected with another person or a group. How did that make you feel?
- Is your current work environment an example of a culture of control, a culture of indifference, or a connection culture? Why?
- Which of the seven universal human needs to thrive at work are being met in your workplace? Which are not being sufficiently met?
- What steps can you take to help meet the seven universal needs for others in your workplace? Commit to taking two actions in the next week to meet others' needs (for example, affirm a colleague for a job well done).

Chapter 3

- Share an example of an organization that you believe exhibits a high degree of the connection culture element of vision.
  - How is this vision communicated?
  - Has the vision produced a shared identity that people connected with the organization feel proud about?

- Share an example of an organization that you believe exhibits a high degree of the connection culture element of value.
  - How do the leaders show that they value employees?
  - Has value in the organization produced a bond of shared empathy among people in the organization?
- Share an example of an organization that you believe exhibits a high degree of the connection culture element of voice.
  - How does the organization encourage employees to provide feedback?
  - Has voice in the organization resulted in a greater shared understanding?
- Which of the 24 character strengths do you believe you exhibit? Which do you believe you need to strengthen?

Part I: Profiles in Connection

- Take a moment to reflect on the stories that you read in this section. Which story did you find most inspiring? Why? Which story challenged you the most? Why?
- Write down three ideas you learned from the leaders highlighted in this section that you would like to implement in your own organization.
- The common theme through each of the profiles is a commitment on the part of the leader or organization to vision, value, and voice. How does your organization or team embody each of those elements? Which element needs to be strengthened?

Chapter 4

- What research presented in this chapter really jumped out at you? How is it relevant to your work and your life outside of work?
- Research clearly shows that connection is critical for our personal health and well-being. On a scale of one to 10 (with 10 being fully connected), how would you rate your current level of personal connection?
- Based on what you learned in this chapter about the importance of using connection to manage stress levels, write down two positive

actions you can take the next time you feel overwhelmed at work. If you are a supervisor, write down two ways you can use connection to help your direct reports feel less stressed.

Chapter 5

- What research presented in this chapter really jumped out at you? How is it relevant to your work and your life outside of work?
- Research clearly shows that connection provides a performance and competitive advantage to organizations. On a scale of one to 10 (with 10 being fully connected), how would you rate your organization's current level of connection?
- Organizations often display two or more of the three types of cultures. Which culture describes your team? Which cultures are present throughout the organization? If your team lacks a connection culture, consider contacting a leader in your organization who is an intentional connector and ask for tips on turning your team's culture around.

Part II: Profiles in Connection

- Take a moment to reflect on the stories that you read in this section. Which story did you find most inspiring? Why? Which story challenged you the most? Why?
- Write down three ideas you learned from the leaders highlighted in this section that you would like to implement in your own organization.
- The common theme through each of the profiles is a commitment on the part of the leader or organization to vision, value, and voice. How does your organization or team embody each of those elements? Which element needs to be strengthened?

Chapter 6

- An important point made in this chapter is that connection occurs in subgroups, including across departments. Which departments or people are most critical for you to have strong relationships with? What is the current state of those relationships?

- This chapter gives many practical tips for implementing a connection culture within your organization. Which three actions do you believe are most critical for your team at this point in time?
- Connection is not just for the workplace. It's critical in all relationships, including community organizations, religious groups, families, and friends. What actions will you personally take to build connection in groups outside work?

Chapter 7

- Can you identify specific individuals you've known who fall into each of the categories of intentional disconnector, unintentional disconnector, and intentional connector?
- Of the factors mentioned in "The Changing Workplace and Future of Work" section, which do you expect might have the most relevance to you over the next three years? What other potential issues do you see on the horizon?
- What are your spheres of influence? What steps can you take to build connection in those local cultures?

Appendix III
Additional Resources

To learn more about connection culture, visit:

- Connection Culture Group, ConnectionCulture.com
- Michael's blog, MichaelLeeStallard.com

You can also subscribe to the monthly email newsletter by visiting either the Connection Culture Group website or Michael's blog.

My colleagues and I give keynote speeches; teach live seminars, workshops, and the online Connection Culture Academy; and offer assessments. To learn more, visit ConnectionCulture.com.

To learn more about MCORE, visit MotivationalCore.com.

References

Introduction to the 2nd Edition

Cigna. 2020. "Loneliness and the Workplace: 2020 U.S. Report." multivu.com /players/English/8670451-cigna-2020-loneliness-index.

Gawande, A. 2020. "Amid the Coronavirus Crisis, a Regimen for Reentry." *New Yorker*, May 13. newyorker.com/science/medical-dispatch/amid-the-coronavirus -crisis-a-regimen-for-reentry.

Holt-Lunstad, J. 2017. "The Potential Public Health Relevance of Social Isolation and Loneliness: Prevalence, Epidemiology, and Risk Factors." *Public Policy & Aging Report*, September. ncbi.nlm.nih.gov/pmc/articles/PMC5598785/pdf /nihms840818.pdf.

Holt-Lunstad, J., T. Robles, and D. Sbarra. 2017. "Advancing Social Connection as a Public Health Priority in the United States." *American Psychologist*, September 1. academic.oup.com/ppar/article/27/4/127/4782506.

Holt-Lunstad, J., T.B. Smith, and J.B. Layton. 2010. "Social Relationships and Mortality Risk: A Meta-Analytic Review." *PLoS Medicine*, July 7. journals.plos .org/plosmedicine/article?id=10.1371/journal.pmed.1000316.

Holt-Lunstad, J., T.B. Smith, M. Baker, T. Harris, and D. Stephenson. 2015. "Loneliness and Social Isolation as Risk Factors for Mortality: A Meta-Analytic Review." *Perspectives on Psychological Science*, October 2. journals.sagepub.com /doi/abs/10.1177/1745691614568352.

Kenner, R. dir. 2018. *Influenza 1918*. PBS American Experience Films, January 2. pbs.org/wgbh/americanexperience/films/influenza.

Kirzinger, A., A. Kearney, L. Hamel, and M. Brodie. 2020. "KFF Health Tracking Poll - Early April 2020: The Impact Of Coronavirus On Life In America." Kaiser Family Foundation, April 2. kff.org/coronavirus-covid-19/report/kff -health-tracking-poll-early-april-2020.

New York Times. 2020a. "Coronavirus in the U.S.: Latest Map and Case Count." Last modified July 16, 2020. nytimes.com/interactive/2020/us/coronavirus -us-cases.html.

New York Times. 2020b. "Coronavirus Map: Tracking the Global Outbreak." Last modified July 16, 2020. nytimes.com/interactive/2020/world/coronavirus -maps.html.

Ozcelik, H., and S. Barsade. 2017. "Work Loneliness and Employee Performance." *Academy of Management Proceedings,* October 5. journals.aom.org/doi/pdf /10.5465/ambpp.2011.65869714.

Schwartz, N.D., B. Casselman, and E. Koeze. 2020. "How Bad Is Unemployment? 'Literally Off the Charts'" *New York Times,* May 8. nytimes.com/interactive /2020/05/08/business/economy/april-jobs-report.html.

Stallard, M., and K. Stallard. 2020. "Connection Is Critical During the Coronavirus Pandemic." ATD Insights, April 8. td.org/insights/connection -is-critical-during-the-coronavirus-pandemic

Chapter 1

American Theatre Editors. 2020. "'Hamilton' Education Program Launches EduHam at Home." American Theatre, April 21. americantheatre.org/2020 /04/21/hamilton-education-program-launches-eduham-at-home.

Ball, D., and J. Reed. 2016. "Lin-Manuel Miranda Immigrant Songs." *NEA Arts Magazine,* March 16. arts.gov/NEARTS/2016v1-telling-all-our-stories-arts -and-diversity/lin-manuel-miranda.

Cacioppo, J.T., and W. Patrick. 2008. *Loneliness: Human Nature and the Need for Social Connection.* New York: W.W. Norton & Company.

Dembin, R.M. 2017. "The Classroom Where It Happens." American Theatre, May 10. americantheatre.org/2017/05/10/the-classroom-where-it-happens.

Espana, E., dir. 2017. *Hamilton: One Shot to Broadway.* Vision Films, DVD.

Fierberg, R. 2019. "6 Things to Know Before You Go to Broadway's Freestyle Love Supreme." Playbill.com, September 29. playbill.com/article/6-things-to -know-before-you-go-to-broadways-freestyle-love-supreme.

Grein, P. 2019. "Lin-Manuel Miranda's First Tony Awards Win: Looking Back at His Big 2008 Moment." Billboard.com, June 10. billboard.com/articles/news /awards/8513535/lin-manuel-miranda-first-tony-award-2008.

Handy, B. 2018. "The Supercalifragilistic Lin-Manuel Miranda." *Vanity Fair,* Holiday 2018/2019, 74–83.

Harrison, K. 2018. *Lin-Manuel Miranda: Composter, Actor, and Creator of Hamilton.* New York: Enslow Publishing.

Jennings, S. 2015. "Notes from the Guy Backstage—Thomas Kail ('99) Returns to Campus." *Methods Magazine,* November 20. method-magazine.com/art/2015 /11/14/ii2mcxhg2yv3bkoh6d3fnkswbg352l.

Jensen, E. 2018. "Kennedy Center Honors 2018: Cher Receives Hilarious Tribute From Whoopi Goldberg, More Highlights." USAToday.com, December 3. usatoday.com/story/life/people/2018/12/03/kennedy-center-honors-2018 -kelly-clarkson-reba-mcentire-cher-hamilton-lin-manuel-miranda/2188095002.

Kail, T., A. Blankenbuehler, A. Lacamoire, and L.-M. Miranda. 2018. "'Hamilton' Creators on Crafting a Revolutionary Musical: Full Interview." Interview by John Dickerson. CBS This Morning video, December 20, 2018. youtube.com/watch?reload=9&v=yCEtUP5w5Y0.

Katz, B. 2020. "What Disney's Execs Are Saying About 'Hamilton' Behind the Scenes." *Observer*, July 10. observer.com/2020/07/hamilton-viewership-disney-plus-subscribers.

Krasinski, J. 2020a. "Some Good News with John Krasinski Ep. 1." Some Good News, Episode 1, March 29, 2020. youtube.com/watch?v=F5pgG1M_h_U.

Krasinski, J. 2020b. "Hamilton Cast Zoom Surprise: Some Good News With John Krasinski (Ep. 2)." Some Good News, Episode 2. April 5, 2020. youtube.com/watch?v=oilZ1hNZPRM.

Lee, A. 2020. "Bringing 'Hamilton' to the Screen: Filming is Easy, Editing's Harder." *Los Angeles Times*, July 2. latimes.com/entertainment-arts/movies/story/2020-07-02/hamilton-movie-disney-changes.

Low, D. 2007. "Scaling the Heights." *Wesleyan University Magazine*, June 20. magazine.blogs.wesleyan.edu/2007/06/20/scaling-the-heights.

Low, D. 2015. "A Musical Revolution on Broadway." *Wesleyan University Magazine*, December 7. magazine.blogs.wesleyan.edu/2015/12/07/a-musical-revolution-on-broadway.

McCarter, J. 2016. "Why Hamilton Matters." BuzzFeedNews.com, April 10. buzzfeednews.com/article/jeremymccarter/saving-america-from-itself.

Mead, R. 2015. "All About the Hamiltons." *The New Yorker*, February 9. newyorker.com/magazine/2015/02/09/hamiltons.

Miranda, L., and J. McCarter. 2016. *Hamilton: The Revolution*. New York: Grand Central Publishing.

Paulson, M. 2019. "Lin-Manuel Miranda's 'Freestyle Love Supreme' Is Coming to Broadway." *New York Times*, June 18. nytimes.com/2019/06/18/theater/lin-manuel-miranda-freestyle-love-supreme-broadway.html.

Paulson, M. 2020. "'Hamilton' Movie Will Stream on Disney Plus on July 3." *New York Times*, May 12. nytimes.com/2020/05/12/movies/hamilton-movie-disney-plus.html.

Rugg, J.E. 2018. "The Connection Value Chain: Impact of Connection Culture and Employee Motivation on Perceived Team Performance." PhD dissertation, Biola University.

Uchino, B.N., J.T. Cacioppo, and J.K. Kiecolt-Glaser. 1996. "The Relationship Between Social Support and Physiological Processes: A Review With Emphasis on Underlying Mechanisms and Implications for Health." *Psychological Bulletin* 119(3): 488–531.

Winfrey, O. 2017b. "This Is Us: Oprah Talks With Lin-Manuel Miranda About America at its Best." *O, The Oprah Magazine*, May.

Chapter 2

Amabile, T., and S. Kramer. 2011. *The Progress Principle: Using Small Wins to Ignite Joy, Engagement, and Creativity at Work.* Boston: Harvard Business Review Press.

Berkman, L., and L. Syme. 1979. "Social Networks, Host Resistance and Mortality: A Nine-Year Study of Alameda County Residents." *American Journal of Epidemiology* 109(2): 186–204.

Bloom J.R., S.L. Stewart, M. Johnson, P. Banks, and P. Fobair. 2001. "Sources of Support and the Physical and Mental Well-Being of Young Women With Breast Cancer." *Social Science and Medicine* 53(11): 1513–1524. sciencedirect .com/science/article/abs/pii/S0277953600004408.

Clifton, J., and J. Harter. 2019. *It's the Manager: Gallup Find the Quality of Managers and Team Leaders Is the Single Biggest Factor in Your Organization's Long-Term Success.* New York: Gallup Press.

CLC (Corporate Leadership Council). 2004. *Driving Performance and Retention Through Employee Engagement.* Washington, DC: Corporate Executive Board.

Csikszentmihalyi, M. 1990. *Flow: The Psychology of Optimal Experience.* New York: Harper & Row.

Devine, D., P.A. Parker, R.T. Fouladi, and L. Cohen. 2003. "The Association Between Social Support, Intrusive Thoughts, Avoidance, and Adjustment Following an Experimental Cancer Treatment." *Psycho-oncology* 12(5): 453–462. ncbi.nlm.nih.gov/pubmed/12833558.

Frankl, V. 1984. *Man's Search for Meaning: An Introduction to Logotherapy.* New York: Simon & Schuster.

Fredrickson, B. 2003. "The Value of Positive Emotions." *American Scientist* 91(4): 330–335.

Gallup. 2017. "State of the American Workplace." gallup.com/workplace/238085/ state-american-workplace-report-2017.aspx.

Hallowell, E. 1999a. *Connect: 12 Vital Ties That Open Your Heart, Lengthen Your Life, and Deepen Your Soul.* New York: Pantheon.

Hallowell, E. 1999b. "The Human Moment at Work." *Harvard Business Review,* January, 58–66.

Institute for American Values. 2013. "Hardwired to Connect: The New Scientific Case for Authoritative Communities." New York: Commission on Children at Risk. americanvalues.org/catalog/pdfs/hwexsumm.pdf.

"Kathryn Purvis Institute of Child Development." n.d. TCU College of Science and Engineering. child.tcu.edu.

Kleiner, A. 2005. *Who Really Matters: The Core Group Theory of Power, Privilege and Success.* New York: Currency Doubleday.

Lekander M., C.J. Fürst, S. Rotstein, H. Blomgren, and M. Fredrikson. 1996. "Social Support and Immune Status During and after Chemotherapy for Breast Cancer." *Acta Oncologica* 35(1): 31–37. 10.3109/02841869609098476.

Levy, S. M., R.B. Herberman, T. Whiteside, K. Sanzo, J. Lee, and J. Kirkwood. 1990. "Perceived Social Support and Tumor Estrogen/Progesterone Receptor Status as Predictors of Natural Killer Cell Activity in Breast Cancer Patients." *Psychosomatic Medicine* 52(1): 73–85. psycnet.apa.org/record/1990-20194-001.

Lieberman, M. 2013. "The Social Brain and Its Superpowers: Matthew Lieberman, PhD at TEDxStLouis." TEDx Talks, video, October 7, 2013. youtube.com/watch?v=NNhk3owF7RQ.

Magner, E. 2017. "Why Your Relationships May Be Key to Your Longevity." WellandGood.com, December 11. wellandgood.com/good-advice/relationships-friends-longevity-telomeres.

Maslow, A.H. 1943. "A Theory of Human Motivation." *Psychological Review* 50:370–396.

Rowe, J.W., and R.L. Kahn. 1998. *Successful Aging.* New York: Pantheon.

Ryan, R., and E. Deci. 2001. "On Happiness and Human Potentials: A Review of Research on Hedonic and Eudaimonic Well-Being." *Annual Review of Psychology* 52:141–166.

Sapolsky, R. 2008. *Stress: Portrait of a Killer. Documentary.* National Geographic Television and Stanford University, September 24.

Schore, A. 2009. "Dr. Allan N. Schore." allanschore.com.

Seligman, M. 2006. *Learned Optimism: How to Change Your Mind and Your Life.* New York: Vintage.

Stallard, M.L. 2007. *Fired Up or Burned Out: How to Reignite Your Team's Passion, Creativity, and Productivity.* Nashville, TN: Thomas Nelson.

Stallard, M.L. 2008. "The Connection Culture: A New Source of Competitive Advantage." ChangeThis. ceo801mstro0h2uinte.blob.core.windows.net/legacyassets/system/manifestos/pdfs/000/000/231/original/44.06.ConnectionCulture.pdf.

Tronick, E. 2009. "Still Face Experiment: Dr. Edward Tronick." UMass Boston, video, November 30, 2009. Excerpt from L. Hudson and J. Lovett. 2007. "Helping Babies From the Bench: Using the Science of Early Childhood in Court." Lovett Productions. youtube.com/watch?v=apzXGEbZht0.

Zaff, J.F., and K.A. Moore. 2002. "Promoting Well-being Among America's Teens: An Executive Summary of Adolescent Development Research Reviews Completed for the John S. and James L. Knight Foundation." Child Trends, October. childtrends.org/wp-content/uploads/2002/10/Child_Trends-2002_10_01_ES_TeenWellbeing.pdf.

Chapter 3

Covey, S. 1989. *Seven Habits of Highly Effective People.* New York: Simon & Schuster.

Crabtree, L. (Southwest Airlines Communications Lead). 2019. Email to the author dated October 11.

Deshpande, R. 2011. "The Ordinary Heroes of the Taj." *Harvard Business Review,* December, 119–123.

Diversity Woman. 2014. "Dr. Frances Hesselbein: Leading with a Purpose." DiversityWoman.com, May 28. diversitywoman.com/dr-frances-hesselbein-leading-with-a-purpose.

Hanessian, B., and C. Sierra. 2005. "Leading a Turnaround: An Interview With the Chairman of D&B." *McKinsey Quarterly,* May. mckinsey.com/insights/strategy/leading_a_turnaround_an_interview_with_the_chairman_of_d_and_.

Hatfield, E., J.T. Cacioppo, and R.L. Rapson. 1994. *Emotional Contagion.* New York: Cambridge University Press.

Hesselbein, F. 2012. *More Hesselbein on Leadership.* San Francisco: Jossey-Bass.

Kearns Goodwin, D. 1994. *No Ordinary Time: Franklin and Eleanor Roosevelt: The Home Front in World War II.* New York: Simon & Schuster.

McCullough, D. 1991. *Brave Companions: Portraits in History.* New York: Prentice Hall.

Mulcahy, A. 2012. Telephone conversation with the author on February 22.

Peterson, C., and M.E.P. Seligman. 2004. *Character Strengths and Virtues: A Handbook and Classification.* Washington, DC: American Psychological Assoc.

Rajgopaul, R. 2010. "Salute to Ratan Tata." Ramana's Musings Blog. April 8. rummuser.com/?p=3182.

Stallard, M.L. 2007. *Fired Up or Burned Out: How to Reignite Your Team's Passion, Creativity, and Productivity.* Nashville, TN: Thomas Nelson.

Tata Group. 2014. *The Tata Way.* Internal Publication.

Tata. 2019. "About Us: Investors Section." tata.com/investors.

The National WWII Museum. 2012. "By the Numbers: Wartime Production." The National WWII Museum, New Orleans. enroll.nationalww2museum.org/learn/education/for-students/ww2-history/ww2-by-the-numbers/wartime-production.html.

West, R. (Southwest Airline's Corporate Historian). 2014. Email to author dated June 11.

Wooden, J. 1997. *Wooden: A Lifetime of Observations and Reflections on and off the Court.* New York: McGraw-Hill.

Chapter 4

Ackerlind, I., and J.O. Hornquist. 1992. "Loneliness and Alcohol Abuse: A Review of Evidence of an Interplay." *Social Science and Medicine* 34:405–414.

Ali, A., and T. Barnagarwala. 2018. "You Are Not the Only One: India Stares at Loneliness Epidemic." IndianExpress.com, April 29. indianexpress.com /article/express-sunday-eye/you-are-not-the-only-one-5154976.

Anderson, G. 2010. "Loneliness Among Older Adults: A National Survey of Adults 45+." AARP, September 26. aarp.org/personal-growth/transitions/info-09 -2010/loneliness_2010.html.

Anderson, J. 2018. "The UK Is Sending Postal Workers Door to Combat Loneliness." QZ.com, October 16. qz.com/1424127/the-uk-is-sending-postal -workers-door-to-door-to-combat-loneliness.

APA (American Psychological Association). 2010. "Stress in America: Stress and Gender." Press release, November 9. apa.org/news/press/releases/stress /2010/gender-stress.pdf.

Baumeister, R.F., C.N. DeWall, N.J. Ciarocco, and J.M. Twenge. 2005. "Social Exclusion Impairs Self-Regulation." *Journal of Personality and Social Psychology* 88:589–604.

Baumeister, R.F., J.M. Twenge, and C.K. Nuss. 2002. "Effects of Social Exclusion on Cognitive Processes: Anticipated Aloneness Reduces Intelligent Thought." *Journal of Personality and Social Psychology* 83:817–827.

Berkman, L., and L. Syme. 1979. "Social Networks, Host Resistance and Mortality: A Nine-Year Study of Alameda County Residents." *American Journal of Epidemiology* 109(2): 186–204.

Brooks, S.K., R.K. Webster, L.E Smith, L. Woodland, S. Wessely, N. Greenberg, G.J. Rubin. 2020. "The Psychological Impact of Quarantine and How to Reduce It: Rapid Review of the Evidence." *Rapid Review* 395(10227): 912–920. thelancet .com/journals/lancet/article/PIIS0140-6736(20)30460-8/fulltext.

Bruhn, J.G., and S. Wolf. 1979. *The Roseto Story.* Norman: University of Oklahoma Press.

Bryant, A. 2011. "Google's Quest to Build a Better Boss." *New York Times*, March 12. nytimes.com/2011/03/13/business/13hire.html.

Cacioppo, J.T., and W. Patrick. 2008. *Loneliness: Human Nature and the Need for Social Connection.* New York: W.W. Norton & Company.

Cai, J. 2018. "Loneliness: The Latest Economic Niche Opening Up in China." SouthChinaMorningPost.com, February 17. scmp.com/news/china/economy /article/2133317/loneliness-latest-economic-niche-opening-china.

CDC (Centers for Disease Control & Prevention). 2012. "An Estimated 1 in 10 U.S. Adults Report Depression." CDC, April 20. cdc.gov/features/dsdepression.

CDC (Centers for Disease Control & Prevention). 2013. "Strategic Direction for the Prevention of Suicidal Behavior: Promoting Individual, Family, and Community Connectedness to Prevent Suicidal Behavior." cdc.gov/ViolencePrevention/pdf /Suicide_Strategic_Direction_Full_Version-a.pdf.

Census of Housing. 2011. "Historical Census of Housing Tables." U.S. Census Bureau, October 31. census.gov/hhes/www/housing/census/historic/livalone.html.

Cigna. 2018a. "New Cigna Study Reveals Loneliness at Epidemic Levels in America." May 1. cigna.com/newsroom/news-releases/2018/pdf/new-cigna-study-reveals -loneliness-at-epidemic-levels-in-america.pdf.

Cigna. 2018b. "U.S. Loneliness Index: Survey of 20,000 Americans Examining Behaviors Driving Loneliness in the United States." multivu.com/players/English /8294451-cigna-us-loneliness-survey/docs/IndexReport_1524069371598 -173525450.pdf.

Cigna. 2020. "Loneliness and the Workplace: 2020 U.S. Report." multivu.com /players/English/8670451-cigna-2020-loneliness-index.

Common Sense Media. 2016. "Plugged-In Parents: Attitudes, Behaviors and Role Models." Infographic, December 6. commonsensemedia.org/plugged-in-parents -of-tweens-and-teens-2016-infographic.

Coric, D., and B.I. Murstein. 1993. "Eating Disorders." *The Journal of Treatment & Prevention* 1(1): 39–51.

CT.gov. 2020. "Executive Orders." The Office of Governor Ned Lamont. portal.ct.gov /Office-of-the-Governor/Governors-Actions/Executive-Orders.

Gladwell, M. 2008. *Outliers: The Story of Success.* New York: Little, Brown.

Global Health Aging. 2016. "Breaking Down the Stigma of Loneliness in Denmark." GlobalHealthAging.com, July 3. globalhealthaging.org/2016/07 /03/breaking-down-the-stigma-of-loneliness-in-denmark.

Goldsmith, S.K., T.C. Pellmar, A.M. Kleinman, and W.E. Bunny. 2002. *Reducing Suicide: A National Imperative.* Washington, DC: National Academy Press.

Goleman, D. 2006. *Social Intelligence: The New Science of Human Relationships.* New York: Random House.

Hallowell, E. 1999a. *Connect: 12 Vital Ties That Open Your Heart, Lengthen Your Life, and Deepen Your Soul.* New York: Pantheon.

Hoffman, M. 2018. "Japan Struggles to Keep Loneliness at Arms' Length." JapanTimes.co.jp, November 10. japantimes.co.jp/news/2018/11/10/national /media-national/japan-struggles-keep-loneliness-arms-length/#.XdcN7C-ZOu5.

Holt-Lunstad, J. 2017. "The Potential Public Health Relevance of Social Isolation and Loneliness: Prevalence, Epidemiology, and Risk Factors." Public Policy & Aging Report, September. ncbi.nlm.nih.gov/pmc/articles/PMC5598785/pdf /nihms840818.pdf.

Holt-Lunstad, J., T. Robles, and D. Sbarra. 2017. "Advancing Social Connection as a Public Health Priority in the United States." *American Psychologist,* September 1. academic.oup.com/ppar/article/27/4/127/4782506.

Holt-Lunstad, J., T.B. Smith, and J.B. Layton. 2010. "Social Relationships and Mortality Risk: A Meta-Analytic Review." *PLoS Medicine,* July 7. journals.plos. org/plosmedicine/article?id=10.1371/journal.pmed.1000316.

Holt-Lunstad, J., T.B. Smith, M. Baker, T. Harris, and D. Stephenson. 2015. "Loneliness and Social Isolation as Risk Factors for Mortality: A Meta-Analytic Review." Perspectives on Psychological Science, October 2. journals.sagepub.com/doi/abs/10.1177/1745691614568352.

Hurley, D. 2013. "Grandma's Experiences Leave a Mark on Your Genes." *Discover*, June 11. discovermagazine.com/2013/may/13-grandmas-experiences-leave-epigenetic-mark-on-your-genes.

Karen, R. 1990. "Becoming Attached." *The Atlantic*, February. theatlantic.com/magazine/archive/1990/02/becoming-attached/308966.

Kiltz, R. 2019. Emails with the author and Katharine Stallard dated October 21–25.

Leszkiewicz, A. 2018. "Netflix's Maniac Is a Moving, Surreal, Sharp Take on Themes From Trauma to Capitalism to Loneliness." Newstatesman.com, October. newstatesman.com/2018/10/maniac-netflix-review-emma-stone-jonah-hill.

Levenson, S. 2017. Liner notes to *Dear Evan Hansen*. Atlantic Records. CD.

Lieberman, M. 2013a. *Social: Why Our Brains Are Wired to Connect.* New York: Crown.

Lieberman, M. 2013b. "The Social Brain and Its Superpowers: Matthew Lieberman, PhD at TEDxStLouis." TEDx Talks, video, October 7, 2013. youtube.com/watch?v=NNhk3owF7RQ.

Lieberman, M. 2019. "Matthew Lieberman: The Social Brain and the Workplace." Talks at Google, video. February 22, 2019. youtube.com/watch?v=h7UR9JwQEYk.

Marche, S. 2012. "Is Facebook Making Us Lonely?" *The Atlantic*, April. theatlantic.com/magazine/archive/2012/05/is-facebook-making-us-lonely/308930.

Marmot, M., and R. Sapolsky. 2014. "Of Baboons and Men: Social Circumstances, Biology, and the Social Gradient in Health." Chapter 16 in *Sociality, Hierarchy, Health: Comparative Biodemography: A Collection of Papers.* National Research Council. Washington, D.C.: National Academies Press. ncbi.nlm.nih.gov/books/NBK242456.

Masnick, G. 2015. "The Rise of the Single-Person Household." Housing Perspectives, May. housingperspectives.blogspot.com/2015/05/the-rise-of-single-person-household.html?m=1.

McCann WorldGroup. 2011. "Truth About Youth." McCann WorldGroup. truthcentral.mccann.com/truth-studies.

Morris, J. 2020. Meeting and correspondence with author.

Noack, R. 2018. "Isolation Is Rising in Europe. Can Loneliness Ministers Help Change That?" *Washington Post*, February 2. washingtonpost.com/news/worldviews/wp/2018/02/02/isolation-is-rising-in-europe-can-loneliness-ministers-help-change-that.

Olds, J., and R. Schwartz. 2009. *The Lonely American: Drifting Apart in the Twenty-First Century.* Boston: Beacon Press.

OneRepublic. 2018. "OneRepublic – Connection." OneRepublic YouTube channel, video. August 28, 2018. youtube.com/watch?v=iJUM11goXAU.

Pedrosa, M. 2018. "OneRepublic Releases Thoughtful Video for 'Connection': Watch." Billboard.com, August 28. billboard.com/articles/columns/pop /8472667/onerepublic-connection-video.

Rath, T., and J. Harter. 2010. *Well Being: The Five Essential Elements.* New York: Gallup Press.

Rocket, I.R.H., M.D. Regier, N.D. Kapusta, J.H. Coben, T.R. Miller, R.L. Hanzlick, K.H. Todd, R.W. Sattin, L.W. Kennedy, J. Kleinig, and G.S. Smith. 2012. "Leading Causes of Unintentional and Intentional Injury Mortality: United States, 2000-2009." *American Journal of Public Health* 102(11): e84–e92. ajph.aphapublications.org/doi/full/10.2105/AJPH.2012.300960.

Rowe, J.W., and R.L. Kahn. 1998. *Successful Aging.* New York: Pantheon.

Russia Beyond. 2018. "Politician Proposed Creating Ministry of Loneliness in Russia." Russia Beyond, February 4. rbth.com/lifestyle/327485-politician -proposed-creating-ministry.

Saad, L. 2017. "Eight in 10 Americans Afflicted by Stress." Gallup.com, December 20. news.gallup.com/poll/224336/eight-americans-afflicted-stress.aspx.

Sapolsky, R. 2008. *Stress: Portrait of a Killer.* Documentary. National Geographic Television and Stanford University, September 24.

Sapolsky, R. 2010. *Stress and Your Body.* Chantilly, VA: The Teaching Company.

Schaef, A.W. 1987. *When Society Becomes an Addict.* New York: Harper Collins.

Shirom, A., S. Toker, Y. Alkaly, O. Jacobson, and R. Balicer. 2011. "Worked Based Predictors of Mortality: A 20-Year Follow-Up of Healthy Employees." *Health Psychology* 30(3): 268–275.

Stacy, A.W., M.D. Newcomb, and P.M. Bentler. 1995. "Expectancy in Mediational Models of Cocaine Abuse." *Personality and Individual Differences* 19(5): 655–667.

Stallard, M.L. 2007. *Fired Up or Burned Out: How to Reignite Your Team's Passion, Creativity, and Productivity.* Nashville, TN: Thomas Nelson.

Stewart, Z. 2018. "All the Lonely People and Dear Evan Hansen." Theater Mania, March 1. theatermania.com/broadway/reviews/all-the-lonely-people-and-dear -evan-hansen-_84285.html.

Stroh, P. 2019. "Feeling Alone? You're Not Alone—and It Could Be Affecting Your Physical Health." CBC News, January 19. cbc.ca/news/health/national -dealing-with-loneliness-1.4828017.

Sussman, S., N. Lisha, and M. Griffiths. 2011. "Prevalence of the Addictions: A Problem of the Majority or the Minority?" *Evaluation & the Health Professions* 34(1): 3–56.

Twenge, J.M. 2017. *iGen: Why Today's Super-Connected Kids Are Growing Up Less Rebellious, More Tolerant, Less Happy—and Completely Unprepared for Adulthood—and What That Means for the Rest of Us.* New York: Simon & Schuster.

Twenge, J.M. 2019. "The Sad State of Happiness in the United States and the Role of Digital Media." Chapter 5 in *The World Happiness Report*, March 20. worldhappiness.report/ed/2019/the-sad-state-of-happiness-in-the-united-states -and-the-role-of-digital-media.

Twenge, J.M., K.R. Catanes, and R.F. Baumeister. 2002. "Social Exclusion Causes Self-Defeating Behavior." *Journal of Personality and Social Psychology* 83:606–615.

Twenge, J.M., R.F. Baumeister, D.M. Tice, and T.S. Stucke. 2001. "If You Can't Join Them, Beat Them: Effects of Social Exclusion on Aggressive Behavior." *Journal of Personality and Social Psychology* 81:1058–1069.

U.S. Census Bureau. 2019. "One-Person Households on the Rise." Census.gov, November 19. census.gov/library/visualizations/2019/comm/one-person -households.html.

Utsey, S., N. Giesbrecht, J. Hook, and P. Stanard. 2008. "Cultural, Sociofamilial, and Psychological Resources that Inhibit Psychological Distress in African Americans Exposed to Stressful Life Events and Race-Related Stress." *Journal of Counseling Psychology* 55(1): 49–62.

Valliant, G.E. 2012. *Triumphs of Experience: The Men of the Harvard Grant Study.* Cambridge, MA: Belknap Press of Harvard University Press.

Vespa, J., J.M. Lewis, and R.M. Kreider. 2013. "America's Families Living Arrangements: 2012." United States Census Bureau, August. census.gov/prod /2013pubs/p20-570.pdf.

Wahlquist, C. 2018. "Loneliness Minister' Proposed to Tackle Australian Social Isolation." *The Guardian*, October 18. theguardian.com/society/2018/ oct/19/loneliness-minister-proposed-to-tackle-australian-social-isolation.

Whiting, K. 2018. "Postal Workers in France Are Helping Elderly People Fight Loneliness." World Economic Forum, November 29. weforum.org/agenda /2018/11/postal-workers-in-france-are-helping-look-after-elderly-people.

Willis Towers Watson. 2020. "Employers Take Aim at Expected Higher Levels of Employee Stress and Anxiety, Willis Towers Watson Survey Finds." Press Release, April 27. willistowerswatson.com/en-US/News/2020/04/employers -take-aim-at-expected-higher-levels-of-employee-stress-and-anxiety-wtw -survey-finds.

Wilson, E.O. 2012. *The Social Conquest of Earth.* New York: Liveright.

Wong, W.L. 2019. "Trending: The Loneliness Issue." *Challenge*, April 16. psd.gov .sg/challenge/ideas/trends/trending-the-loneliness-issue.

Woolf, S.H., and L. Aron, eds. 2014. *U.S. Health in International Perspective: Shorter Lives, Poorer Health.* Washington, DC: The National Academies Press.

Zachary, S. 2018. "All the Lonely People and *Dear Evan Hansen*." Theater Mania, March 1. theatermania.com/broadway/reviews/all-the-lonely-people-and-dear-evan-hansen-_84285.html.

Chapter 5

Amabile, T., and S. Kramer. 2011. *The Progress Principle: Using Small Wins to Ignite Joy, Engagement, and Creativity at Work.* Boston: Harvard Business Review Press.

Brooks, D. 2011. *The Social Animal: The Hidden Sources of Love, Character and Achievement.* New York: Random House.

Bryant, A. 2011. "Google's Quest to Build a Better Boss." *New York Times*, March 12. nytimes.com/2011/03/13/business/13hire.html.

Clarridge, C. 2020. "Costco to Require Masks for Shoppers to Protect Against Coronavirus." *Seattle Times*, April 30. seattletimes.com/seattle-news/health/costco-to-require-masks-for-shoppers-starting-monday.

Clifton, J., and J. Harter. 2019. *It's the Manager: Gallup Find the Quality of Managers and Team Leaders Is the Single Biggest Factor in Your Organization's Long-Term Success.* New York: Gallup Press.

CLC (Corporate Leadership Council). 2004. *Driving Performance and Retention Through Employee Engagement.* Washington, DC: Corporate Executive Board.

Costco. 2020. "Updates and Coronavirus Response." costco.com/covid-updates.html

Csikszentmihalyi, M. 1990. *Flow: The Psychology of Optimal Experience.* New York: Harper & Row.

de Geus, A. 1997. "The Living Company." *Harvard Business Review*, March-April, 51–59.

Duhigg, C. 2016. "What Google Learned from Its Quest to Build the Perfect Team." *New York Times*, February 25. nytimes.com/2016/02/28/magazine/what-google-learned-from-its-quest-to-build-the-perfect-team.html.

Ferrie, J., ed. 2004. "Work Stress and Health: the Whitehall II Study." London: Public and Commercial Services Union. ucl.ac.uk/whitehallII/pdf/Whitehallbooklet_1_.pdf.

Fleming, J.H., C. Coffman, and J.K. Harter. 2005. "Manage Your Human Sigma." *Harvard Business Review*, July-August.

Frankl, V. 1984. *Man's Search for Meaning: An Introduction to Logotherapy.* New York: Simon & Schuster.

Gallup. 2017. "State of the American Workplace." gallup.com/workplace/238085/state-american-workplace-report-2017.aspx.

Gibbons, J. 2007. "Finding a Definition of Employee Engagement." *The Conference Board Executive Action Series*, June.

Hall, T. 2015. "Three Ways to Promote Psychological Safety in Your Team." ConnectionCulture.com, September 12. connectionculture.com/post/3-ways -to-promote-psychological-safety-in-your-team.

Harrell, M., and L. Barbato. 2018. "Great Managers Still Matter: The Evolution of Google's Project Oxygen." re:Work, February 27. rework.withgoogle.com/blog /the-evolution-of-project-oxygen.

Harter, J.K., F.L. Schmidt, J.W. Asplund, E.A. Killham, and S. Agrawal. 2010. "Causal Impact of Employee Work Perceptions on the Bottom Line of Organizations." *Perspectives on Psychological Science* 5(4): 378–389.

Hay Group. 2010. "Creating High Performing Organizations: Being an Employer of Choice." Hay Group. docplayer.net/21618378-Creating-high-performing -organizations-being-an-employer-of-choice.html.

Heath, C., and D. Heath. 2010. *Made to Stick: How to Change Things When Change Is Hard*. New York: Crown.

Hewitt Associates. 2004. "Research Brief: Employee Engagement Higher at Double-Digit Growth Companies." Hewitt Associates, May. mckpeople.com.au/SiteMedia /w3svc161/Uploads/Documents/016fc140-895a-41bf-90df-9ddb28f4bdab.pdf.

Idris, M.A., M.F. Dollard, and M.R. Tuckey. 2015. "Psychosocial Safety Climate as a Management Tool for Employee Engagement and Performance: A Multilevel Analysis." *International Journal of Stress Management* (22)2: 183–206. psycnet.apa.org/doiLanding?doi=10.1037%2Fa0038986.

Jelinek, C. 2017. Telephone call with the author on November 6.

Kaufman, J., R. Markey, S. Dey Burton, and D. Azzarello. 2013. "Who's Responsible for Employee Engagement?" Bain & Company, December 11. bain.com /publications/articles/whos-responsible-for-employee-engagement.aspx.

Kiel, F. 2013. "Psychopaths in the C-Suite: Fred Kiel at TEDxBGI." TEDx Talks, video, February 4, 2013. youtube.com/watch?reload=9&v=vqBPZR63vfA.

Kiel, F. 2015. *Return on Character: The Real Reason Leaders and Their Companies Win*. Boston: Harvard Business Review Press.

Martin, R. 2007. *The Opposable Mind: How Successful Leaders Win Through Integrative Thinking*. Boston: Harvard Business School Publishing.

Ozcelik, H., and S.G. Barsade. 2018. "No Employee and Island." *Academy of Management Journal* 61(6). journals.aom.org/doi/abs/10.5465/amj .2015.1066.

Pfeffer, J. 2018. *Dying for Paycheck: How Modern Management Harms Employee Health and Company Management—and What We Can Do About It*. New York: Harper Collins.

re:Work. 2016. "Guide: Understand Team Effectiveness." re:Work with Google, August 13. rework.withgoogle.com/guides/understanding-team -effectiveness/steps/introduction.

Rugg, J.E. 2018. "The Connection Value Chain: Impact of Connection Culture and Employee Motivation on Perceived Team Performance." PhD dissertation, Biola University.

Ryan, R., and E. Deci. 2001. "On Happiness and Human Potentials: A Review of Research on Hedonic and Eudaimonic Well-Being." *Annual Review of Psychology* 52:141–166.

Sherman, G.D., J.J. Lee, A.J.C. Cuddy, J. Renshon, C. Oveis, J.J. Gross, and J.S. Lerner. 2012. "Leadership Is Associated With Lower Levels of Stress." *Proceedings of the National Academy of Sciences of the United States of America* 109(44): 17903–17907.

Sinegal, J. 2017. Emails and telephone calls with the author from June 28, 2017 through November 3, 2017.

Stallard, M.L. 2007. *Fired Up or Burned Out: How to Reignite Your Team's Passion, Creativity, and Productivity.* Nashville, TN: Thomas Nelson.

Stallard, M.L. 2020. "America's Loneliness Epidemic: A Hidden Systemic Risk to Organizations." ATD Insights, February 26. td.org/insights/americas -loneliness-epidemic-a-hidden-systemic-risk-to-organizations.

Temkin Group. 2013. "Employee Engagement Benchmark Study 2013." Temkin Group Research, January. temkingroup.com/research-reports/employee -engagement-benchmark-study-2013.

Valet, V. 2019. "America's Best Employers 2019." *Forbes*, April 17. forbes.com /sites/vickyvalet/2019/04/17/americas-best-employers- 2019/#57fcbafb7c23.

Weber, B. 2019. Conversations with the author.

Zimmerman, A. 2004. "Costco's Dilemma: Be Kind to Its Workers, or to Wall Street?" *Wall Street Journal*, March 26. wsj.com/articles/ SB108025917854365904.

Chapter 6

APA (American Psychological Association). 2010. "Stress in America: Stress and Gender." Press release, November 9. apa.org/news/press/releases/stress/2010 /gender-stress.pdf.

Behar, H. 2009. "Starbucks: It's Not About the Coffee." Interview by M.L. Stallard. BrightTalk, March 27. brighttalk.com/webcast/89/2408.

Behar, H., and J. Goldstein. 2007. *It's Not About the Coffee: Lessons on Putting People First from a Life at Starbucks.* New York: Portfolio.

Chapman, G., and P. White. 2011. *The 5 Languages of Appreciation in the Workplace: Empowering Organizations by Encouraging People.* Chicago: Northfield Publishing.

Derrick, S., and K. Wooley. 2009. Meetings with Scott Derrick and Kitty Wooley of 13L.

Dorsey, D. 2000. "Positive Deviant." *Fast Company,* November 30. fastcompany
.com/42075/positive-deviant.

Duhigg, C. 2016. "What Google Learned from Its Quest to Build the Perfect
Team." *New York Times,* February 25. nytimes.com/2016/02/28/magazine
/what-google-learned-from-its-quest-to-build-the-perfect-team.html.

Dutton, J. 2003. *Energize Your Workplace: How to Create and Sustain High
Quality Connections at Work.* San Francisco: Jossey-Bass.

Flash Mentoring. n.d. "What Is Flash Mentoring?" www.flashmentoring.com.

Fredrickson, B. 2009. *Positivity: Top-Notch Research Reveals 3-to-1 Ratio That Will
Change Your Life.* New York: Three Rivers Press.

Fredrickson, B. 2013. "Your Phone vs. Your Heart." *New York Times,* March 24.
nytimes.com/2013/03/24/opinion/sunday/your-phone-vs-your-heart.html.

Fredrickson, B., and T. Joiner. 2002. "Positive Emotions Trigger Upward Spirals
Toward Emotional Well-Being." *Psychological Science* 13(2). unc.edu/peplab
/_publications/Fredrickson_Joiner_2002.pdf.

Fredrickson, B., K.M. Grewen, K.A. Coffey, S.B. Algoe, A.M. Firestine, J.M.G.
Arevalo, J. Ma, and S.W. Cole. 2013. "A Functional Genomic Perspective on
Human Well-Being." *Proceedings of the National Academy of Sciences* 110(33):
13684–13689.

Goldsmith, M. 2007. *What Got You Here Won't Get You There: How Successful
People Become Even More Successful!* New York: Hyperion.

Goleman, D. 2006. *Social Intelligence: The New Science of Human Relationships.*
New York: Random House.

Google. 2009. Meetings with executives at Google's Googleplex headquarters in
Mountain View, CA, on July 28.

Gottman, J. 1994. *Why Marriages Succeed or Fail.* New York: Simon & Schuster.

Grant, A. 2020. "Yes, Even Introverts Can Be Lonely Right Now." *New York
Times,* April 16. nytimes.com/2020/04/16/smarter-living/coronavirus
-introverts-lonely.html.

Hardin, A.E. 2018. "Getting Acquainted: How Knowing About Colleague's Personal
Lives Impacts Workplace Interactions." *Academy of Management Journal,* July 9.
journals.aom.org/doi/abs/10.5465/AMBPP.2018.14989abstract.

Harris, I. 2015. "WOW Stories: How Ritz-Carlton Brings Its Stories to Life."
Gatehouse, April 27. gatehouse.co.uk/wow-stories-how-ritz-carlton-brings-its
-values-to-life.

Hsieh, T. 2010. Conversation with Tony Hsieh, Zappo's CEO, in a meeting with
the author on September 15.

Morris, J. 2020. Meeting and correspondence with author.

Pennebaker, J. 1997. *Opening Up: The Healing Power of Expressing Emotions.* New
York: Guilford Press.

Pfeffer, J., and R. Sutton. 2000. *The Knowing-Doing Gap: How Smart Companies Turn Knowledge into Action*. Cambridge, MA: Belknap Press of Harvard University Press.

Soames, M. 1999. *Speaking for Themselves: The Private Letters of Sir Winston and Lady Churchill. Black Swan.* Quoted in Lee, N., and S. Lee. 2000. *The Marriage Book*. London: Alpha International.

Southwest Airlines. n.d. "Culture." careers.southwestair.com/culture.

Spiegelman, P. 2012. *Smile Guide: Employee Perspectives on Culture, Loyalty, and Profit*. Dallas: Brown Books.

Stallard, M.L. 2007. *Fired Up or Burned Out: How to Reignite Your Team's Passion, Creativity, and Productivity*. Nashville, TN: Thomas Nelson.

Stallard, M.L. 2010. "Has Jim Goodnight Cracked the Code on Corporate Culture?" Michael Lee Stallard blog, June 18. michaelleestallard.com/has-jim-goodnight-cracked-the-code-of-corporate-culture.

Stallard, M.L., and K.P. Stallard. 2015. "Creating a Culture That Connects." *AMA Quarterly*, Summer: 38–41.

Sutton, R. 2007. *The No Asshole Rule: Building a Civilized Workplace and Surviving One That Isn't*. New York: Warner Business Books.

Utsey, S., N. Giesbrecht, J. Hook, and P. Stanard. 2008. "Cultural, Sociofamilial, and Psychological Resources that Inhibit Psychological Distress in African Americans Exposed to Stressful Life Events and Race-Related Stress." *Journal of Counseling Psychology* 55(1): 49–62.

Chapter 7

Baldwin, R. 2019. *The Globotics Upheaval: Globalization, Robotics and the Future of Work*. New York: Oxford University Press.

Berger, S. 2017. "Side Hustle Nation: Millennials Are Making Major Money with Side Gigs." Bankrate.com, July 12. bankrate.com/personal-finance/smart-money/side-hustles-survey.

Bloom, N., and J. Liang, J. Roberts, Z.J. Ying. 2015. "Does Working From Home Work? Evidence From a Chinese Experiment." *Quarterly Journal of Economics* 130(1): 165–218. ideas.repec.org/a/oup/qjecon/v130y2015i1p165-218.html.

BLS (Bureau of Labor Statistics). 2019. "29 Percent of Wage and Salary Workers Could Work at Home in Their Primary Job in 2017–18." TED: The Economics Daily, BLS, September 30. bls.gov/opub/ted/2019/29-percent-of-wage-and-salary-workers-could-work-at-home-in-their-primary-job-in-2017-18.htm

Brenan, M. 2020. "U.S. Workers Discovering Affinity for Remote Work." Gallup, April 3. news.gallup.com/poll/306695/workers-discovering-affinity-remote-work.aspx.

Christakis, N. 2019. "How AI Will Rewire Us." *The Atlantic*, April. theatlantic .com/magazine/archive/2019/04/robots-human-relationships/583204.

Coutu, D. 2004. "Putting Leaders on the Couch." *Harvard Business Review*, January. hbr.org/2004/01/putting-leaders-on-the-couch.

Crockett, Z. 2018. "The Most Lucrative Side Hustles." TheHustle.com, October 13. thehustle.co/the-highest-and-lowest-paying-side-hustles.

Dignan, L. 2020. "CFOs Looking to Make Remote Work, Telecommuting More Permanent Following COVID-19, Says Gartner Survey." ZD Net, April 6. zdnet.com/article/cfos-looking-to-make-remote-work-telecommuting-more -permanent-following-covid-19-says-gartner-survey.

Gallup. 2017. "State of the American Workplace." gallup.com/workplace/238085 /state-american-workplace-report-2017.aspx.

George, D.T. 2013. *Untangling the Mind: Why We Behave the Way We Do.* New York: HarperOne.

George, D.T. 2019. Conversations and emails to author.

Global Workplace Analytics. 2019. "Latest Telecommuting/Mobile Work/Remote Work Statistics." globalworkplaceanalytics.com/telecommuting-statistics.

Hickman, A., and J. Robison. 2020. "Is Working Remotely Effective? Gallup Research Says Yes." Gallup, January 24. gallup.com/workplace/283985 /working-remotely-effective-gallup-research-says-yes.aspx.

Jones, S. 2017. *Finding Heart in Art: A Surgeon's Renaissance Approach to Healing Modern Medical Burnout.* Charleston, SC: Advantage.

Lancer, D. 2018. "Beware of the Malevolent Dark Triad." *Psychology Today*, December 10. psychologytoday.com/us/blog/toxic-relationships/201812 /beware-the-malevolent-dark-triad.

Lieberman, D., and M. Long. 2018. *The Molecule of More: How a Single Chemical in Your Brain Drives Love, Sex, and Creativity—and Will Determine the Fate of the Human Race.* Dallas, TX: BenBella Books.

LinkedIn Learning. 2019. "Workplace Learning Report: Why 2019 Is the Breakout Year for the Talent Developer." learning.linkedin.com/content/dam/me /business/en-us/amp/learning-solutions/images/workplace-learning-report -2019/pdf/workplace-learning-report-2019.pdf.

Lustig, R. 2017. *The Hacking of the American Mind: Inside the Sugar-Coated Plot to Confuse Pleasure With Happiness.* New York: Penguin Random House.

Maslach, C., and M.P. Leiter. 2016. "Understanding the Burnout Experience: Recent Research and Its Implications for Psychiatry." *World Psychiatry* 15(2): 103–111. ncbi.nlm.nih.gov/pmc/articles/PMC4911781.

Pfeffer, J., and R. Sutton. 2000. *The Knowing-Doing Gap: How Smart Companies Turn Knowledge into Action.* Cambridge, MA: Belknap Press of Harvard University Press.

Plews, L. 2019. "Older Americans in the Workforce." United Income, April 22. unitedincome.com/library/older-americans-in-the-workforce.

Reistad-Long, S. 2008. "Older Brain May Be a Wiser Brain." *New York Times,* May 20. nytimes.com/2008/05/20/health/research/20brai.html.

Saporito, T. 2012. "It's Time to Acknowledge CEO Loneliness." *Harvard Business Review,* February 15. hbr.org/2012/02/its-time-to-acknowledge-ceo-lo.

Schiraldi, G. 2017. *The Resilience Workbook: Essential Skills to Recover From Stress, Trauma, and Adversity.* Oakland, CA: New Harbinger Publications.

SHRM (Society for Human Resource Management). 2016. "Telecommuting Has Increased Threefold in 20 years, SHRM Survey Shows." Press Release, July 13. shrm.org/about-shrm/press-room/press-releases/pages/telecommuting -up-over-past-20-years.aspx.

SIA (Staffing Industry Analysts). 2018. "US Gig Economy Grows to USD $864 Billion." SIA Press Release, October 2. staffingindustry.com/eng/About /Media-Center/Press-Releases/Press-Release-Archives/2018/US-Gig -Economy-Grows-to-USD-864-Billion.

SIA (Staffing Industry Analysts). n.d. "Human Cloud." *The Lexicon: The Global Language of the Workforce Solutions Ecosystem,* SIA. lexicon.staffingindustry .com/alphabets/h.

Side Hustle Nation. 2019. "2019 Side Hustle Statistics and Survey Results: Income Levels, Most Popular Gigs, and Common Struggles." sidehustlenation.com /side-hustle-statistics-2019.

Sussman, S., N. Lisha, and M. Griffiths. 2011. "Prevalence of the Addictions: A Problem of the Majority or the Minority?" *Evaluation & the Health Professions* 34(1): 3–56.

Toossi, M., and E. Torpey. 2017. "Older Workers: Labor Force Trends and Career Options." Bureau of Labor Statistics, May. bls.gov/careeroutlook/2017/ article/older-workers.htm.

Useem, J. 2017. "When Working From Home Doesn't Work." *The Atlantic,* November. theatlantic.com/magazine/archive/2017/11/when-working-from -home-doesnt-work/540660.

Waber, B. 2017. "Whether You Can Work Well From Home Depends on These Three Things." Quartz at Work, November 10. qz.com/work/1125093 /should-i-work-from-home-today.

Willis Towers Watson. 2020. "Employers Take Aim at Expected Higher Levels of Employee Stress and Anxiety, Willis Towers Watson Survey Finds." Press Release, April 27. willistowerswatson.com/en-US/News/2020/04/employers -take-aim-at-expected-higher-levels-of-employee-stress-and-anxiety-wtw -survey-finds.

Woolworth, J. 2018. *The Waterwheel: Practical Wisdom for 64 Common Concerns.* Greenwich, CT: Cardinal Flower Publishing.

Profiles in Connection

Restoring Navy Pride

Clark, V. 2002. "Presence, Power, Precision: The United States Navy in the 21st Century." *Sea Power*, April.

Clark, V. 2003. "Admiral Vern Clark Remarks." United States Naval Institute's 129th Annual Meeting & 13th Annapolis Seminar Luncheon at the Alumni Hall, United States Naval Academy, Annapolis, MD, April 3.

Clark, V. 2014. Telephone conversation with the author on April 4.

Herdt, J., T. Lafluer, C.W. Moore Jr., F. Pandolfe, and F. Thorpe. 2008–2010. Personal meetings, telephone interviews, and emails to author about CNO Adm. Vern Clark and his leadership of the U.S. Navy. October 6, 2008, to June 10, 2010.

U.S. Navy. 2005. "Top Five Priorities, Articles, Speeches, Interviews, etc. of Admiral Vern Clark, Chief of Naval Operations, USN." U.S. Department of the Navy, reviewed August 1, 2009. navy.mil/navydata/nav_legacy.asp?id=215.

Connecting on and off the Court

Ballard, C. 2016. "Why Steph Curry and Steve Kerr Are Among the World's Greatest Leaders." *Fortune*, March 24. fortune.com/2016/03/24/steph -curry-steve-kerr-golden-state-warriors-great-leaders.

Cowherd, C. 2019. "Steph Curry Could Be the Best Leader in NBA, 76ers Need to Make Tough Choices | NBA |THE HERD." The Herd with Colin Cowherd, video, May 13, 2019. youtube.com/watch?reload=9&v=ME4UsNbWThI.

Deb, S. 2019. "Hitting Pause, but Only on Basketball." *New York Times*, June 22.

Dunkyard. 2016. "Stephen Curry Documentary 'The Journey.'" Dunkyard video. March 13, 2016. youtube.com/watch?v=y_q2-zai8zU.

Lopresti, M. 2018. "March Madness: A Look Back at Davidson, Stephen Curry's Run in 2008." NCAA.com, March 12. ncaa.com/news/basketball-men/article /2018-03-12/march-madness-look-back-davidson-stephen-currys-run-2008.

Medina, M. 2019. "How Stephen Curry Helped the Warriors Keep Everything Together." Mercury News, March 27. mercurynews.com/2019/03/27/how -stephen-curry-helped-the-warriors-keep-everything-together.

Peter, J. 2019. "A Look Inside What Makes Steph Curry a Special Leader for Golden State Warriors." *USA Today*, June 4. usatoday.com/story/sports/nba /warriors/2019/06/04/nba-finals-steph-curry-special-leader-golden-state /1346551001.

Piotrekzprod. 2017. "NBA Players on Stephen Curry." YouTube video, July 8, 2017. youtube.com/watch?v=ZGsJ0pkCvls.

Principled Pragmatist

Bennhold, K. 2020. "A German Exception? Why the Country's Coronavirus Death Rate Is Low." *New York Times*, May 6. nytimes.com/2020/04/04 /world/europe/germany-coronavirus-death-rate.html.

CFR (Council on Foreign Relations). 2015. "Power Profile: Angela Merkel." Uncorrected transcript, November 20. cfr.org/event/power-profile-angela -merkel.

Davidson, J. 2020. "The Leader of the Free World Gives a Speech, and She Nails It." *New York Magazine Intelligencer*, March 18. nymag.com/intelligencer /2020/03/angela-merkel-nails-coronavirus-speech-unlike-trump.html.

Dempsey, J. 2020. "Why Merkel's Coronavirus Address Matters." Carnegie Europe, March 24. carnegieeurope.eu/2020/03/24/why-merkel-s-coronavirus -address-matters-pub-81357.

Gallu, J., and A. Delfs. 2020. "Merkel's Frankness and Clarity Beats Trump's Virus Bluster." *Bloomberg Businessweek*, April 28. bloomberg.com/news/articles /2020-04-28/how-trump-s-and-merkel-s-leadership-against-coronavirus -compare.

Hill, J. 2018. "Angela Merkel's Quiet Power." BBC News, October 29. bbc.co.uk /news/resources/idt-sh/angela_merkel.

Marr, A. 2013. "The Making of Merkel With Andrew Marr." BBC Two documentary. bbc.co.uk/programmes/b03bspsz.

Merkel, A. 2019. "German Chancellor Angela Merkel's Address | Harvard Commencement 2019." Harvard University YouTube channel, May 30. youtube.com/watch?v=9ofED6BInFs&t=10s.

Miller, S. 2020. "The Secret to Germany's COVID-19 Success: Angela Merkel Is a Scientist." *The Atlantic*, April 20. theatlantic.com/international/archive/2020 /04/angela-merkel-germany-coronavirus-pandemic/610225.

News Wires. 2020. "Merkel Shines in Handling of Germany's Coronavirus Crisis." France 24, March 29. france24.com/en/20200329-merkel-shines-in-handling -of-germany-s-coronavirus-crisis.

Packer, G. 2014. "The Quiet German." *New Yorker*, November 24. newyorker.com /magazine/2014/12/01/quiet-german.

Qvortrup, M. 2016. *Angela Merkel: Europe's Most Influential Leader.* New York: Overlook Duckworth.

Vick, K. 2015. "Person of the Year: Chancellor of the Free World." *Time*, December 21. time.com/time-person-of-the-year-2015-angela-merkel.

The Soul of Starbucks

Behar, H. Emails and telephone calls the author had with Howard Behar from 2013 to 2019.

Behar, H., and J. Goldstein. 2007. *It's Not About the Coffee: Lessons on Putting People First from a Life at Starbucks.* New York: Portfolio.

Carr, A. 2015. "The Inside Story of Starbucks's Race Together Campaign, No Foam." *Fast Company,* June 15. fastcompany.com/3046890/the-inside-story -of-starbuckss-race-together-campaign-no-foam.

"Howard Behar." 2016. Greenleaf Center for Servant Leadership. greenleaf.org /team/Howard-Behar.

Schultz, H. 2018. "'I Love You, Howard Behar': Howard Schultz Pays Tribute to Starbucks President in Heartfelt Speech." *Seattle Business Magazine,* video, March 13, 2018. youtube.com/watch?v=wH2MR5VmyXE.

Somaiya, R. 2015. "Starbucks Ends Conversation Starters on Race." *New York Times,* March 22. nytimes.com/2015/03/23/business/media/starbucks-ends -tempestuous-initiative-on-race.html.

Healing Connections

Berg, S. 2018. "4 Lessons Mayo Clinic Learned from Group Meetings to Cut Burnout." AMA, April 4. ama-assn.org/practice-management/physician -health/4-lessons-mayo-clinic-learned-group-meetings-cut-burnout.

Brangham, W. 2020. "An ICU Nurse on Wavering Between Confidence and Fear." PBS NewsHour, April 24. pbs.org/newshour/show/an-icu-nurse-on-wavering -between-confidence-and-fear.

Burns, K., E. Ewers, and C.I. Ewers, dirs. 2018. *The Mayo Clinic: Faith, Hope and Science.* Documentary, PBS. pbs.org/kenburns/the-mayo-clinic.

Haskell, B., M. Schroer, and M. Zsamboky. 2020. "Easing the Psychological Impact of COVID-19 for Nurses." *American Nurse,* April 13. myamericannurse.com/easing-the-psychological-impact-of-covid-19-for-nurses

Kane, J. 2020. "'Do Not Call Me a Hero.' Listen to an ICU Nurse's Plea for Fighting the Coronavirus." PBS News Hour, April 24. pbs.org/newshour /health/do-not-call-me-a-hero-read-an-icu-nurses-plea-for-fighting-the -coronavirus.

Mayo Clinic. 2019. "Mayo Clinic Mission and Values." mayoclinic.org/about-mayo -clinic/mission-values.

McLean, R. 2020. "Dr. McLean's Presidential Address." American College of Physicians. acponline.org/membership/physician-membership/acp-fellowship /dr-mcleans-presidential-address.

MD Anderson Cancer Center. 2019. "Quick Facts 2019." PDF accessed in 2019; now updated to 2020 Quick Facts on the MD Anderson Cancer Center website.

Pardes, H. 2014. "Herbert Pardes, M.D.—2014 Inaugural Pardes Humanitarian Prizewinner." Brain and Behavior Research Foundation, October 27, 2014. youtube.com/watch?v=OPHNjlCNKgw.

Stallard, M.L., and J. Pankau. 2007. "Strengthening Human Value in Organizational Cultures." *Leader to Leader* 47:18–23.

Stodghill, R. 2007. "The Doctor Is In." *New York Times,* January 7. nytimes.com /2007/01/07/business/yourmoney/07hospital.html?.

Swensen, S., and C. West. 2016. "Getting Back to Medicine as a Community." NEJM Catalyst, July 21. catalyst.nejm.org/getting-back-medicine-community.

Watkins, A., M. Rothfeld, W.K. Rashbaum, and B.M. Rosenthal. 2020. "Top E.R. Doctor Who Treated Coronavirus Patients Dies by Suicide." *New York Times,* April 27. nytimes.com/2020/04/27/nyregion/new-york-city-doctor-suicide -coronavirus.html.

What Oprah Knows for Sure

Koehn, N. 2011. *Oprah, Leading With Heart.* Self-Published by New Word City.

Muller, R. 2019. "Oprah Says These 3 Questions Will Improve Your Relationship." ThriveGlobal.com, January 9. thriveglobal.com/stories/oprah-question-trick -relationship-argument-improve.

O Media Kit. 2020. "2020 Media Kit Download." omediakit.com/hotdata /publishers/oprahmaga3395825/omediakit7535/pdfs/2020_MK _DOWNLOAD-03.pdf.

Tiede, B. 2019. *Now That's a Great Question.* Self-published.

Winfrey, O. 2014. "Oprah Winfrey on Career, Life, and Leadership." Student-led interview at Stanford Graduate School of Business, April 28, 2014. youtube.com/watch?v=6DlrqeWrczs.

Winfrey, O. 2017a. "The Academy." Oprah Winfrey Leadership Academy for Girls. owlag.co.za/academy.

Winfrey, O. 2019. *The Path Made Clear: Discovering Your Life's Direction and Purpose.* New York: Flatiron Books.

Main Street Connectors

Muchnick, J. 2018. "Kneaded Bread Celebrates 20 Years in Port Chester." Lohud .com, June 19. lohud.com/story/life/food/restaurants/2018/06/19/port -chester-kneaded-bread/698297002.

Stallard, E. 2019. Email to the Katharine Stallard dated October 28.

Horned Frog Family

Bartosek, N. 2011. "Why TCU Is the Hottest School in Texas." *Fort Worth Magazine,* July.

Boschini, V. 2018. "Chancellor's Remarks: Texas Christian University Fall Convocation." September 11. chancellor.tcu.edu/wp-content/uploads/2018 /11/Convocation-Fall-2018.pdf.

Osborne, R. 2012. "Victor Boschini." *Image* 43(Fall): 28–33.

TCU (Texas Christian University). 2010–2019. Meetings, emails, and telephone calls the author had with TCU administrators, faculty, and students from 2010 to 2019.

TCU and UNTHSC School of Medicine. 2019. "Empathetic Scholar: Communication." mdschool.tcu.edu/empathetic-scholar/communication.

One

Assayas, M. 2005. *Bono: In Conversation with Michka Assayas*. New York: Penguin Group.

Bono, The Edge, A. Clayton, L. Mullen Jr., and N. McCormick. 2006. *U2 by U2*. New York: HarperCollins.

Garrett, G. 2009. *We Get to Carry Each Other: The Gospel According to U2*. Louisville, KY: Westminster John Knox Press.

Grammy.com. 2013. "The Recording Academy Announces 2014 Grammy Hall of Fame Inductees." Press release, December 3. grammy.com/recording-academy /press-release/the-recording-academy-announces-2014-grammy-hall-of-fame -inductees.

Grammy.com. 2014. "U2: Past Grammy Awards." July 19. grammy.com/artist/u2.

Martin, R. 2019. "Ed Sheeran Sets Record for Highest-Grossing Tour." *Morning Edition*. NPR, August 7. npr.org/2019/08/07/748972080/ed-sheeran-sets -record-for-highest-grossing-tour.

Stevens, H. 2011. "Did U2 Just Surpass the Rolling Stones as the Greatest Band Ever?" *The Atlantic*, August 3. theatlantic.com/entertainment/archive/2011 /08/did-u2-just-surpass-the-rolling-stones-as-the-greatest-band-ever/242943.

Miracle in Motor City

Mulally, A., and R. Kirkland. 2013. "Leading in the 21st Century: An Interview with Ford's Alan Mulally." *McKinsey & Company Insights and Publications*, November. mckinsey.com/insights/strategy/leading_in_the_21st_century _an_interview_with_fords_alan_mulally.

Stallard, M.L. 2004. "7 Practices of Alan Mulally That Helped Ford Pass Competitors." Foxbusiness.com, January 22. foxbusiness.com/markets/2014 /01/22/7-practices-alan-mulally-that-helped-ford-pass-competitors.

Vlasic, B. 2014. "Complete U-Turn: The Head of Ford Retires, Having Rejuvenated the Carmaker." *New York Times*, May 1. nytimes.com/2014 /05/02/business/ford-motor-chief-to-retire.html.

Saving the Girl Scouts

Berry, J. 2018. "Endorphins: Effects and How to Increase Levels." Medical News Today, February 6. medicalnewstoday.com/articles/320839.php.

Bourg Carter, S. 2014. "Helper's High: The Benefits (and Risks) of Altruism." Psychology Today, September 4. psychologytoday.com/us/blog/high-octane -women/201409/helpers-high-the-benefits-and-risks-altruism.

Byrne, J.A. 1990. "Profiting from the Nonprofits." *Business Week*, March 26.

"Girl Scouts." 2019. Encyclopedia.com, November 3. encyclopedia.com/sports- and-everyday-life/social-organizations/private-organizations/girl-scouts.

Hadjian, A. 1995. "Follow the Leader." *Fortune*, November 27, 96.

Helgesen, S. 1995. *The Female Advantage: Women's Ways of Leadership*. New York: Doubleday.

Hesselbein, F. 2002. *Hesselbein on Leadership*. San Francisco: Jossey-Bass.

Hesselbein, F. 2012. *More Hesselbein on Leadership*. San Francisco: Jossey-Bass.

McKinney, M. 2011. "Frances Hesselbein: To Serve Is to Live." Leadership Now, February 16. leadershipnow.com/leadingblog/2011/02/frances_hesselbein _to_serve_is.html.

Coach K's Aha Moment

GoDuke.com. "Men's Basketball: Mike Krzyewski." goduke.com/sports/mens -basketball/roster/coaches/mike-krzyewski/3607.

Sokolove, M. 2006. "Follow Me." *New York Times Magazine*, February 5. nytimes.com/2006/02/05/magazine/05coachk_96_101 116_117_.html?.

Designing Connection Into Culture

Baehrend, J. 2016. "100,000 Lives Campaign: Ten Years Later." IHI, June 17. ihi.org/communities/blogs/100000-lives-campaign-ten-years-later.

Bisognano, M. 2018–2019. Telephone calls and emails to author.

IHI (Institute for Healthcare Improvement). n.d. "Vision, Mission, and Values." ihi.org/about/pages/ihivisionandvalues.aspx.

"Maureen Bisognano." n.d. Harvard School of Public Health. hsph.harvard.edu /ecpe/faculty/maureen-bisognano.

Roth, N. 2019. "Creating an Intentional Culture." GetRealLeadership.com, October 10. getrealleadership.com/2019/10/10/creating-an-intentional-culture.

Prescribing Connection

ACGME (Accreditation Council for Graduate Medical Education). 2019. "2019 Marvin R. Dunn Keynote Address." Keynote presentation at the 2019 ACGME Annual Educational Conference, video. Posted March 26, 2019. vimeo.com/326640280.

Atlantic Live. 2018. "Addressing the Public Health Crisis of Loneliness." *The Atlantic*, video, December 12, 2018. youtube.com/watch?v=0xW30YXOctQ.

Murthy, V. 2020. *Together: The Healing Power of Human Connection in a Sometimes Lonely World*. New York: HarperCollins Publishers, 281.

Murthy, V., and F. Collins. 2017. "A Nation Under Pressure: The Public Health Consequences of Stress in America." Stephen E. Straus Distinguished Lecture hosted by the National Center for Complementary and Integrative Health on September 7, 2017. NIHOD YouTube channel, video. youtube.com/watch ?time_continue=14&v=_SGT1yi-fNo.

Schawbel, D. 2017. "Vivek Murthy: How to Solve the Work Loneliness Epidemic." Forbes, October 7. forbes.com/sites/danschawbel/2017/10/07/vivek-murthy -how-to-solve-the-work-loneliness-epidemic-at-work/#5784effb7172.

Vivek Murthy.com. "Biography." vivekmurthy.com/about.

Called to Connect

Brandt, Ralph, and Rich Brandt. Meetings, telephone calls, and emails to author from 2018 to 2019.

RDR Group. n.d. "Connecting with Others." Training Program. rdrgroup.com /training-topics/diversity-inclusion/connecting-with-others.

Claiming Culture as the Advantage

GreatPlacetoWork.com. n.d. "Progressive Insurance." Accessed November 17, 2019. greatplacetowork.com/certified-company/1000270.

Illinois State University staff. 2019. "Business Alumna Breaks Barriers." Illinois State University, May 19. news.illinoisstate.edu/2019/04/business-alumna -breaks-barriers.

Progressive. n.d. "Core Values." progressive.com/about/core-values.

Progressive. n.d. "Leadership." progressive.com/about/leadership.

Progressive. 2019. "Progressive Investor Relations: Our Culture Is Our Foundation Q4 2018." Accessed November 18, 2019. investors.progressive. com/static-files/2978ff4a-606a-4b33-953b-1ffe10c96213.

Shookman, S. 2019. "Progressive Moves in 2019: One-on-one with CEO Tricia Griffith." WKYC.com, February 20. wkyc.com/article/news/progressive-moves -in-2019-one-on-one-with-ceo-tricia-griffith/95-3ab55128-5677-4c0e-9278- a918608f2a2b.

"Tricia Griffith | Businessperson of the Year 2018." *Fortune*. fortune.com /businessperson-of-the-year/2018/tricia-griffith.

Connecting During a Time of Change

AMFS (Aspen Music Festival and School). n.d. "About the AMFS." aspenmusicfesti-val.com/about/about-the-aspen-music-festival-and-school.

Ardern, J. 2020a. "As promised, here's the latest instalment of our COVID-19 podcast with none other than Suzy Cato." Facebook Live video, April 29, 2020. facebook.com/jacindaardern/videos/2580446498911869.

Ardern, J. 2020b. "Evening everyone. Thought I'd jump online and answer a few questions as we all prepare to stay home for the next wee while. Join me if you'd like!" Facebook Live video, March 25, 2020. facebook.com /jacindaardern/videos/147109069954329.

Ardern, J. 2020c. "If you missed the update on the next steps for shifting alert levels here in New Zealand - join me for a shorter version of today's press conference!" Facebook Live video, May 11, 2020. facebook.com /jacindaardern/videos/533402127325199.

Borchardt, J., and J. Balmert. 2020. "First Came the Pandemic, Then Came the Politics: Why Amy Acton Quit." Cincinnati Equirer, June 15. dispatch.com /news/20200615/first-came-pandemic-then-came-politics-why-amy-acton-quit.

Cave, D. 2020. "Jacinda Ardern Sold a Drastic Lockdown with Straight Talk and Mom Jokes." *New York Times*, May 24. nytimes.com/2020/05/23/world /asia/jacinda-ardern-coronavirus-new-zealand.html.

Cuomo, A. 2020a. "Gov. Andrew Cuomo Provides Daily Coronavirus Update: May 1." *USA Today*, video. May 1, 2020. youtube.com/watch?v=toOIJ jt5MIk&t=1334s.

Cuomo, A. 2020b. "Governor Cuomo Holds Briefing on COVID-19 Response." Governor Andrew M. Cuomo YouTube channel. April 3, 2020. youtube.com/watch?v=uwMYunTbdPU.

Dosani, S., and A. Westbrook 2020. "The Leader We Wish We All Had." *New York Times,* video, May 5, 2020. nytimes.com/video/opinion/10000000 7111965/coronavirus-ohio-amy-acton.html.

Editorial Board. 2020. "In a Crisis, True Leaders Stand Out." Opinion, *New York Times*, April 30. nytimes.com/2020/04/30/opinion/coronavirus -leadership.html.

Fletcher, A. 2020. "Season Cancelation Notice." Aspen Music Festival and School, May 4. aspenmusicfestival.com/season-cancellation-notice.

Friedman, T.L. 2020. "We Need Great Leadership Now, and Here's What It Looks Like." *New York Times*, April 21. nytimes.com/2020/04/21/opinion/covid -dov-seidman.html?.

Gordon, K. 2020. "Amy Acton Is Calming Leader in Coronavirus Crisis." *The Columbus Dispatch*, March 13. dispatch.com/news/20200313/amy-acton-is -calming-leader-in-coronavirus-crisis.

Hancock, L. 2020. "New Ohio House Bill Would Make Feb. 26 Dr. Amy Acton Day." Cleveland.com, July 14. cleveland.com/open/2020/07/new-ohio-house -bill-would-make-feb-26-dr-amy-acton-day.html.

Mosby, C. 2020. "Amy Acton Resigns as Director of Ohio Department of Health." MSN Money, June 11. msn.com/en-us/money/careersandeducation/amy -acton-resigns-as-director-of-ohio-department-of-health/ar-BB15mdSR.

Neuman, S. 2020. "With No Current Cases, New Zealand Lifts Remaining COVID-19 Restrictions." NPR, June 8. npr.org/sections/coronavirus-live -updates/2020/06/08/871822321/with-no-current-cases-new-zealand-lifts -remaining-covid-19-restrictions.

Roberts, S. 2020. "Embracing the Uncertainties." *New York Times*, April 7. nytimes .com/2020/04/07/science/coronavirus-uncertainty-scientific-trust.html.

Weber, L., A.M. Barry-Jester, M.R. Smith. 2020. "Public Health Officials Face Wave of Threats, Pressure Amid Coronavirus Response." The Associated Press; Kaiser Health News, June 12. khn.org/news/public-health-officials-face-wave-of- threats-pressure-amid-coronavirus-response.

Witte, G. 2020. "Ohio's Amy Acton Inspires Admiration, and a Backlash, With Tough Coronavirus Response." *Washington Post*, May 18. washingtonpost.com /national/a-white-coated-hero-or-a-medical-dictator-ohios-amy-acton-inspires -admiration-and-a-backlash-with-tough-coronavirus-response/2020/05/17 /fa00cd1c-96d4-11ea-82b4-c8db161ff6e5_story.html.

Index

In this index, f denotes figure and t denotes table.

J

Jelinek, Craig, 93–94
Jim (Starbucks store manager), 55
Jones, Shawn C., 174
Judgment Index, 168

K

Kail, Thomas, 6–7, 8–9, 10, 11
Kaiser Family Foundation, xiii
Kasner, Herlind, 49
Kasner, Horst, 49
Kerr, Steve, 45, 48
Kiltz, Riley, 88–89
King, Martin Luther, Jr., 35, 65, 110
Kneaded Bread, 67
knowing-doing gap, 182–183
knowledge flows sessions, 158–159
knowledge traps, 96–98, 96*f*
Kohl, Helmut, 50
Kohn, Jeffrey, 67
Krasinski, John, 10
Kräusslich, Hans-Georg, 52
Krzyzewski, Mickie, 117–118
Krzyzewski, Mike (Coach K), 117–118

L

Lacamoire, Alex, 6–7, 8–9
languages of appreciation, 156
"Leader lacks humility" trap, 96–97
leadership
    COVID-19 pandemic, 52, 133–141
    defined, 36
    qualities, 134
    training, 149, 153–154
learned helplessness, 16
Lee, Damion, 47–48
Levenson, Steven, 81
Lieberman, Daniel Z., 169–170
listening, 56, 66, 115, 158. *See also* voice
living alone, 84
"Living Company, The" (de Geus),
    100–101
loneliness, x, 80, 82–83, 125, 170
Long, Michael E., 169–170
Loren, Allan, 32
Lustig, Robert H., 170, 170*t*

M

"Main Street" connectors, 67–68
Maniac, 82
Mass General Brigham, xiv
Mayo, Charlie, 60
Mayo Clinic, 59–61
McCann Worldgroup, 88
McKillop, Bob, 46
McLean, Robert, 63
MD Anderson Cancer Center, 59, 146
meaning, 25
Medina, Mark, 48
Medley, Nick, 20, 21
meetings, 113, 114, 148, 159, 160,
    183–184
Memorial Sloan Kettering Cancer
    Center, 20–22, 31, 58
Mendoza, KP, 62–63
mental health, xii–xiii, 137
mentors, 32, 43, 71, 122, 153–154, 164
Merkel, Angela, 48–52
mindset, 156, 161–162
Miranda, Lin-Manuel, 4–9, 10, 11
mirror neurons, 155
mission, 31–32
Molecule of More, The (Lieberman &
    Long), 169–170
monoculturalism, 129
Montpelier Command Philosophy, 148
motivation, employee, 104, 107*f*
Mulally, Alan, 112–114, 148
Mulcahy, Anne, 33–34
Mullen, Larry, Jr., 109–111
multi-generational workforce, 122,
    179–180
multitasking, 171
Mumbai terrorist attack, 32
Murthy, Vivek, 123–127

N

names, remembering, 119
National Academy of Medicine, 86
National Research Council, 86
nature, 172
Nazis, 31, 34
needs, universal human, 23–25, 102–103
negotiating, 156

About the Author and Contributors

Michael Lee Stallard is co-founder and president of E Pluribus Partners and Connection Culture Group. He is a keynote speaker, workshop leader, coach, and consultant for a wide variety of organizations, including Costco, Federal Reserve Bank of San Francisco, Memorial Sloan Kettering Cancer Center, NASA, Texas Christian University, Turner Construction, the U.S. Air Force, Qualcomm, the U.S. Department of Treasury, and Yale New Haven Health. He is the author of *Connection Culture*, the primary author of *Fired Up or Burned Out: How to Reignite Your Team's Passion, Creativity, and Productivity*, and a contributor to several books including *What Managers Say, What Employees Hear: Connecting with Your Front Line (So They'll Connect With Customers)* and the *ASTD Management Development Handbook*.

Articles written by Michael or about his work have appeared in *Financial Times, Wall Street Journal, New York Times, Leader to Leader, HR Magazine, Human Resource Executive, Leadership Excellence*, FoxBusiness.com, *Training Industry Quarterly, Training Magazine, Capital* (Dubai), *Rotman* (Canada), *Economic Times* (India), *Developing HR Strategy* (UK), *Shukan Diayamondo* (Japan), and *Outlook Business or Decision Makers* (India). He has spoken at conferences organized by the Association for Talent Development, Conference Board, the Corporate Executive Board, the Human Capital Institute, *Fortune* magazine, the Innovation Council, and the World Presidents Organization. He is a faculty member of the Institute for Management Studies (IMS), and he has been a guest lecturer at many universities including the University of Virginia's Darden Graduate School of Business, Texas Christian University, and University of Toronto's Rotman School of Management.

Prior to founding E Pluribus Partners and Connection Culture Group, Michael was chief marketing officer for businesses at Morgan Stanley and Charles Schwab. The programs his team identified and implemented at Morgan Stanley contributed to doubling a business unit's revenues during a two-and-a-half year period. The practices he and his team developed became the genesis for his approach to elevating the productivity and innovation of individuals and organizations. Michael has also worked as an executive in marketing and finance positions at Texas Instruments, Van Kampen Investments, and Barclays Bank, PLC. He received a bachelor's degree in marketing from Illinois State University, a master's degree in business administration from the University of Texas, Permian Basin, and a JD from DePaul University Law School. He was admitted to the Illinois bar in 1991. Michael is married and has two daughters.

 **Todd W. Hall, PhD,** is co-founder and chief scientist of Connection Culture Group and a professor of psychology at Biola University. He has more than 25 years' experience helping individuals and teams thrive. Todd's consulting work focuses on helping leaders build a connection culture and leverage people's core motivations to elevate engagement and performance. He is a regular contributor to the Human Capital Institute, and his writing and work have been featured by *Entrepreneur*, Execunet.com, the Association for Talent Development, and AppreciationAtWork.com.

Todd has consulted with universities, start-ups, government agencies, nonprofits, and for-profit organizations, including the National Institute for Mental Health, Northwestern Medicine, McDonald's, and the New York City Leadership Center. He earned a bachelor's and master's degree from Biola University, a master's degree from UCLA, and a doctorate in clinical psychology from Biola University, as well as a doctoral specialization in measurement and psychometrics from UCLA. He is a licensed psychologist in California.

Prior to teaching and consulting, Todd served on active duty in the army as a clinical psychologist. He is married and has two sons.

Katharine P. Stallard is a partner at E Pluribus Partners and Connection Culture Group. She is a gifted connector, speaker, and teacher who brings diverse experience in marketing, administration, business, and nonprofit organizations to her role. Audiences and seminar participants enjoy her sense of humor and practical advice. She has co-authored articles appearing in *Leader to Leader* and *HR Magazine*. Katie has worked in marketing for Tyndale House Publishers, a leading global Christian book publisher; for a Forbes 400 family helping to manage their diverse holdings; and for a highly regarded church in Connecticut in the area of communications. She also has extensive experience helping and serving on the boards of education and social sector organizations. Katie has a bachelor's degree in business administration from the University of Illinois. She is married and has two daughters.

Jason Pankau is a co-founder and partner at E Pluribus Partners. He speaks, teaches, coaches, and consults for the firm's clients. He has also guest lectured at the University of Virginia's Darden Graduate School of Business and has spoken or taught seminars at a wide variety of organizations, including Arkansas Electric, General Dynamics, Gen Re, Johnson & Johnson, the MD Anderson Cancer Center, NASA, and Scotiabank. He wrote *Beyond Self Help* and contributed to *Fired Up or Burned Out: How to Reignite Your Team's Passion, Creativity, and Productivity* and *What Managers Say, What Employees Hear: Connecting With Your Front Line (So They'll Connect With Customers)*, as well as articles for *Leader to Leader* and *Leadership Excellence*.

Jason is also the president of Life Spring Network, a Christian organization that trains and coaches pastors and church leaders. He teaches seminars on leadership, marriage, and discipleship throughout North America and has started churches and served as a pastor focused on mentoring and leadership development. He currently leads Hope Church in inner city Chicago.

Jason has a bachelor's degree from Brown University in business economics and organizational behavior/management. While there, he was captain and pre-season All-American linebacker in football, school record holder in discus, and national qualifier in track. Jason has a master's of divinity from Southern Theological Seminary and has completed the required coursework for a doctorate in leadership at Gordon-Conwell Theological Seminary. He is married and has two daughters and two sons.